IMAGES
of America

MEXICANS IN TEMPE

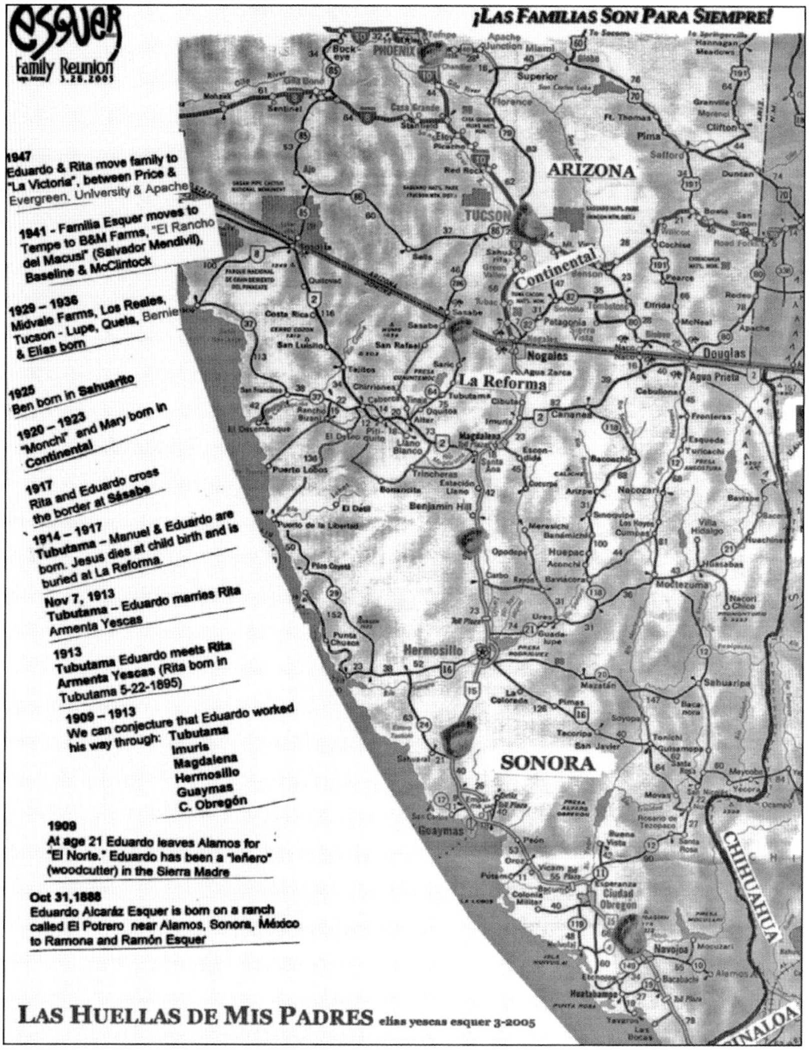

Eduardo Alcaraz Esquer was born to Ramona and Ramón Esquer on October 31, 1888, on a ranch called El Potrero, near Alamos, Sonora, Mexico. Eduardo eventually married his wife, Rita, and immigrated north to Continental and, later, to Tucson. Eduardo and Rita with their family then settled in Tempe in Victory Acres (La Victoria Barrio) in 1941. This map is called *Huellas*, or "footprints," of not only the Esquer family, but also of countless other families that came north from Mexico to help build the United States by working in agriculture, mining, railroads, construction, and, in time, a variety of different careers in the trades and professions. (Elias and Cecilia D. Esquer.)

On the Cover: In 1908, Antonio Celaya halted the horses and paused to enjoy Papago Park's scenery. A relative of the family assumed that the woman dressed in white and standing in the center of the wagon was Lupe, Antonio's wife. Standing on Lupe's left is Ines Escalante, born in 1895 in Tempe; sitting at the end of the wagon is Maria Escalante, born in 1899 in Tempe, who was a teacher there. Both Ines and Maria were daughters of Manuel and Espetacion (Celaya), sister of Antonio. The Escalante girls were cousins to Antonio and Lupe's children, who were in the wagon, and their names were Ophelia, who worked for the city of Tempe most of her life; Ida, a teacher; Lupe; Laura; and Olivia. The others in the wagon are unidentified. (Clara Y. Urbano.)

IMAGES
of America

MEXICANS IN TEMPE

Santos C. Vega, Ph.D.

Arizona Historical Foundation

ARCADIA PUBLISHING

ISBN 978-0-7385-7056-3

Published by Arcadia Publishing
Charleston SC, Chicago IL, Portsmouth NH, San Francisco CA

Printed in the United States of America

Library of Congress Catalog Card Number: 2008936424

For all general information contact Arcadia Publishing at:
Telephone 843-853-2070
Fax 843-853-0044
E-mail sales@arcadiapublishing.com
For customer service and orders:
Toll-Free 1-888-313-2665

Visit us on the Internet at www.arcadiapublishing.com

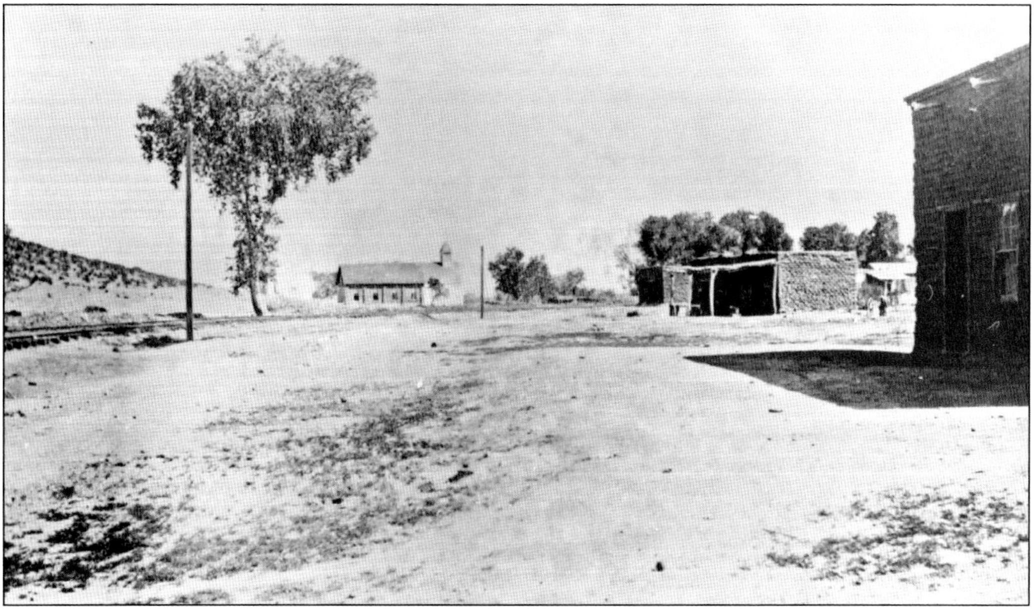

In the 1890s, San Pablo Barrio, with its agricultural canal, provided the desert fields with water and its residents with crops of hay, vegetables, and fruits of the earth to help create a community. Immigration north from New Spain (Mexico) had begun in the early 1600s into the northern territory of New Mexico, of which Arizona was part of and included in the Provincias Internas (Internal Provinces) of Spain. The Internal Provinces became part of Mexico after its 1821 independence. Mexico's northern territories became part of the United States in 1848 by the Treaty of Guadalupe Hidalgo. Mexicans continued to immigrate north, contributed to the founding of the Arizona Territory in 1862, and helped create the communities of San Pablo and, later, Tempe. Mexican labor helped build and support industries, including agriculture, ranching, and mining, in what became the state of Arizona in 1912. From those early times, Mexican pioneers and early settlers have continued to build, support, and defend the United States of America. (Arizona State University.)

Contents

Acknowledgments

Foremost, this work of nonfiction oral history based on true legacies, experience, and memories of Tempe families (Tempeneños) became a reality because of the contributions made by persons, families, and institutions. They provided CDs with photographs and related data. I thank Joe Arredondo, Barney S. Peralta, Jesus and Elizabeth Rivera, Albert and Susana Marquez, and H. Z. and Mary Compoy. Thanks to persons who provided pictures, annuals to be scanned, and encouragement: Clarita Urbano, Norma C. Pinate, Elias and Cecilia D. Esquer, Josie O. Solis, Gilbert Orantia, Jess Valenzuela, Lisa Moss, Robert Martinez, George Escalante, Lynn and JoAnn Pigg, Narcisa Espinoza, Rachel Hernandez Pollack, Sammy and Pat Obregon, Joe Obregon, Mardy Olivas, and Los Amigos de Tempe. Thanks to the Department of Archives and Special Collections Arizona State University (ASU), Arizona Historical Foundation (AHF), Tempe History Museum, and Tardeada Commission of the City of Tempe. All photographs came from Irene Gomez Hormell's personal collection if not otherwise noted. She related historical information with each picture and donated countless hours to the project. I also give heartfelt thanks to my editor at Arcadia Publishing, Jared Jackson, for his guidance and assistance when requested. Thanks to my nephew Danny Valenzuela for assisting me in technical computer work when necessary. I give my sincere appreciation to my wife, Josie R. Vega, for her love, patience, and encouragement on this and other projects. Finally, thanks to God for all blessings given to Tempeneños in their heritage and for making this book project possible.

INTRODUCTION

The area where Tempe is located, along with the rest of Arizona, provided a passageway for ancient Aztec trade with northern tribes of Arizona. The Aztec people and the Hopi people of Arizona are related linguistically. The passageways continue to the present time. In the late 1500s, Spanish missionaries worked in Arizona with the Pima and Tohono O'odham tribes in Maricopa and Pima Counties. The state of Arizona was part of the New Mexico territory. All the states that comprise the Southwest were part of the Internal Provinces of Spain, governed by the viceroy in New Spain before it became Mexico. The allure of the north began with the search for the Seven Cities of Cibola ("gold"), and attraction has continued for people to come north from Mexico. In the early 1800s, Mexican pioneers and settlers moved north into the Tempe area, first from Sonora and other parts of Mexico, from Tubac and Tucson, and also from New Mexico, California, Texas, and other southwestern states. Thus the first photograph in this pictorial book is a map. This is symbolic, showing the footprints of prospectors, miners, ranchers, farmers, and others who followed the footprints of those who came before, such as the conquistadores, the expeditionary leaders: Juan de Oñate, who founded Santa Fe, New Mexico, in 1598; and Capt. Juan de Anza, who led the expedition from Sonora to found San Francisco in 1776. The passage of immigrants was ancient in time, broad in space, and demanding in the struggle to survive. The names of the early settlers in Tempe are the same names of those who sailed the Atlantic from Spain to settle in Mexico and other parts of the Americas and to move north to the United States. Wherever they went and settled, they brought with them the ancient culture, heritage, and traditions of Spain and Mexico. Their photographs in this book tell their story. It is a story that is truly American because they as a people blended with the Native American people of Mexico. Thus Aztec and other native tribal people are now blended into a new American ethnic group combining the middle-eastern and European genetic makeup and culture: the Mexican American. Their family photographs tell this part of their story, except that now the new blended Anglo-American culture and cultures of other European, Asian, and Afro American people expand and improve their heritage and traditions. The photographs of the Mexican American people illustrate a remarkable transition, a genuine new American citizen of the future.

The second chapter begins the story with early Mexican immigrants who left their impressions on Tempe. Present-day descendants of these early settlers call themselves Tempeneños. These early Mexican families arrived in Tempe from various geographical points with a mission of survival, growth, and improvement for their new home along the Salt River. They built a settlement at the base of the butte near the Salt River and called their community San Pablo. The photograph on page four shows how San Pablo looked in the 1890s. A more settled San Pablo can be seen in the picture on page nine. Mexican settlers constructed their church, Nuestra Senora del Carmen (Our Lady of Mount Carmel), at the foot of the butte. The hardworking and industrious Mexican pioneers in the Tempe area cultivated various agricultural fields. Mexican labor helped Winchester Miller build the Tempe Canal. They worked with Charles Trumbull Hayden to help complete his enterprises of a canal and flour mill by 1872. After the establishment of Fort McDowell in 1865, the marketing of agricultural foods to the U.S. government spurred the growth of agriculture in the area. The immigrants continued to work in the meatpacking industry, dairy farms, and creamery located in Tempe. The settlers of San Pablo cultivated fields in what is today the campus and sports complex of Arizona State University. In time, the population of San Pablo was forced to relocate through eminent domain, and they moved to other areas of Tempe such as Escalante in the late 1950s, Mesa, Phoenix, Victory Acres, and other surrounding areas to the east and west. In this way, they contributed to the growth of construction and work in the roads and streets, buildings, and houses of the areas to which they had moved. In later years, they participated more in the trades and services through their work, and their contributions increased and continued to the present time. Their youth graduated from the schools, earned degrees, and entered professions, businesses, and trades. They fought in the First and Second World Wars and in other wars and conflicts that followed to keep their country free and prosperous. All the most informative data about the Mexicans in Tempe was obtained from oral history interviews and the photographs shown in this book.

Chapters two, three, four, and five tell the story of the Mexican people in Tempe, of their traditions, celebrations, work, military service, organizations, their children, education, and sports. Chapter six concludes the story with photographs aimed at their legacy and remembrances. These chapters are intended to tell the story of Tempeneños: Who were they? Where did they come from? What customs and survival skills did they bring? How did they construct their community to meet their cultural, economic, social, and religious needs? What were their faith beliefs? What social practices did they follow? What traditions have they kept? How did they fuse with other cultures when they experienced encounters? All this is depicted in their photographs.

In addition, of special interest are the influences of place: their approximately 18 barrios show influences of early homes compared to later homes, early streets compared to present streets, and how modes of transportation compared over the years. The change of place helped shape the residents of Tempe through the years. As Tempe changed, the Mexican American way of life changed. It would require extensive research and a large textbook to show the Tempeneños' transition into modern culture and present-day language, how they reached for the past to tie the present and future together in a life in daily transformation. This is not possible in this book, but one photograph tells a story of 1,000 words. In this way, this book is a treasure for those blessed with discernment. There is no doubt, however, that the Mexicans in Tempe climbed the "Lord's Mountain." They saw, in their own perspective, their future not only in Tempe, but also in the universe from where they were in the 1800s and from where they are today. The development of their God-given potential as recounted by their photographs and oral history interviews is confirmed through their family life story.

One

Impressions of Place and People

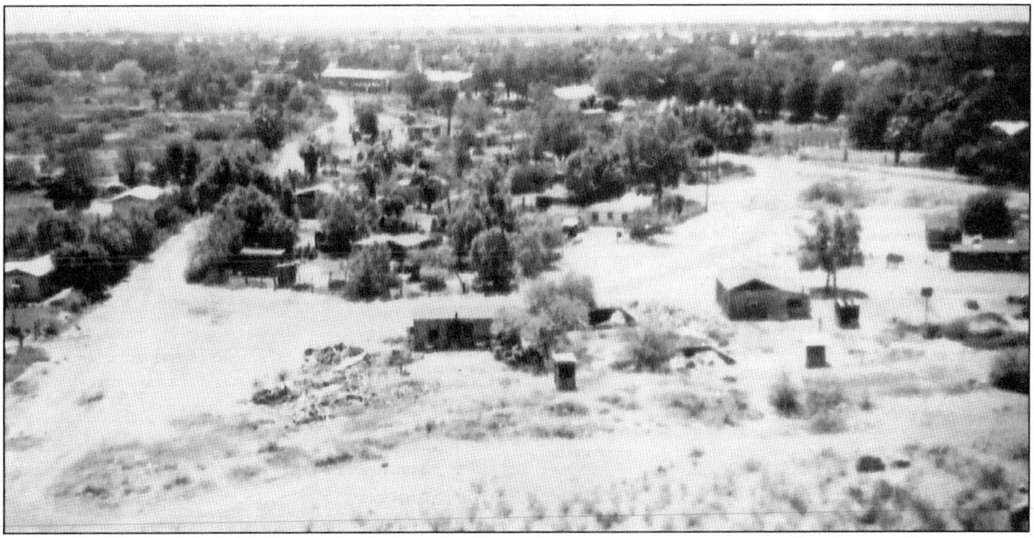

A view shows the barrio Mickey Mouse, a name later given to an area adjacent to the original barrio San Pablo at the foot of the buttes. (Norma C. Pinate.)

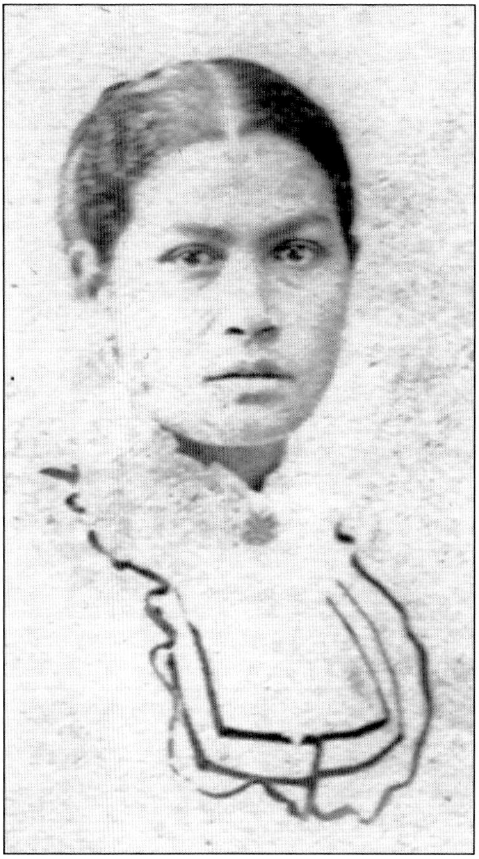

Alcaria Montoya Jones was born on December 12, 1846, in Altar, Sonora, Mexico, and died on August 21, 1923, in Phoenix, Arizona. She is the mother of the Jones girls, including Kate Jones Gomez, mother of John Floyd Jones Gomez and great-grandmother of Irene Gomez Hormell, as well as other family members in Tempe. (Irene Gomez Hormell.)

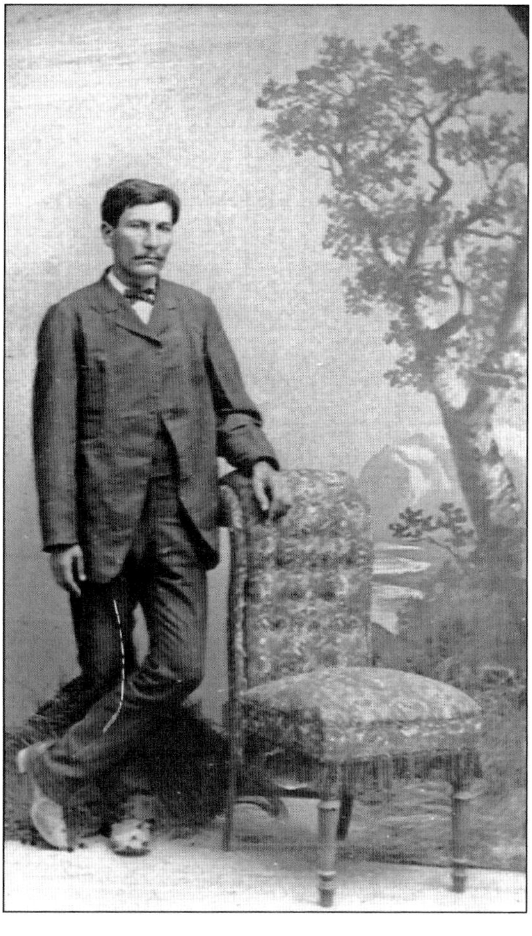

Francisco Monroy, known as Uncle "Tio" Monroy, was born in the mid-1800s. He was related to Alcaria Montoya Jones and was employed by Dr. Walter Wilson Jones, an early territorial pioneer, as a vaquero on his ranch, Blue Point Ranch, east of Tempe. Ranch work demonstrated by vaqueros and learned by younger generations, in time, led to the cowboy ranch work and culture. Monroy taught John Floyd Gomez Sr., Dr. Jones's grandson, the work of a desert vaquero when John Floyd was 11 years old. (Irene Gomez Hormell.)

Joaquina "Quina" Jones, born in 1877, was a sister of Kate Jones. She later married Adolpho Romo Sr. (Irene Gomez Hormell.)

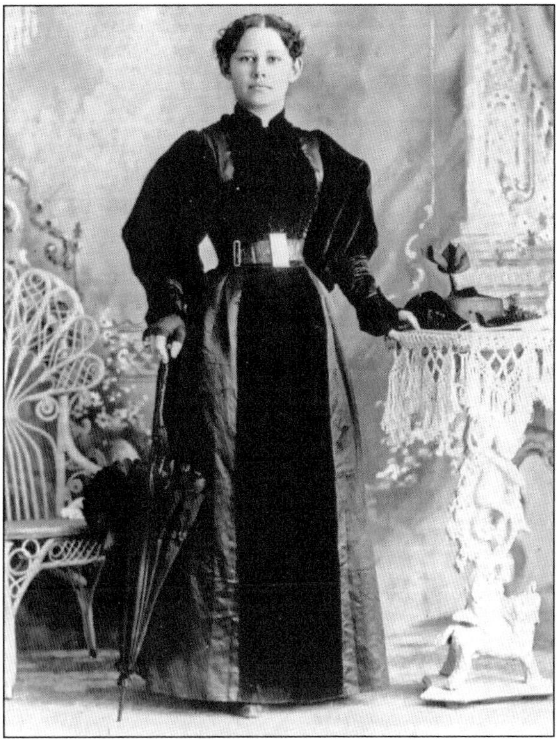

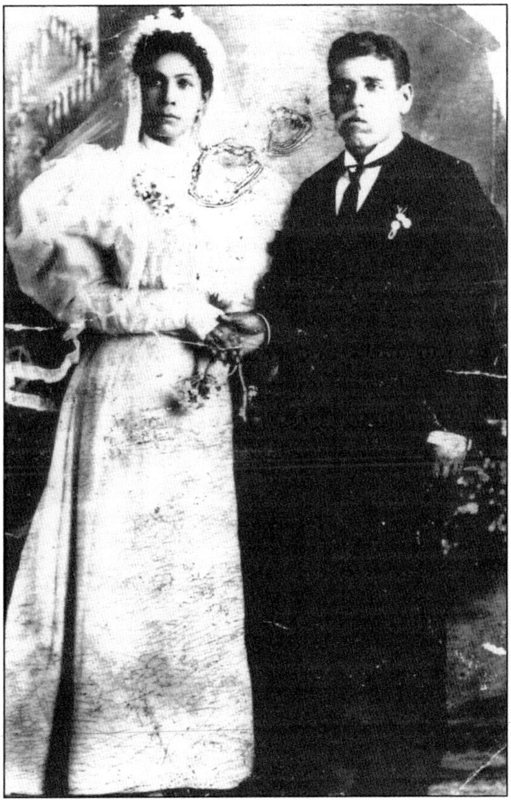

This photograph shows Kate Jones and Jesus Aros Gomez. Kate Jones, a daughter of Alcaria Montoya Jones and sister of Joaquina "Quina" Jones, was born on June 7, 1875. Later she married Jesus Aros Gomez. Jesus and Kate were the parents of John Floyd Jones Gomez Sr., who was the father of Irene Gomez Hormell.

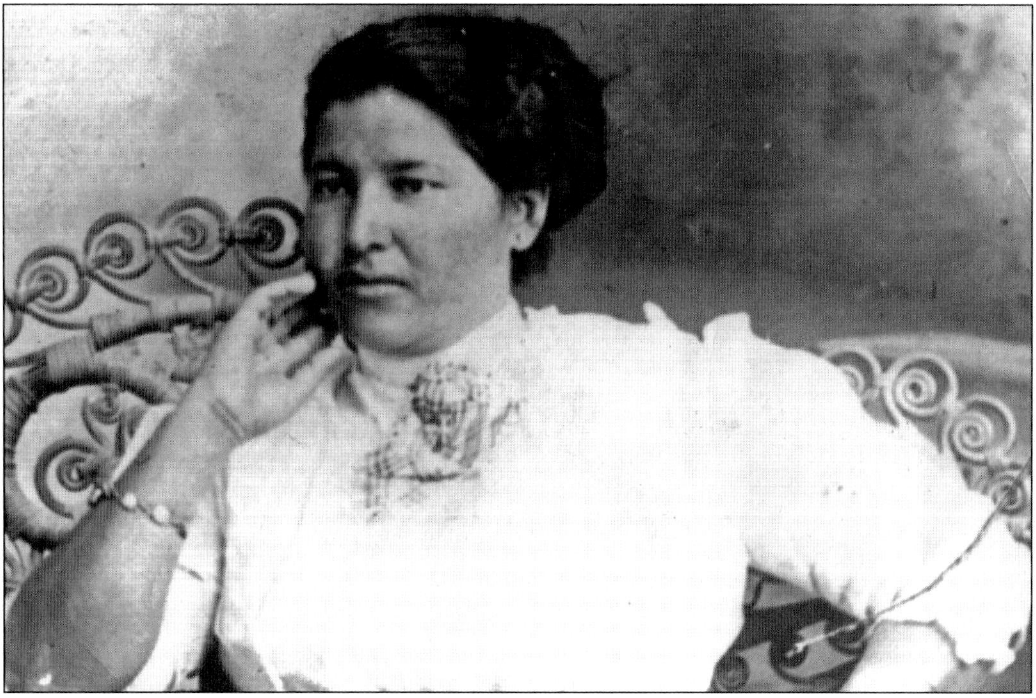

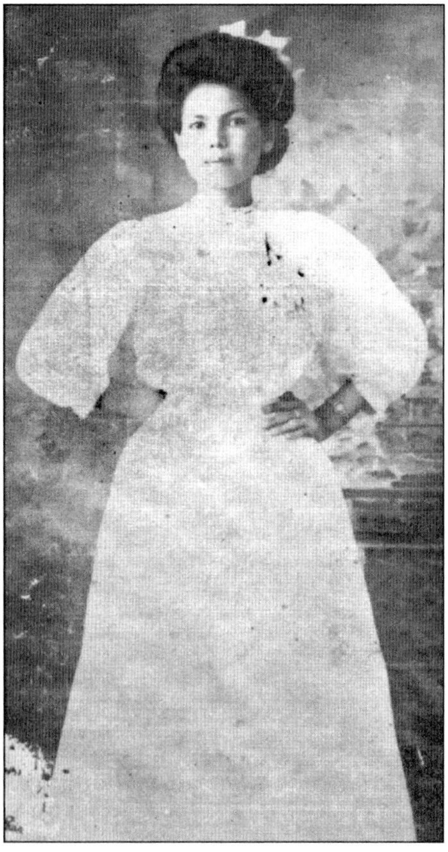

Margarita Monreal was one of the pioneer settlers of Arizona. She was born in Tucson on March 10, 1882. Later she moved to Tempe to live with her daughter Narcisa Espinoza. (Narcisa Espinoza.)

This *c.* 1906 picture shows Elizabeth Cruz Rodriguez in Tempe, Arizona. She is the grandmother of Elizabeth Rodriguez Montanez de Rivera. (Elizabeth M. Rivera.)

This photograph shows "Babe" Adolpho Romo Sr. (seated) and his brother Miguel Romo. Babe is noted for being the first meat butcher in Tempe. Babe was born in Seville, Spain, in the mid-1800s. Babe Romo is also remembered for having fought the practice of segregated schools in Tempe.

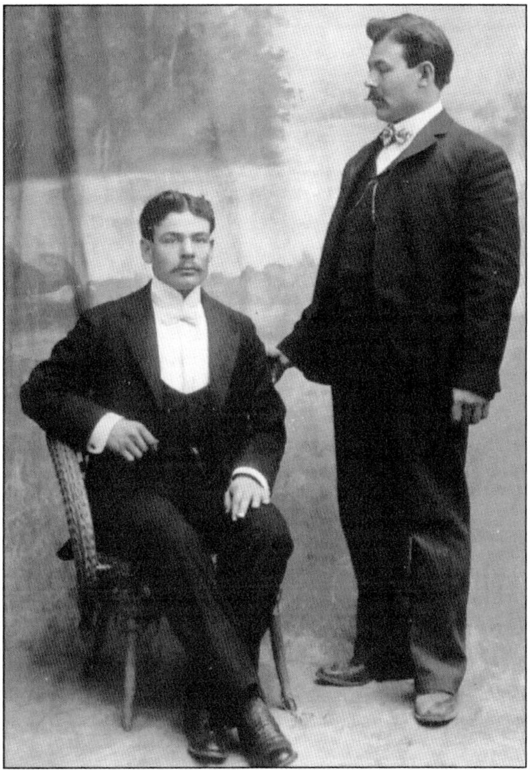

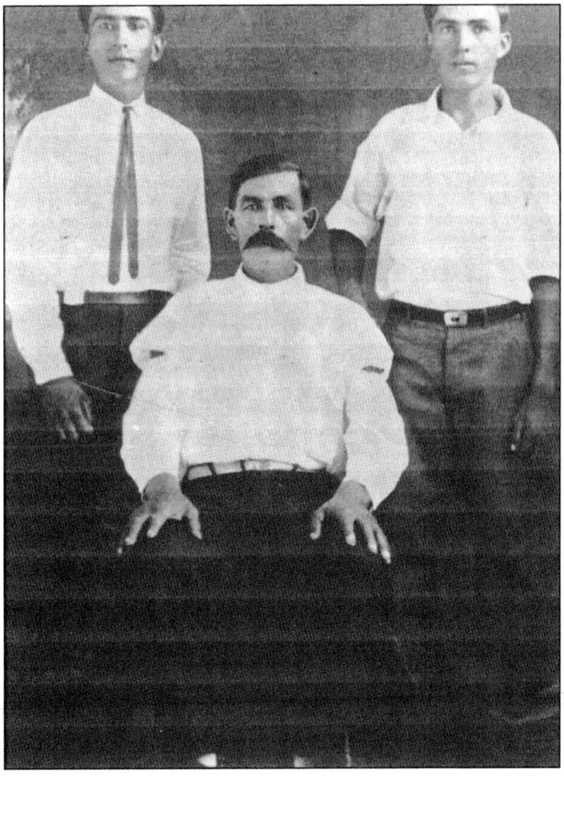

From left to right are Mike Romero Leon Jr., Miguel Leon Sr., and Eugenio "Gene" Romero Leon. The year was 1911. Years later, Miguel worked for the Reynolds Aluminum Plant in Phoenix. Mike and Eugenio "Gene" Leon worked for the Hayden Flour Mill in Tempe.

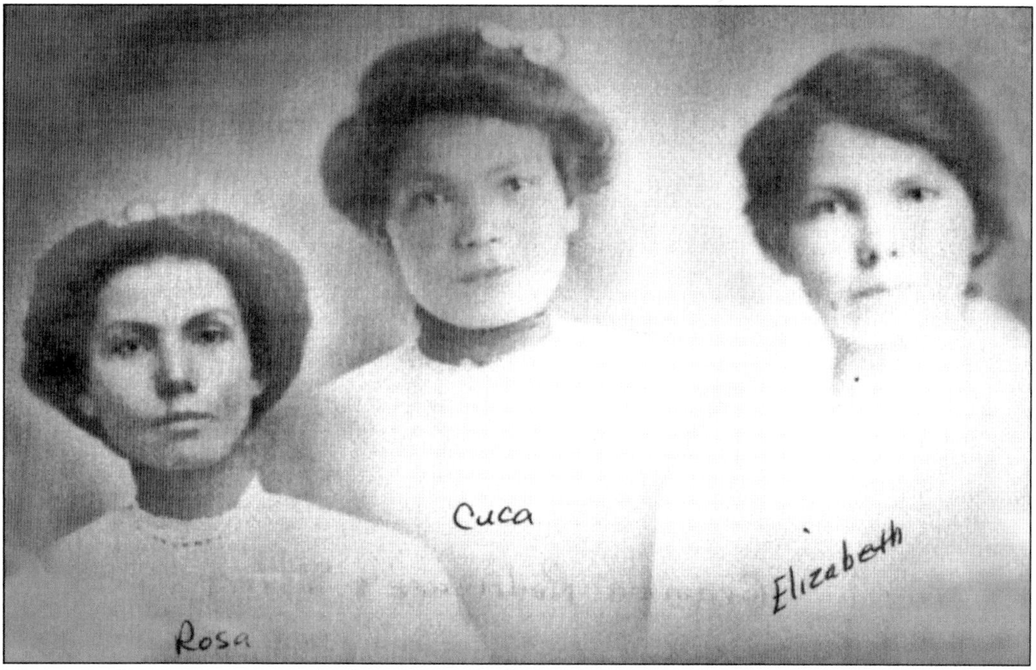

Three Rodriguez sisters in the late 1800s included Rosa (left), Cuca (center), and Elizabeth Rodriguez (right). Elizabeth was the grandmother of Elizabeth Rodriguez Montanez de Rivera. (Rev. Mardy Olivas.)

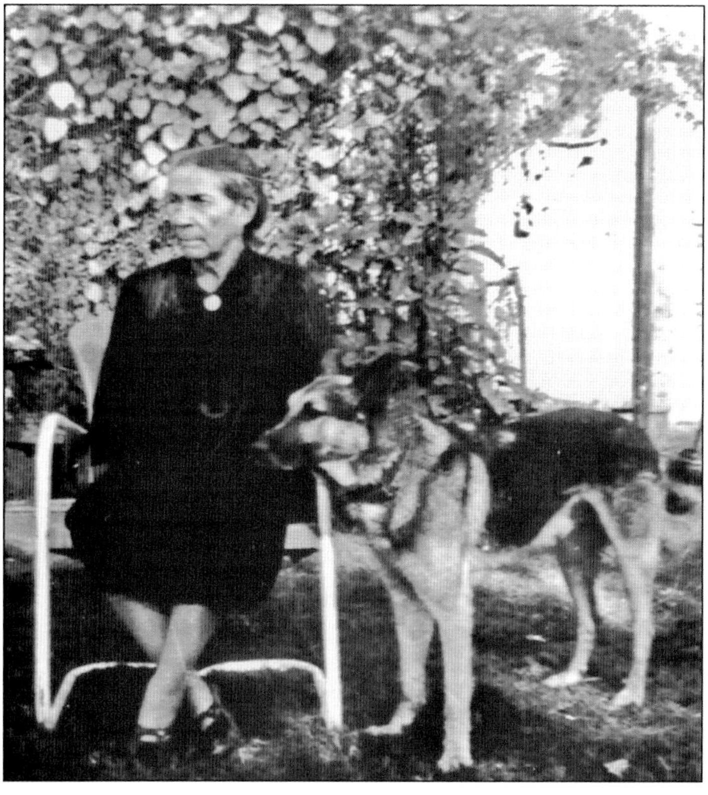

Kathryn "Kate" Jones Gomez sits in front of the big Gomez Ranch, located at what is today the intersection of Fifty-eighth Street and University Drive, when the area was vast and empty of population and homes. Jesus Aros and Kate Gomez were the parents of John Floyd (born on September 15, 1900), Mary, Inez, George, and Ralph Gomez. These early family members helped build Tempe.

This photograph shows Margaret "Big Maggie" Jones Frank's children in the 1900s. From left to right are Margaret "Little Maggie," Walter, and Nellie Frank.

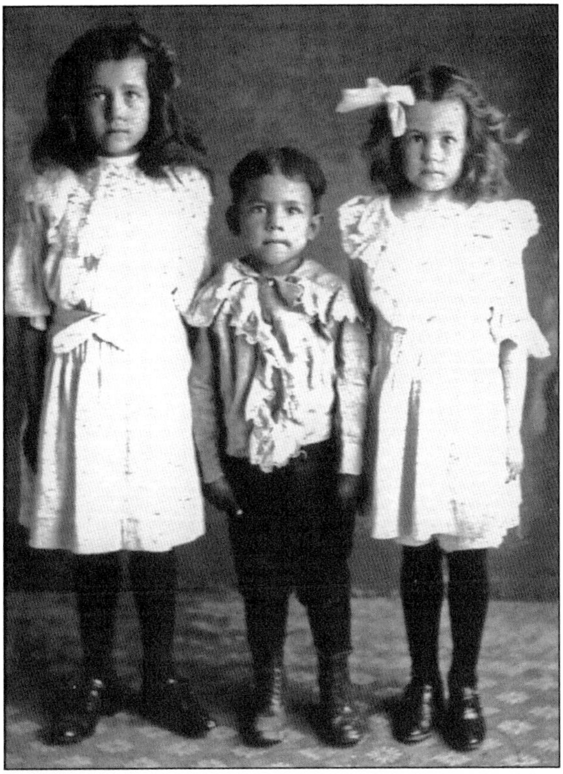

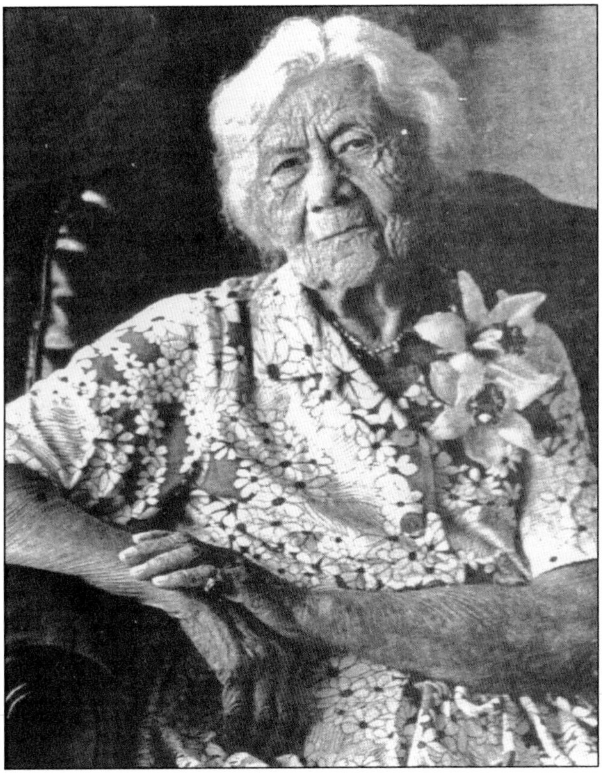

Margaret "Big Maggie" Jones Frank, born on August 24, 1880, celebrated her 100th birthday in 1980 with her son Dick Frank.

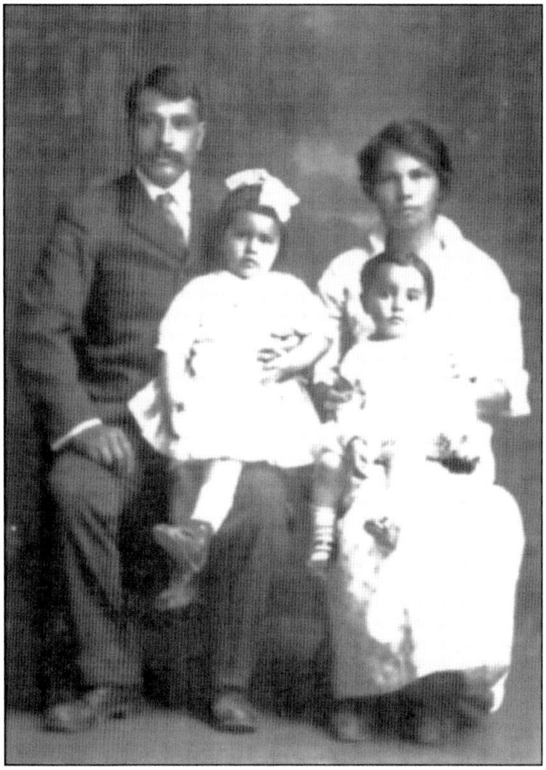

Jose Maria Rodriguez and Elizabeth Cruz Rodriguez, pictured around 1906 in Tempe, hold their children Anita (on Jose's lap) and Abraham "Abe." Jose Maria had at first settled in Florence but moved his family to Tempe around 1888. (Elizabeth M. Rivera.)

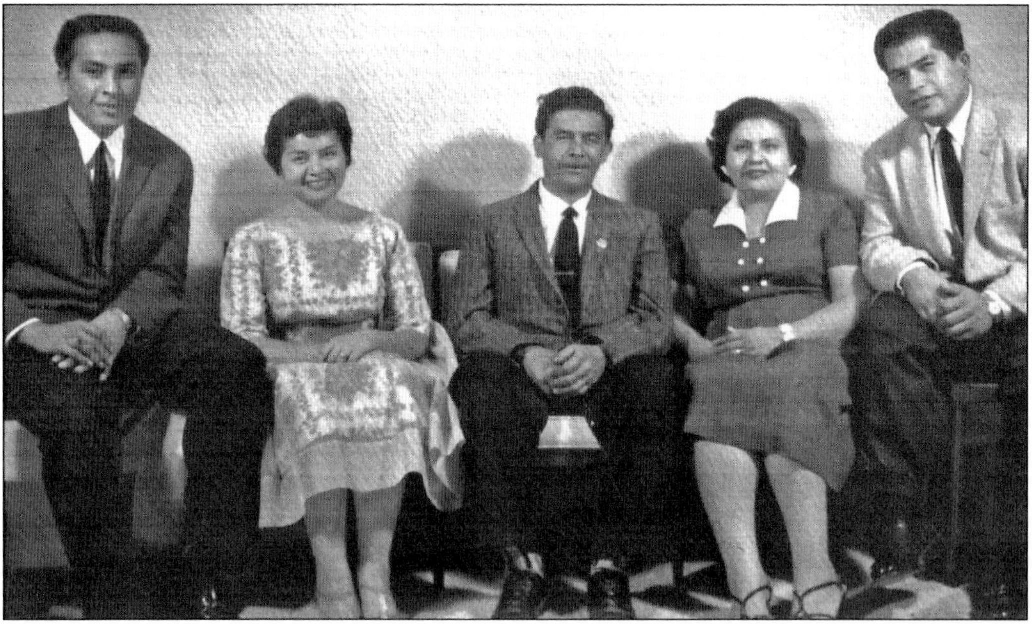

A family picture of Elizabeth M. Rivera (second from the left) shows her parents, Ysa Montanez (third from the left) and Anita Rodriguez Montanez (fourth from the left). The others are Isaac (far left) and Ben (far right). The family resided in Tempe for many years but moved to California, where they now live and work. But like many other former Tempeneños, they keep informed about Tempe and return to visit on special occasions. (Elizabeth M. Rivera.)

John Floyd Jones Gomez is pictured at age three wearing his new boots. John was born on September 15, 1900, as the first child of Kate Jones and Jesus Aros Gomez. Kate was the daughter of Dr. Walter Wilson Jones and Alcaria Montoya. Jesus had origins in the Presidio at Tubac when the land area that is now Arizona was a territory called the Provincias Internas, ruled by Spain. Jesus A. Gomez was a vaquero in the Tubac area and came to the Tempe area when he was hired by Dr. Jones. Jesus met Kate and married her, and they had five children: John Floyd, George, Ralph, Mary, and Inez Gomez.

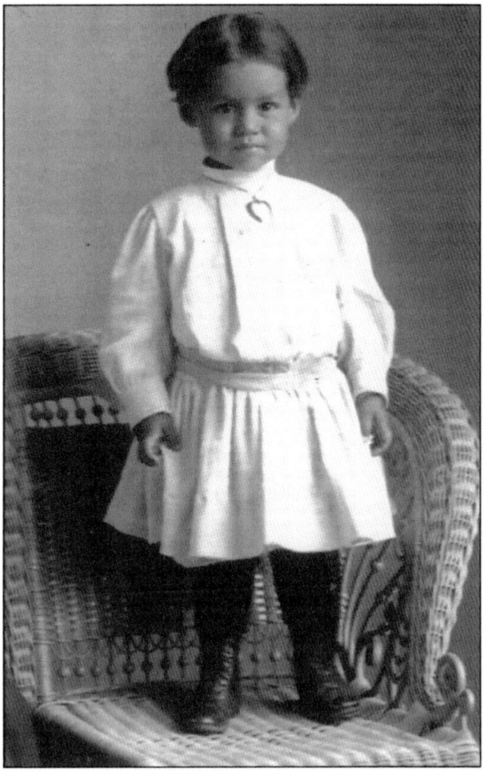

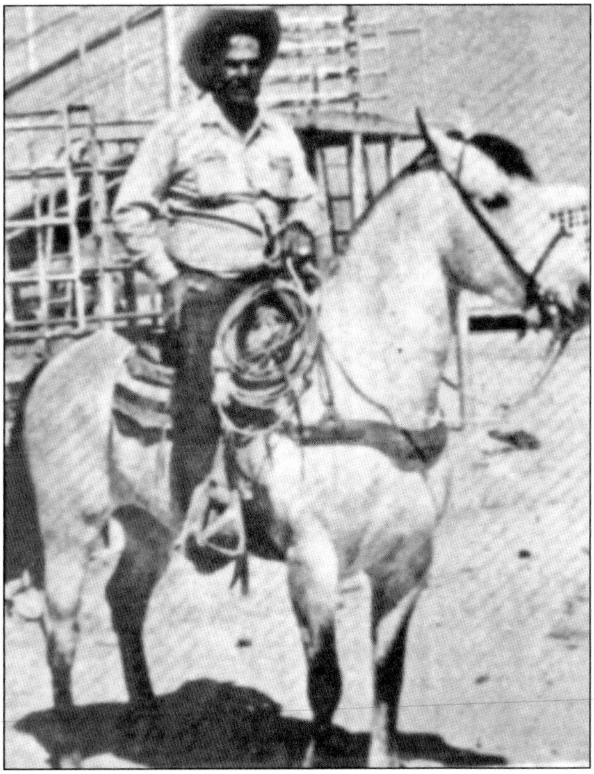

John Floyd Gomez Sr.'s life's ambition was to grow up and be a vaquero. He became a vaquero—later in English a "cowboy." Floyd Gomez Sr. worked and lived in Tempe but also started and worked his ranch in Casa Grande around 1960. Vaqueros had initiated the ranching industry in what is today the southwest United States in the early 1600s. From their ranching heritage emerged the cattle industry.

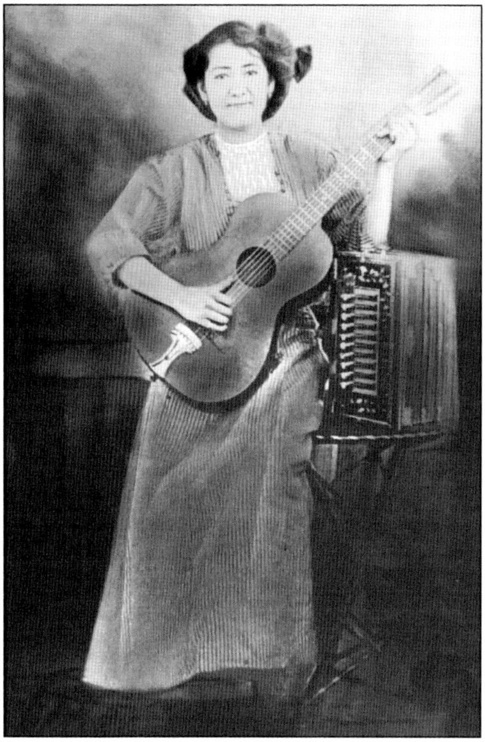

Marina Rojo was born in 1893. She and her husband, John Martinez, were the parents of John Rojo Martinez. John attended Tempe High School, where he gained recognition as being good in sports. John was the father of Johnny Martinez, who years later played quarterback on Tempe High School's football team in 1956, when they won the state championship. (Johnny Martinez.)

A 1947 family picture shows John Rojo Martinez, his wife, Margarita Guerra Martinez, and their children. From left to right are (first row) Barbara Jean Martinez, Cecilia Martinez, and Richard Martinez; (second row) Robert "Bobby" Martinez, John R. Martinez, and Margarita G. Martinez. The family lived at the time on 410 Ash Avenue in Tempe. (Johnny Martinez.)

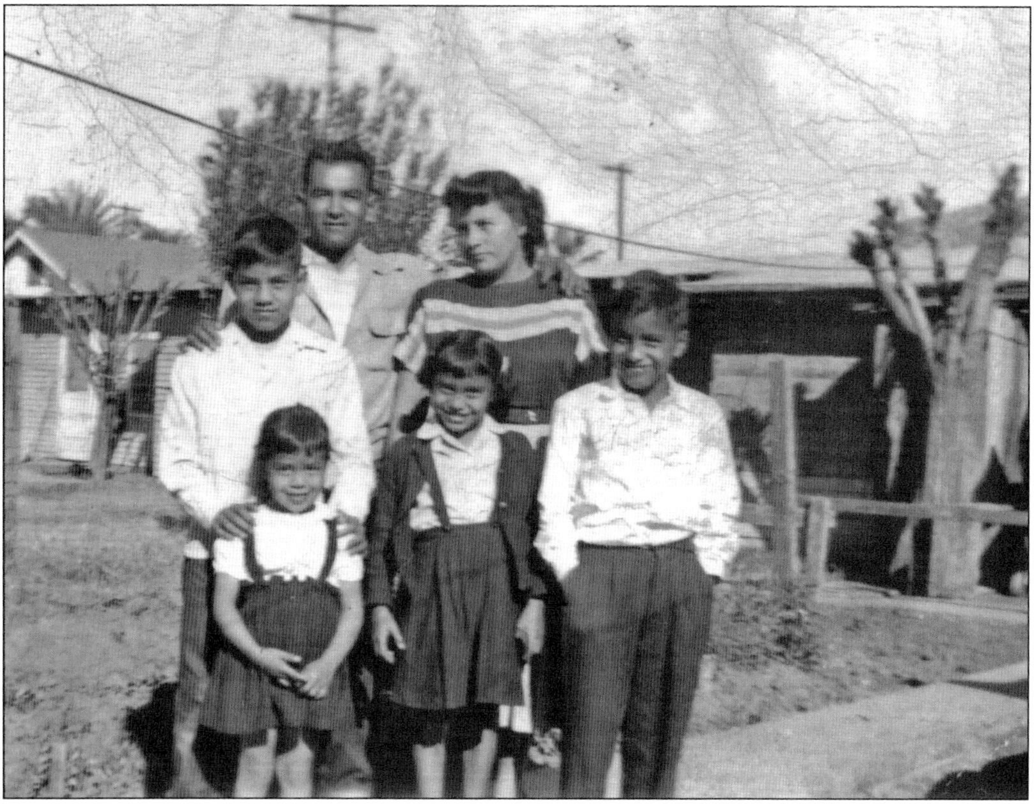

Cresencio Varela, a Tempe resident, was the first Mexican worker employed by the City of Tempe. Cresencio, pictured in 1905, came from Mesilla, New Mexico. He worked for the city watering down the unpaved dirt streets at the time. His first wife died in childbirth. Later he met and married Guadalupe Acedo, and they established their family home on Sixth Street across from where the state constructed the National Guard Building. Their granddaughter Ramona Varela was the first Mexican American to pursue a religious vocation from Mount Carmel Parish in Tempe. She became a Benedictine religious cloistered nun and now is the prioress of her Tucson order.

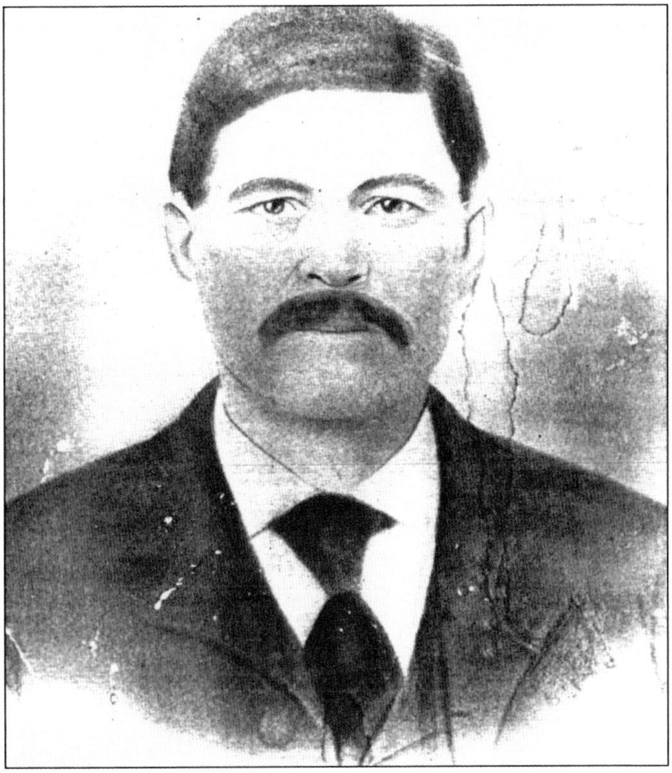

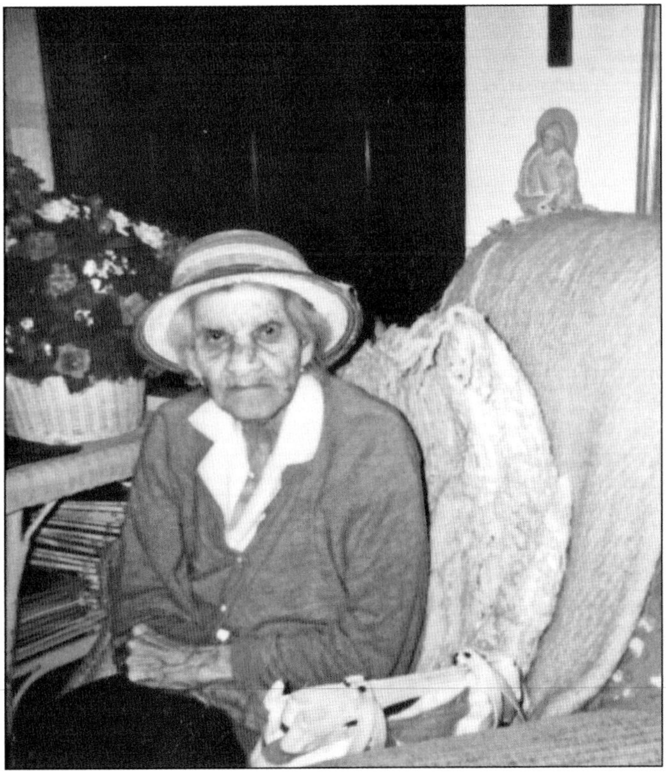

Flora and Juan Martinez lived in the Mickey Mouse barrio in the 1950s. She was considered the barrio storyteller. This was an important part of the barrios prior to television and affordable movies. Flora worked in the fields doing hard farm work. After the end of her work day, she would return home, sweep the dirt area under the large tree, and prepare for the barrio children to sit. Then they would listen to her stories. It is said that grandmothers (*abuelitas*) taught religious practice to their children. Flora Martinez taught the children heritage and culture through stories. Her husband, Juan, worked in construction. Flora lived more than 100 years. She was born in Texas but moved to Tempe in 1917.

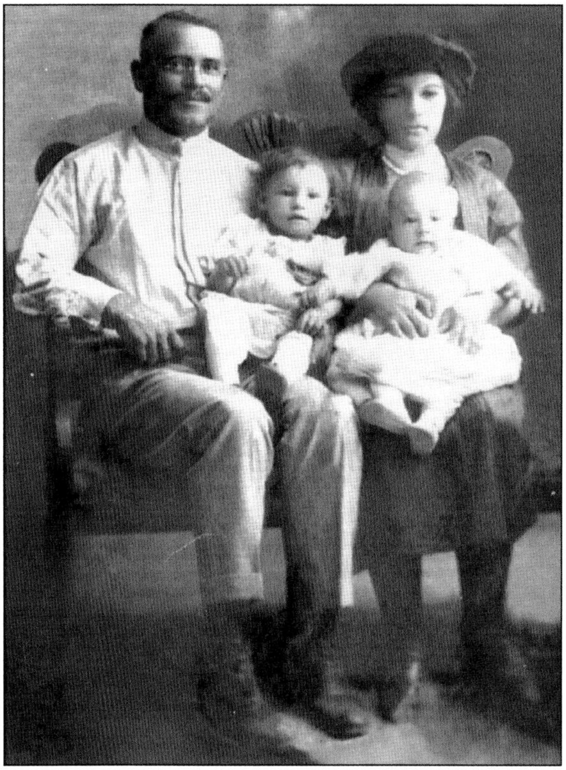

Juan Rodriguez Jimenez and his wife, Gertrudes (called "Tula"), hold their children, Mary (left) and baby John Jr. Mary was also called "Tulita Marta." The father, Juan, was called "Caballos" ("horses") because he was a horse trader. Thus his popular name was Juan Caballos.

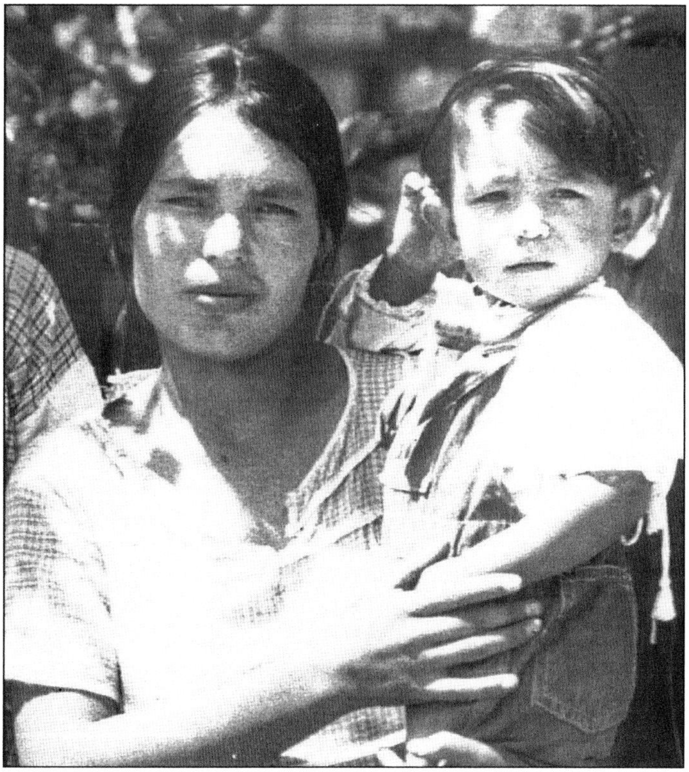

Eutimia Villagomez Hernandez holds her baby boy Encarnacion Hernandez when he was two years old. Eutimia was born on December 18, 1907, and Encarnacion was born in 1927. (Rachel Hernandez Pollack.)

Philomena Rico Dominguez, born in the 1860s, was the great-grandmother of Josie Rodriguez Ortega Solis. (Josie O. Solis.)

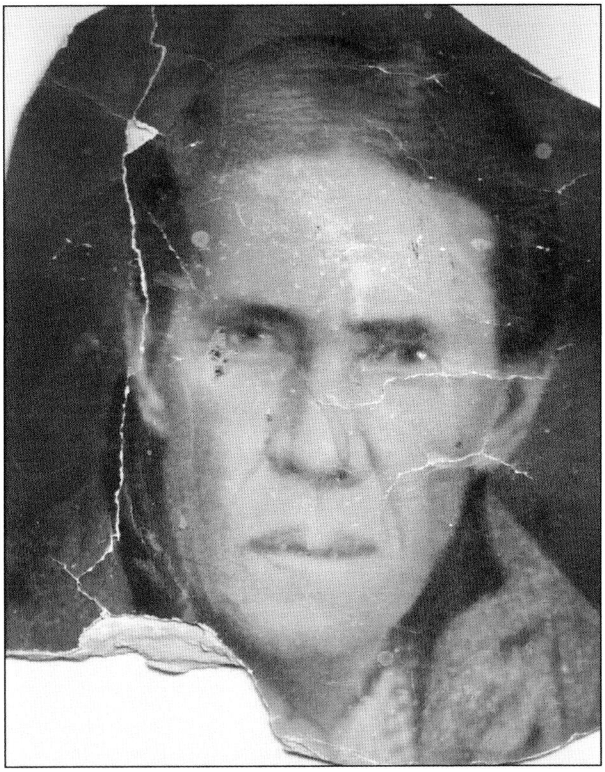

In the photograph below, Carmen Ortega Solis (left) and Josephina Ortega Enriquez (right) are two sisters sitting in the park in the mid-1970s. Philomena Rico Dominguez, pictured at right, was their mother. Carmen Ortega Solis was Josephine Ortega Solis's mother. Josephine Ortega Solis earned a master's degree in psychology from Arizona State University. This story line, like other stories told by these photographs, illustrates how heritage, culture, and potential are passed along through time and space in the lives of Tempeneños.

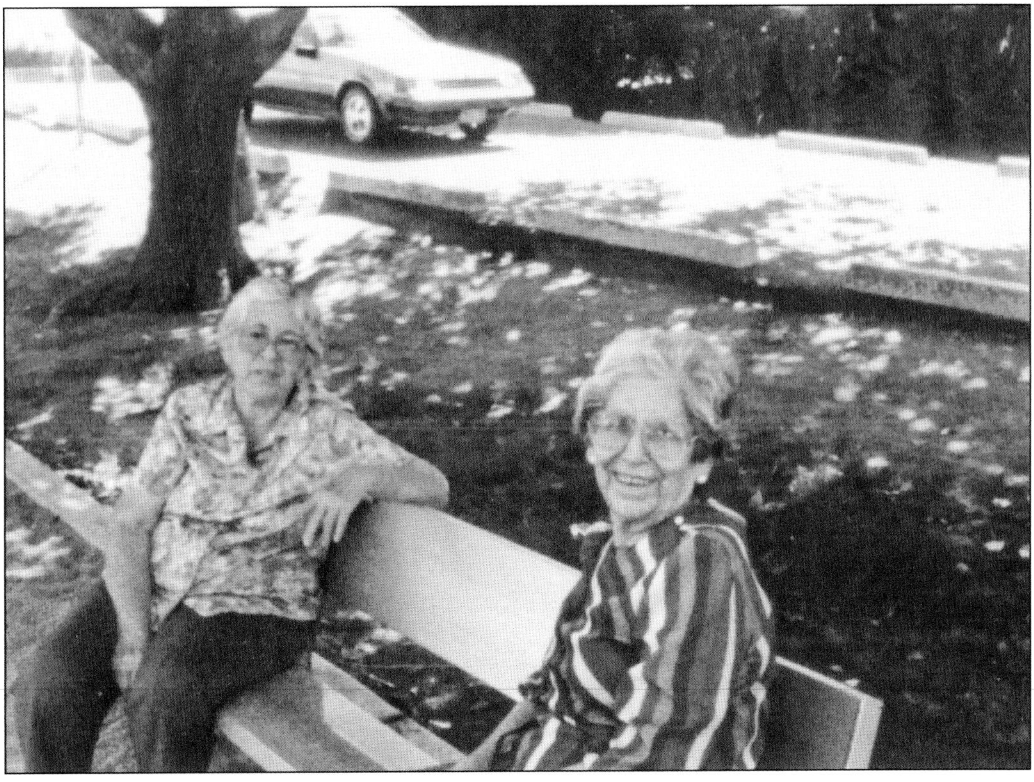

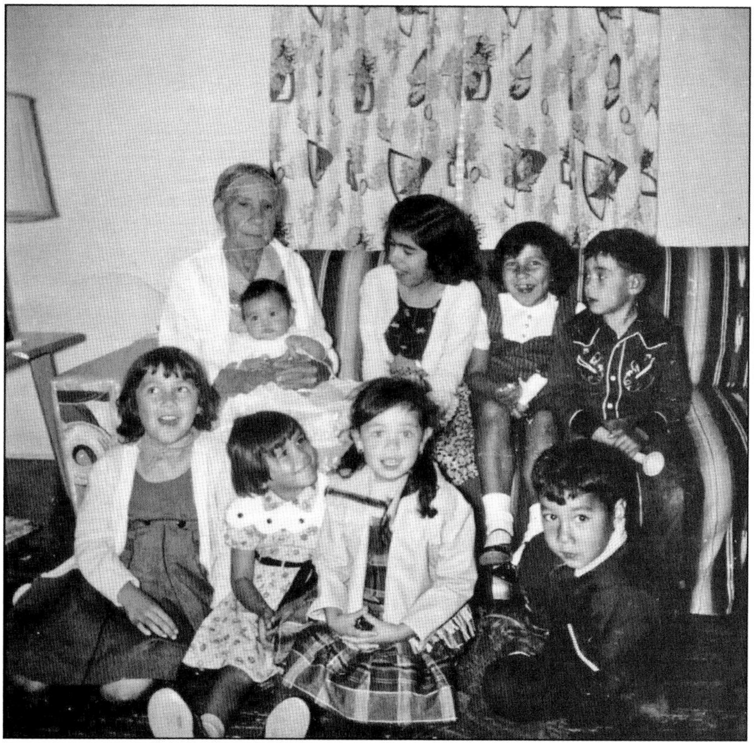

Francisca Dominguez Ortega is shown in this photograph with her grandchildren in October 1955. From left to right are (first row) Yolanda Berumen, Margie Berumen, Josie Solis, and Valentino Sanchez; (second row) Francisca Dominguez Ortega holding baby Carmen Solis, Adelita Sanchez, Rachel Berumen, and Leo Enriquez. (Josie O. Solis.)

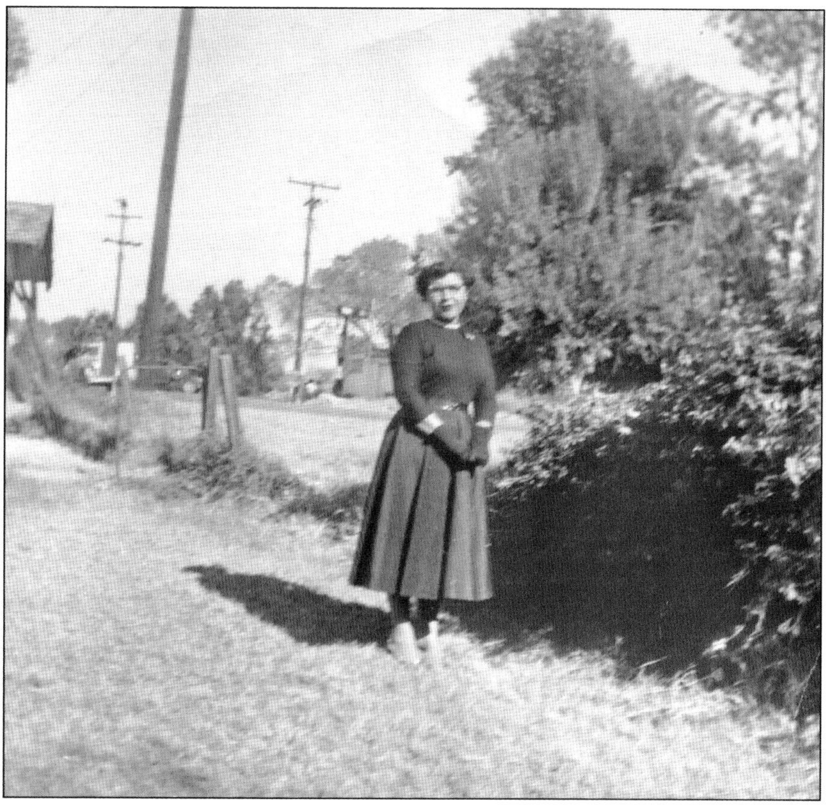

Mary Sterling Peralta poses in front of her home on Rural Road and Tyler Street in 1936. (Barney S. Peralta.)

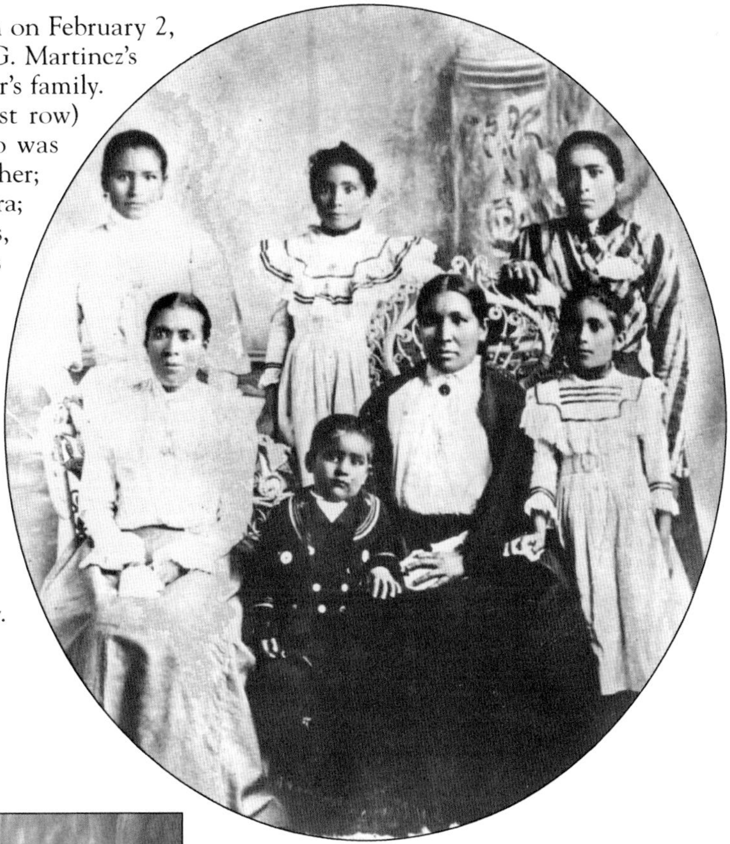

This photograph was taken on February 2, 1889. Pictured are Johnny G. Martinez's maternal great-grandmother's family. From left to right are (first row) Lazara Flores Guerra, who was Johnny's maternal grandmother; Elias Flores, brother of Lazara; Dominga Contreras Flores, Lazara's mother and Johnny's great-grandmother; and Maria Flores; (second row) Dominga Flores, daughter of Dominga Contreras Flores; unidentified; and Juanita Flores. Johnny Martinez worked for the City of Tempe in water maintenance for years, and the city named a building the Johnny G. Martinez Water Management Facility. (Johnny G. Martinez.)

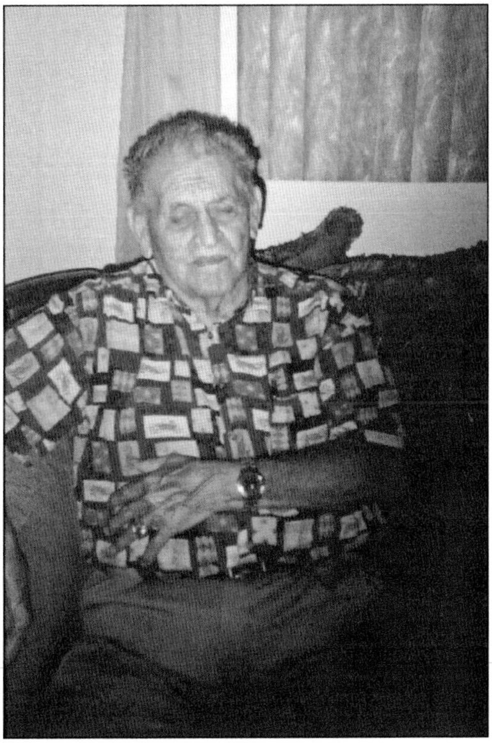

Jose "Joe" Vicerra Ruiz is a member of an early Tempe settler family that helped build the railroad in the late 1880s. The family lived in Maricopa for some time, moved to Tempe and then Phoenix, working on the railroad. They were called the railroad people; they lived in railroad housing sections (Secciónes) or homes provided by the railroad company for workers. Ruiz is also noted for his military service; he served in four wars to help keep the United States of America safe: World War II, Korea, Vietnam, and Desert Storm. By his railroad work and his service, he helped support his family. The family owns the water spring east of Apache Junction.

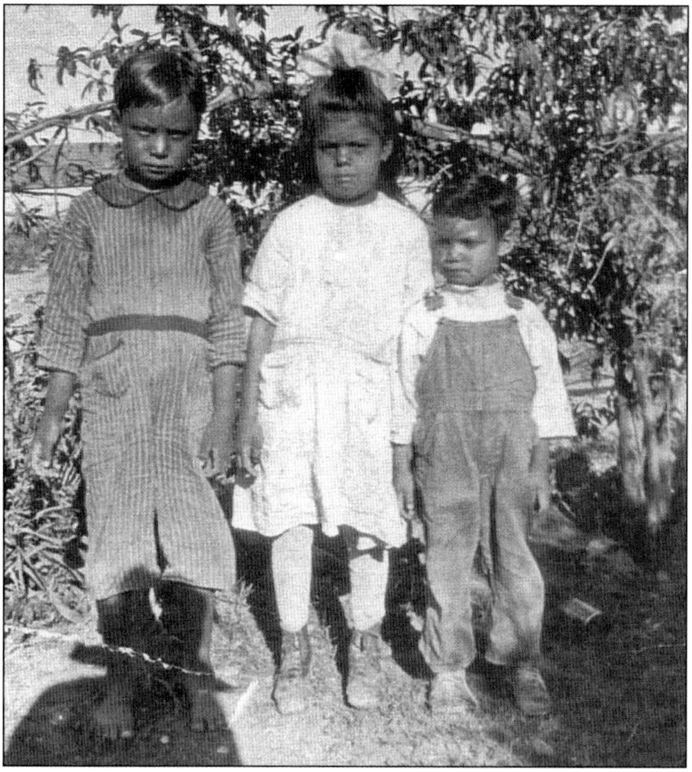

This photograph shows three young children who developed their God-given potential as they grew up. From left to right are Juan Lopez, Leonor Lopez, and Jose Maria Lopez. They came to Tempe in 1910 as orphaned children raised by an aunt named Margaret Chavarria. Juan served his country well in World War II, died overseas, and is buried in Italy. Jose Maria died when he was hit by a train. Leonor married Victor Arroyo Sr. and is the mother of Victor Jr., Rudy, Bertha, Tony, Rueben, and Aelia. The Arroyo families have populated Tempe and continue to grow. When Leonor became a widow, she started her own tamale and dough *masa* shop in Tempe in the 1960s.

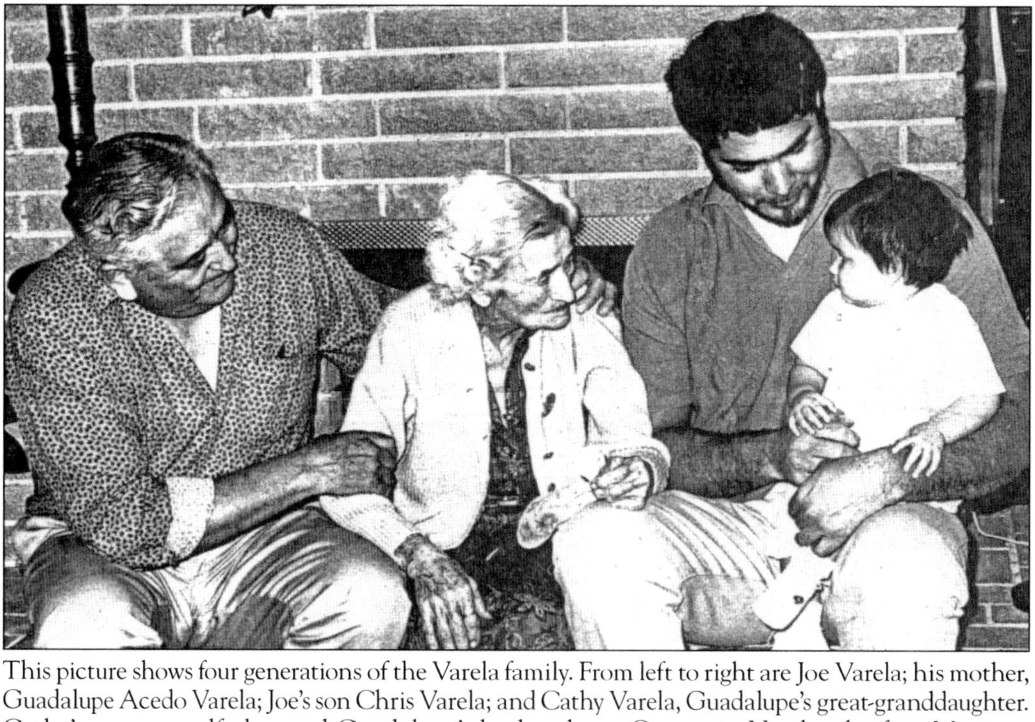

This picture shows four generations of the Varela family. From left to right are Joe Varela; his mother, Guadalupe Acedo Varela; Joe's son Chris Varela; and Cathy Varela, Guadalupe's great-granddaughter. Cathy's great-grandfather and Guadalupe's husband was Cresencio Varela, the first Mexican American hired by the City of Tempe, who watered the unpaved dirt streets of Tempe.

H. Z. and Mary Gray Compoy celebrated their anniversary of 44 years of marriage in 1990. The couple came to live in Tempe from the Ray/Sonora, Arizona, area. Well known in Tempe, they reside in Casa Grande.

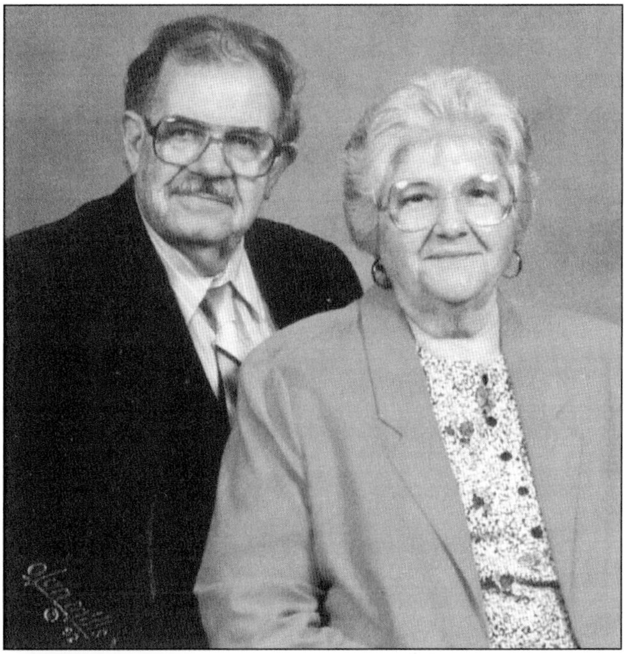

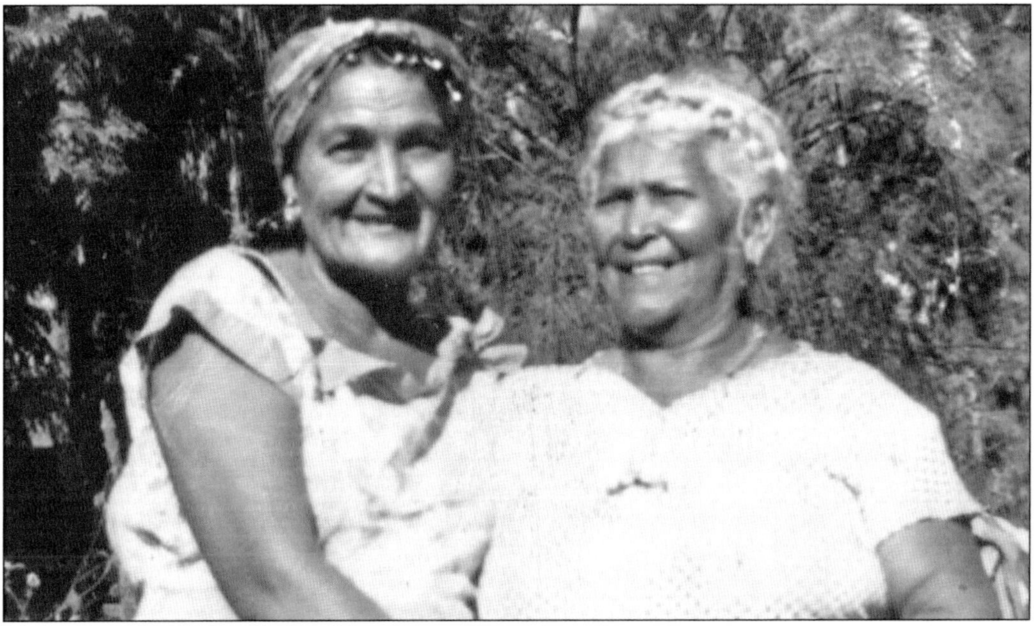

This 1953 photograph shows Teles Granillo Tobin Escalante (left) and Marina Ceballos Soto. Marina served the barrios in Tempe as a clothes peddler (*fayuquera*) when stores were scarce. Before people ordered from catalogues, Marina walked the neighborhoods taking orders from households for clothes and such. She then made trips to the Los Angeles Garment District and negotiated at good prices for the ordered goods. She delivered the ordered items to barrio residents. In this way, she helped support her family. There were an estimated 20 barrios in and about Tempe during her time. Marina served a necessary task before the arrival of clothing stores in Tempe. Her granddaughter Irene Gomez Hormell says that Marina was the first woman to plant cotton in the area, using seed from the federal government. She carried out her enterprises in and after 1917.

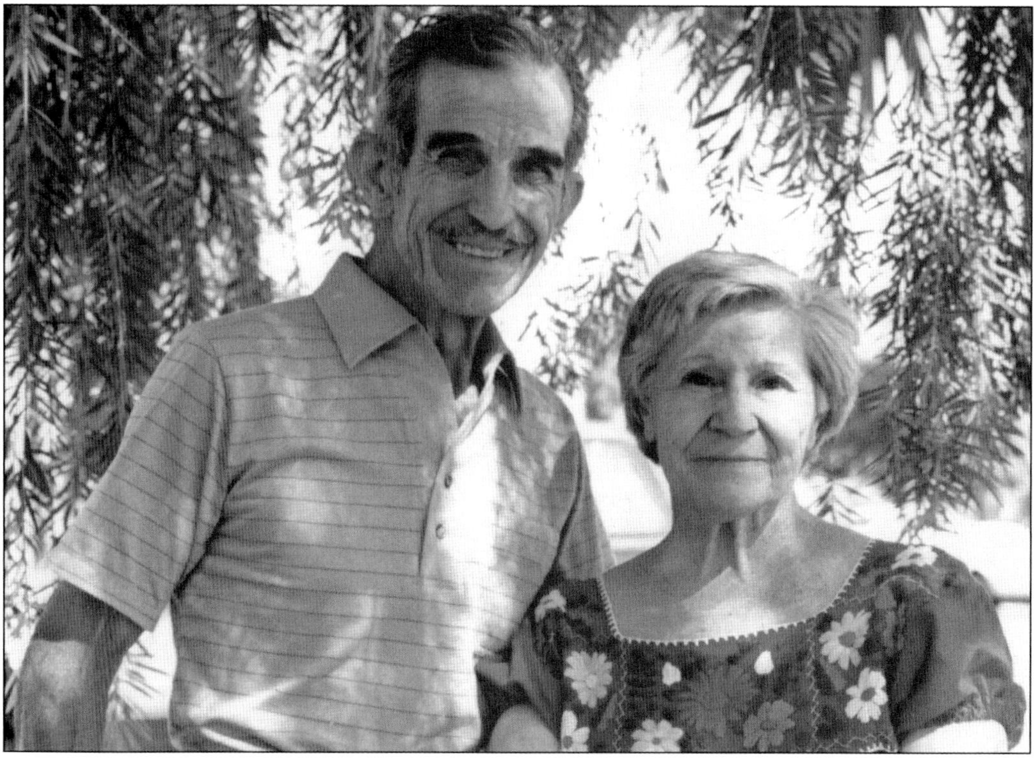

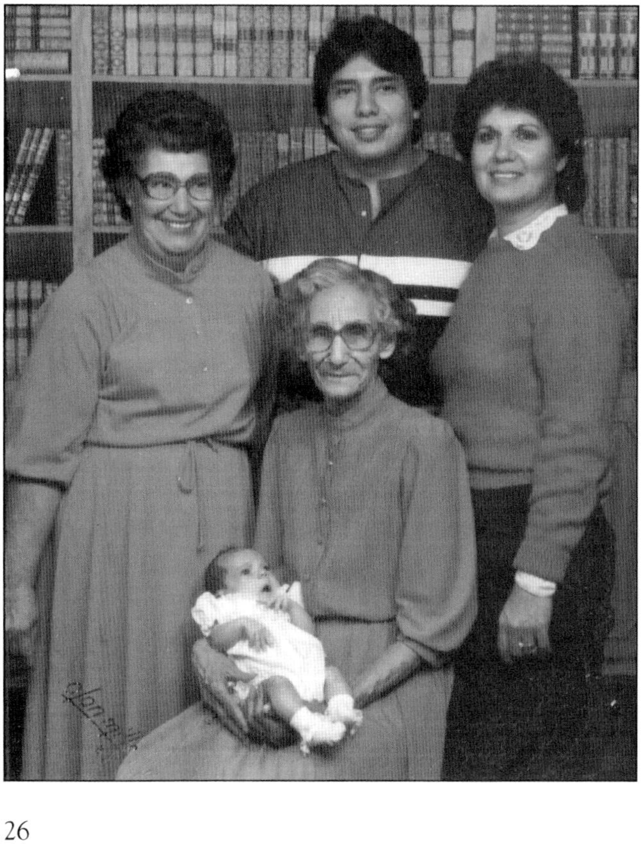

Felo and Helen Guaderrama migrated to Tempe from New Mexico. Mexican pioneers had settled New Mexico in the late 1500s. Felo had a heavy-duty trucking business in New Mexico. In Tempe, he was the first Mexican American to found a Schwinn bicycle business. Youths from all over the barrios came to his shop seeking bicycle parts and to repair broken bicycles. This photograph was taken on May 18, 1986.

Five generations of the family of Juliana Gonzalez Burgos (seated) are pictured in this 1983 photograph. Standing from left to right is Juliana's daughter Mary Burgos Kinlock, grandson Chris Arroyo, and Rachel Arroyo, Chris's mother. The baby, Anika, the fifth generation, held by great-grandmother Juliana, adds to the longtime Tempe family.

Two

TRADITIONS

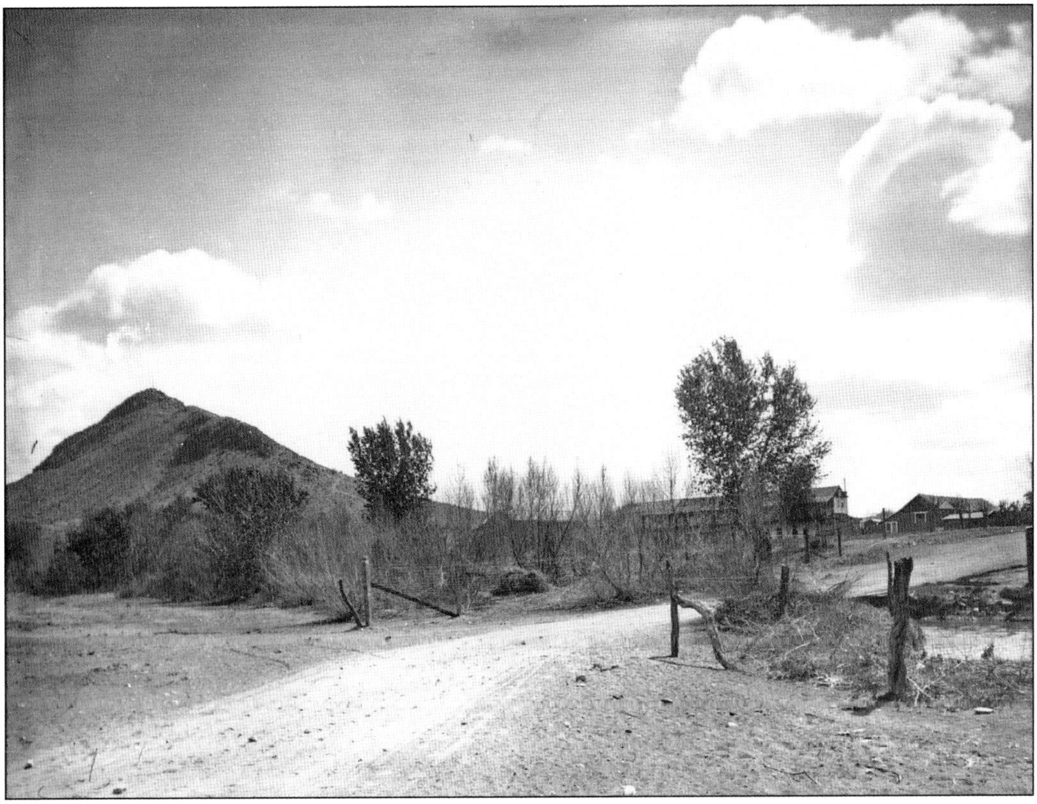

This 1890s picture of San Pablo shows the road called El Pasillo, which leads both ways in and out. This reflects the theme of "Huellas" or "footprints" in the first picture of the book. People, heritage, and culture come in and go out, ever changing. San Pablo gave rise to the Mickey Mouse barrio, and then as the Mexican immigrant population grew, the number of barrios grew and the amount of land expanded. San Pablo was the first barrio, settled in the mid-1800s by Yaqui and other Native Americans from Mexico and by Mexican people. Ancient Native American tribal people had inhabited the San Pablo barrio at the foot of the butte in the unrecorded past. San Pablo itself in time disappeared through the process of governmental public eminent domain laws to provide land space for what today is the Arizona State University campus. Indeed, El Pasillo served as the walkway from one way to another. (AHF.)

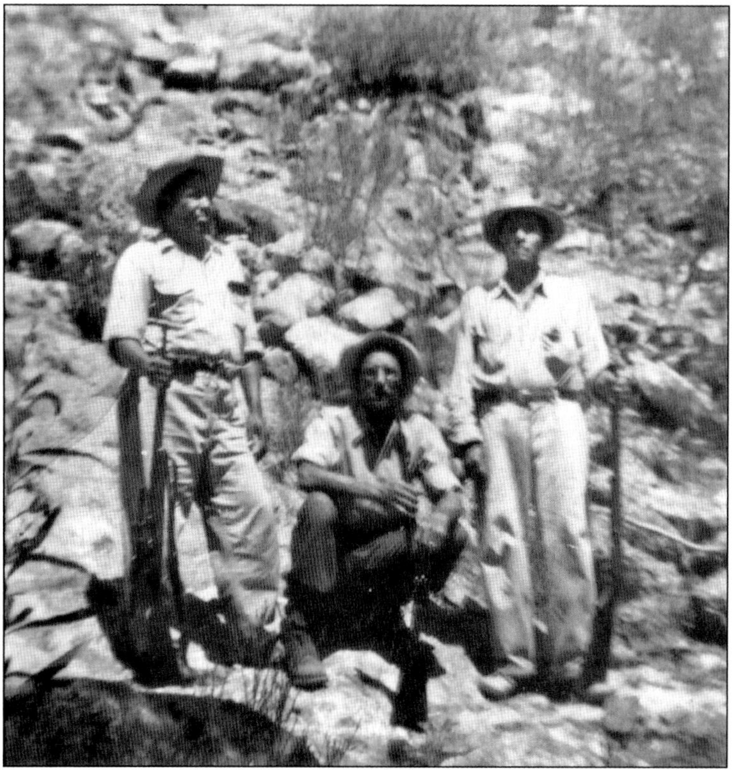

In the 1940s, Ramon Carbajal (left) participates in his annual deer hunt with friend Francisco "Chino" Gonzales (sitting on a rock) and an unidentified person on the right. Both Ramon and Francisco resided in San Pablo. (Norma C. Pinate, Carbajal family collection.)

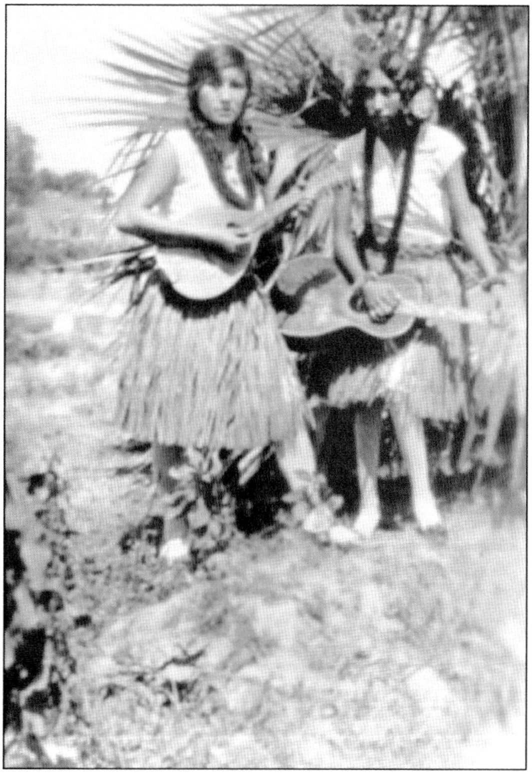

In the San Pablo barrio, in September 1932, Artemisa Carbajal (right), then 19 years old, and her unidentified friend spent a fun time playing music and singing during a Sunday afternoon. They dressed up in their Hawaiian skirts and leis. The music instruments, a guitar and a mandolin, belonged to Artemisa's brother Jose. (Norma C. Pinate, Carbajal family collection.)

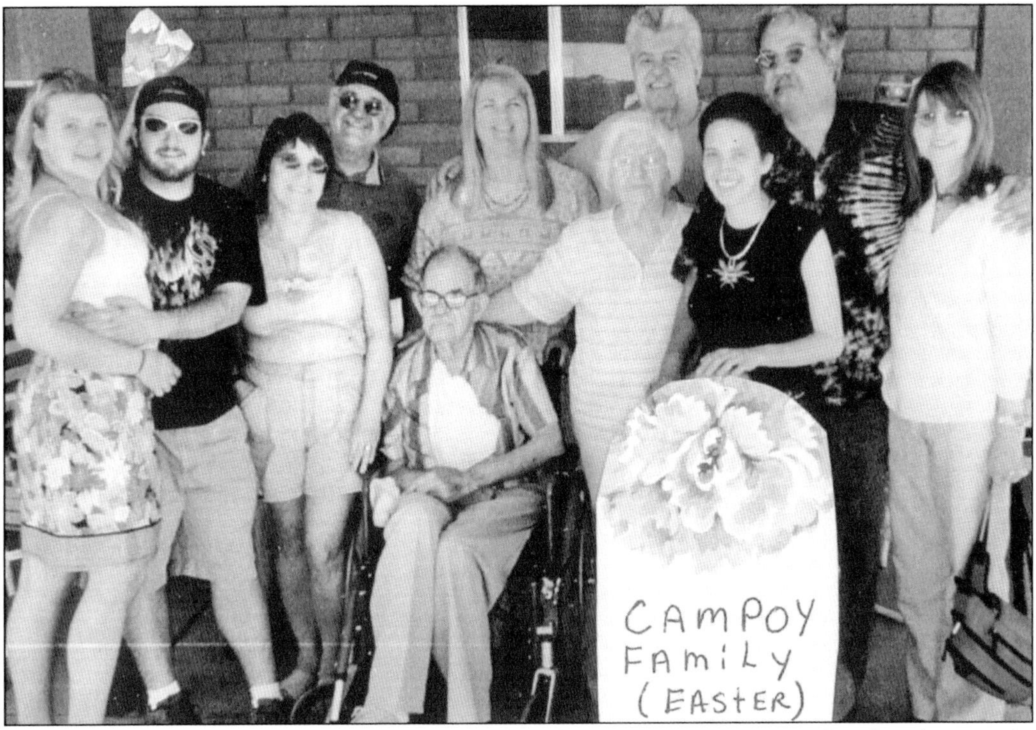

Mary Gray Compoy (standing sixth from the left) is of the 1920s generation, and in this photograph, she and her husband, H. Z. Compoy (seated in wheelchair), are shown celebrating a family reunion in 2004. Mary Gray actively participated in the Mexican Methodist Church, located in a barrio. The family gathered together during Easter, April 11, 2004. In the early times, barrio festivities such as barrio *tardeadas*, with outdoor dancing on dirt floors, encouraged family get-togethers.

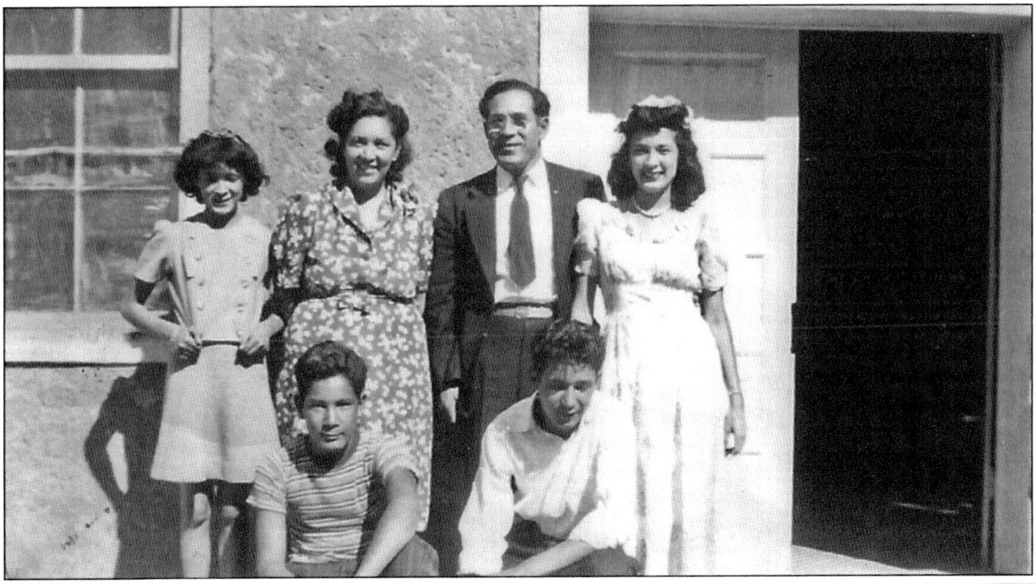

Mexican Methodist pastor Rev. William Portillo (standing, second from the right), his wife, Virginia (far right), and some of their children stand in front of the Methodist church. (Rev. Mardy Olivas.)

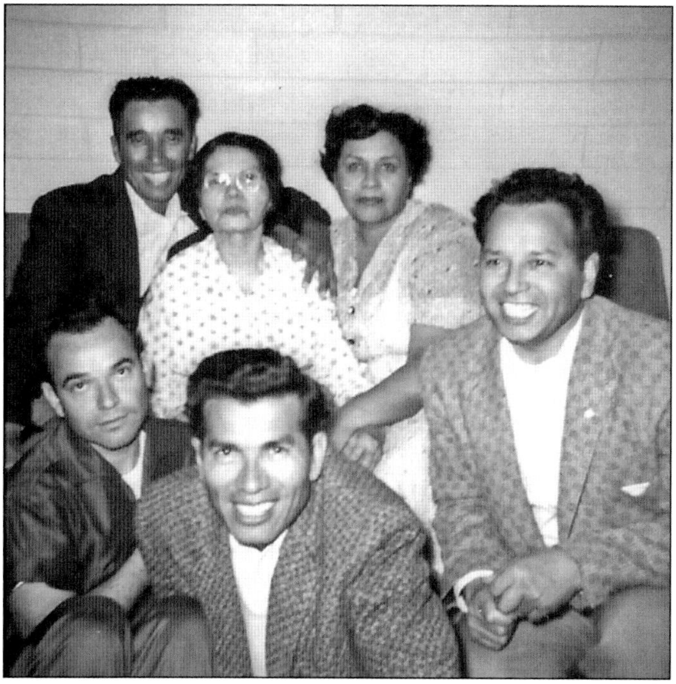

Ben Rodriguez's grandparents Jose Maria Rodriguez and Francisca Ortiz de Rodriguez migrated to Arizona in the late 1880s. The family moved to Tempe in the early 1900s. In the family photograph are, from left to right, (first row) David Rodriguez, Ben Rodriguez, and Daniel Rodriguez; (second row) Abraham Rodriguez, Isabel Rodriguez, and Anna Rodriguez. The family continued to reside in Tempe for some years, attended grade and high schools, and served in the military, but they later moved to California because of employment opportunities. (Elizabeth Rodriguez Montanez de Rivera.)

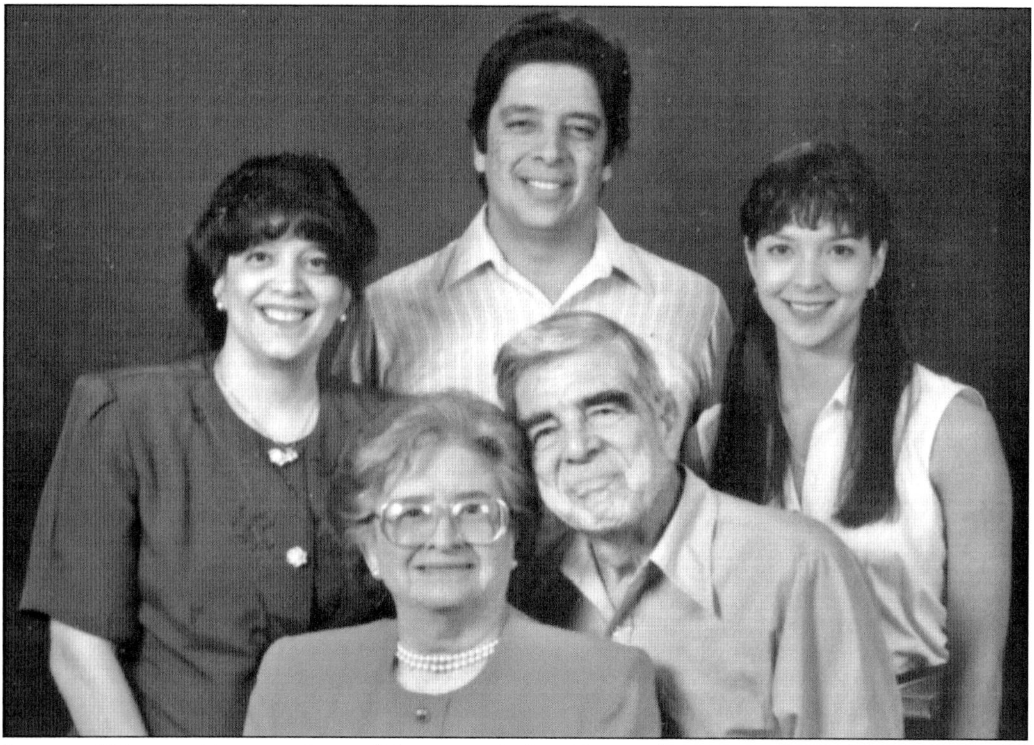

Jesus and Narcisa Espinoza (seated) have resided in Tempe for many years. They came to the Tempe area from Coolidge, Pinal County, into Phoenix, and then to Tempe. Standing from left to right are Cynthia, Thomas, and Elizabeth. The picture was taken on November 4, 1995. (Narcisa Espinoza.)

The Adrian and Cecilia Varela Mendez family has deep roots in Tempe. Cecilia worked for a local bank, and she is noted for her many years of active participation in Our Lady of Mount Carmel Parish.

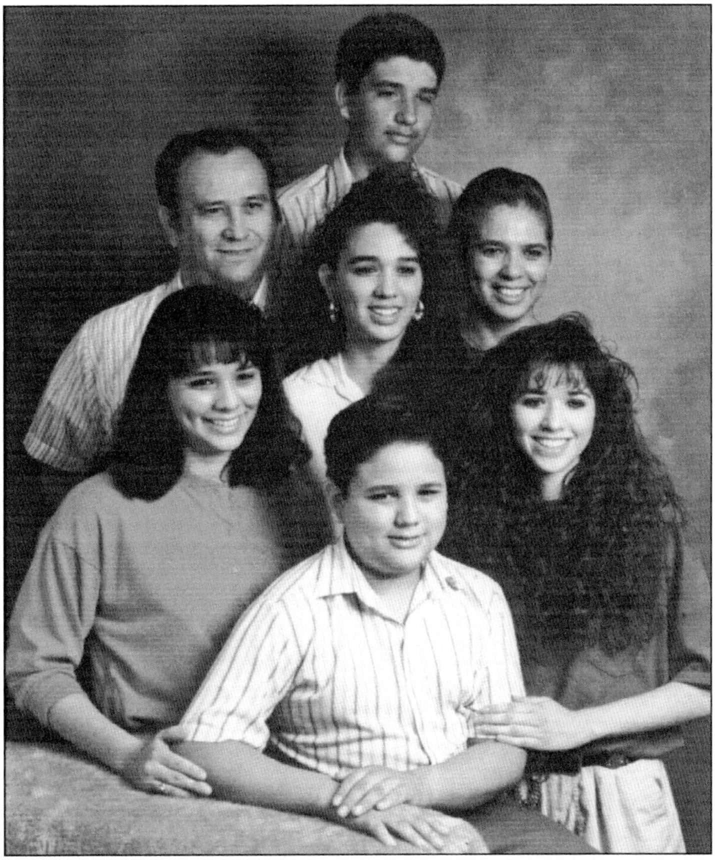

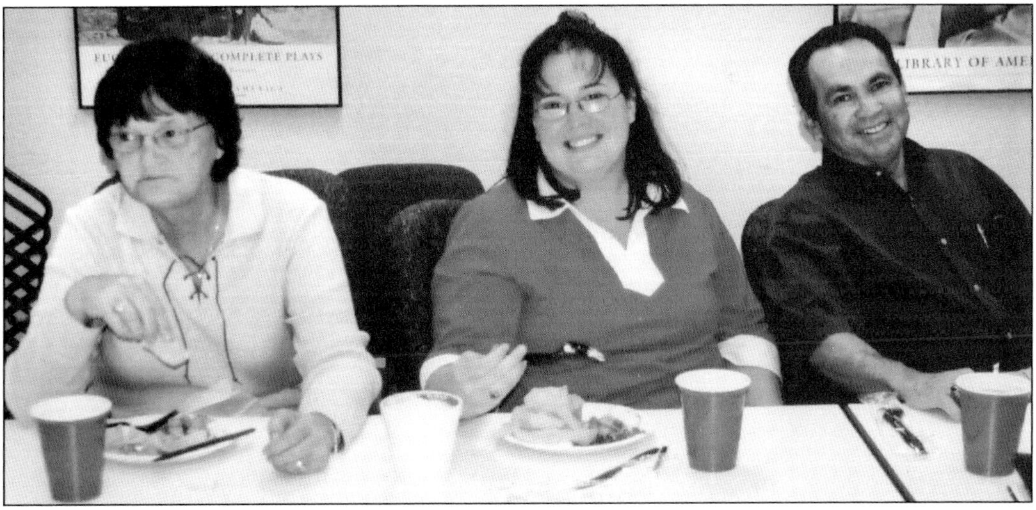

The Joe Arredondo family is well known in Tempe and has served the community in many respects over the years. Pictured here from left to right are Karen, who is married to Joe and has resided in Tempe since 1958; JoLyn Arredondo-Gibbons, who was born and raised in Tempe; and Joe Arredondo, a third-generation born and raised Tempeneño. Joe has served in various city boards and commissions, and at present serves, along with Karen and JoLyn, in the Tempe Tardeada Commission. (Joe Arredondo.)

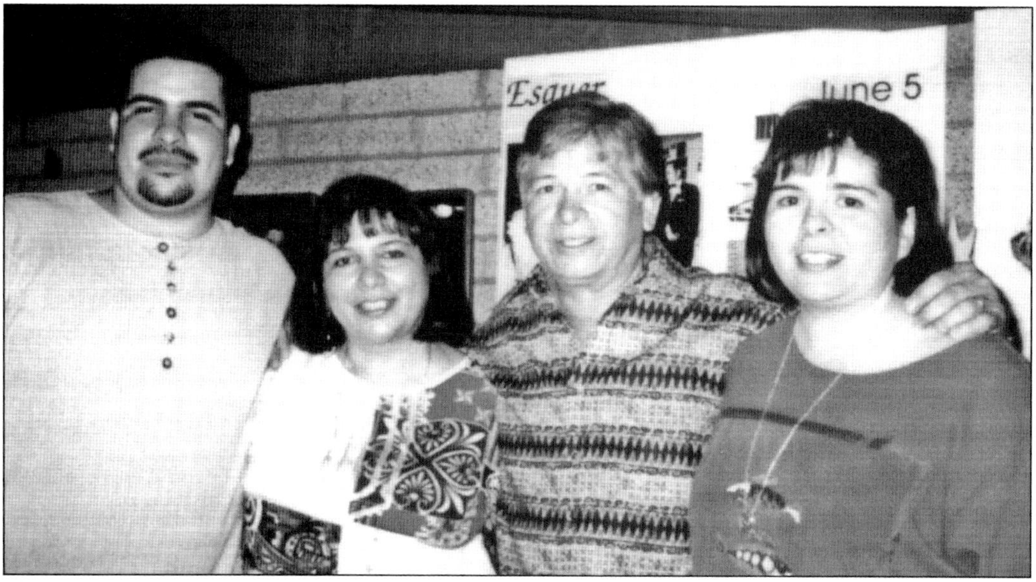

Elias and Cecilia D. Esquer celebrated their 30th wedding anniversary in June 1995. In the picture are, from left to right, son Marcos, Cecilia, Elias, and daughter Andrea Esquer. The Esquer family is active in Tempe by helping people to help themselves through education and politics. (Elias and Cecilia D. Esquer.)

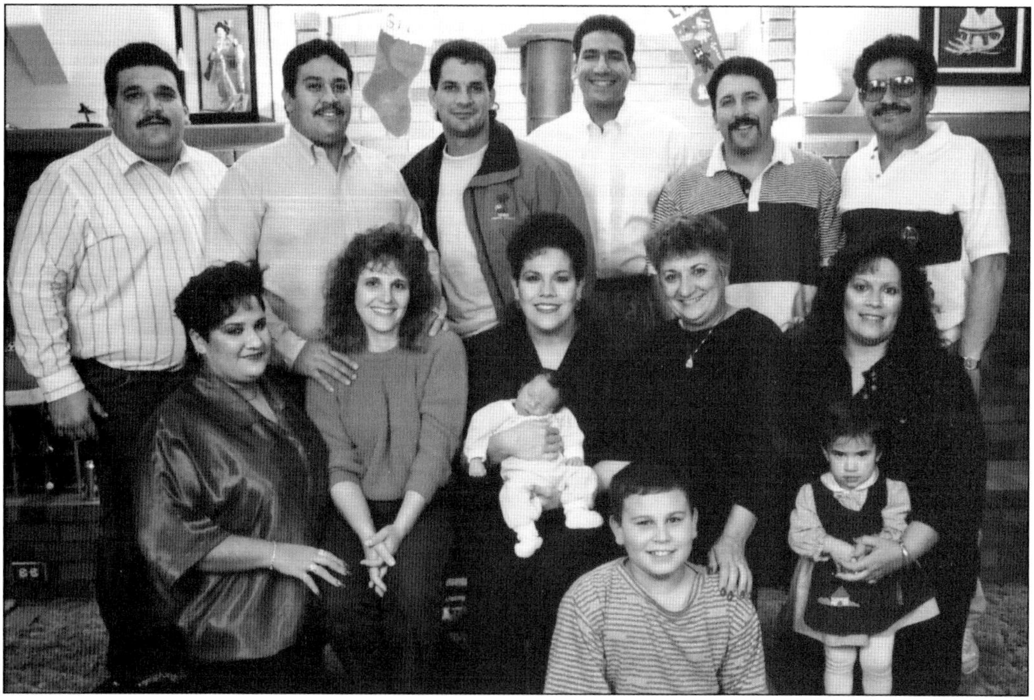

This photograph shows the Gilbert Montanez family. Pictured from left to right are (first row) Robert Montanez; (second row) Julie Montanez; Lisa Montanez; Anne Montanez holding Craig; Rosalie Montanez, wife of Gilbert Montanez Sr.; and Maria Montanez holding Kristina; (third row) John Montanez; Gilbert Montanez Jr.; Michael Montanez; Paul Montanez; Mark Montanez; and Gilbert Montanez Sr., the postmaster of Tempe. (Gilbert Montanez Jr.)

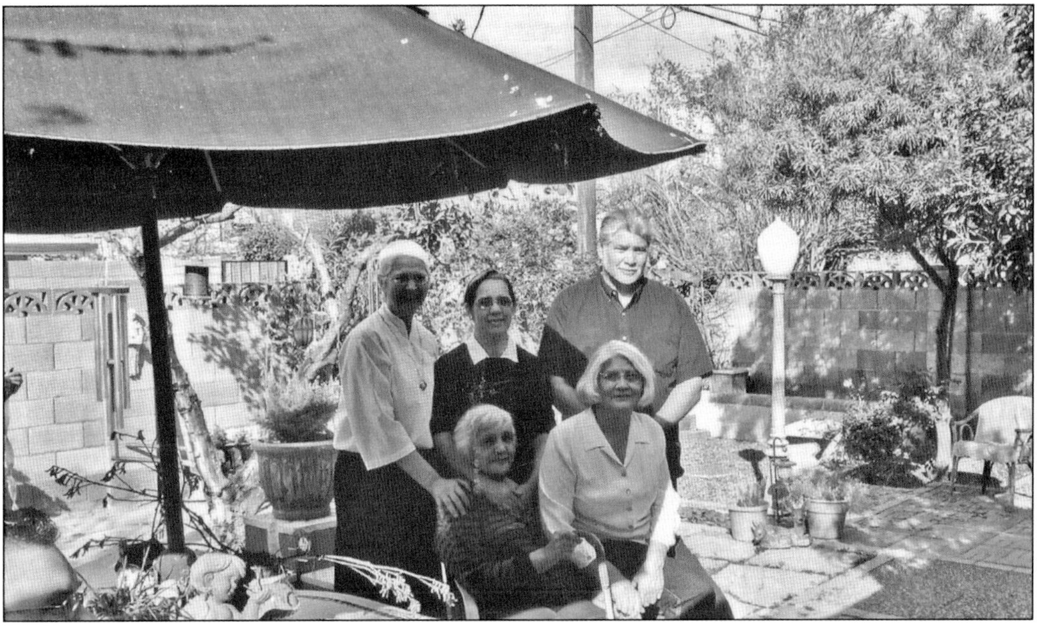

Cresencio and Guadalupe Varela's family reunion served as a bonding time in their backyard on January 1, 2005. From left to right are (first row) Carmela Varela and Virginia Varela Rollins; (second row) Benedictine Sister Ramona Varela, Cecilia Varela Mendez, and Chris Varela.

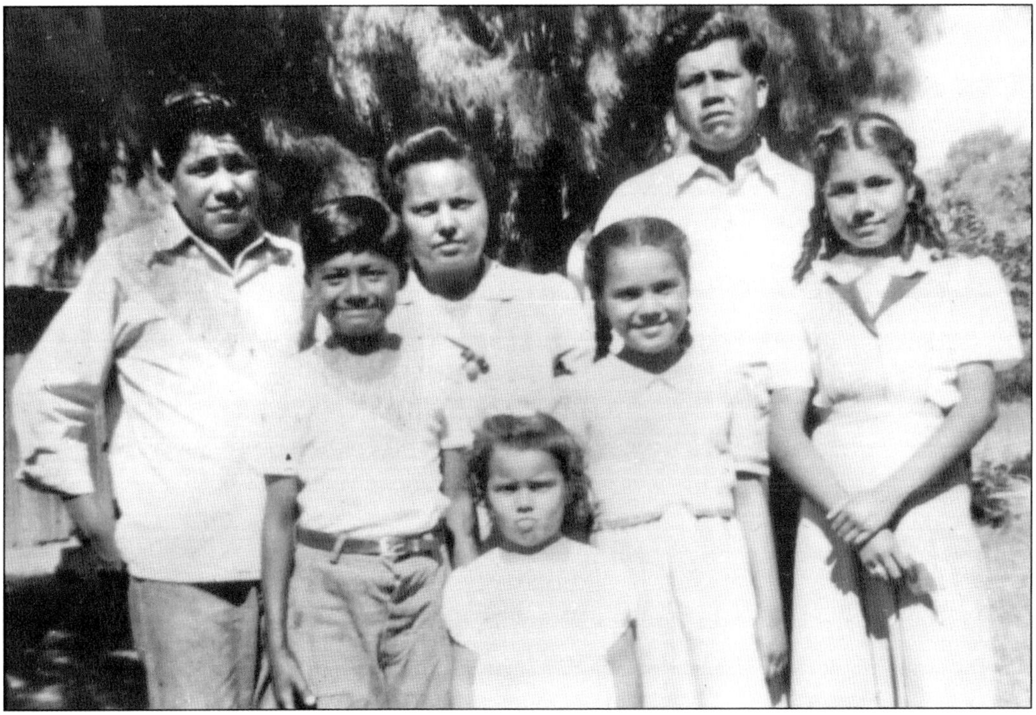

The Obregon family stands by the buttes and next to the canal in Tempe around 1944. From left to right are (first row) Rachel; (second row) Benjamin, Rebecca, and Esther; (third row) Samuel, mother Rebecca Olivas, and father Rosario P. In time, members of the family moved away from Phoenix, but they continue to return and visit. (Samuel Obregon.)

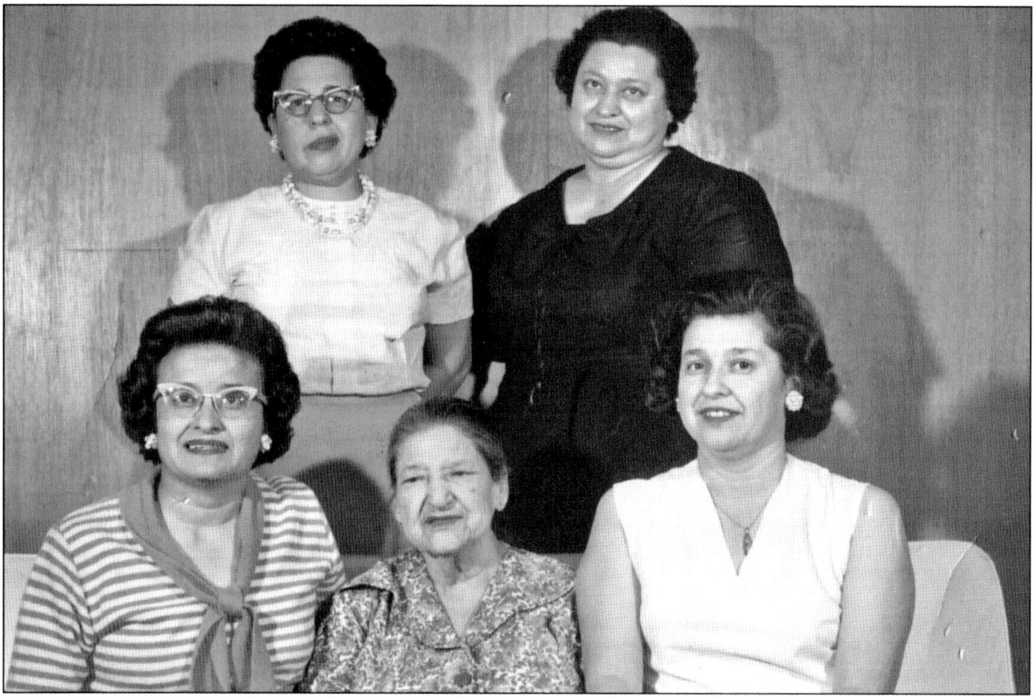

Margarita Monreal and her four daughters are shown in this picture, taken on March 10, 1965. From left to right are (first row) Narcisa Monreal (later Espinoza after her marriage to Jesus Espinoza), Margarita Monreal, and Sophia Monreal; (second row) Maria Luisa Monreal and Josephine Monreal. (Narcisa M. Espinoza.)

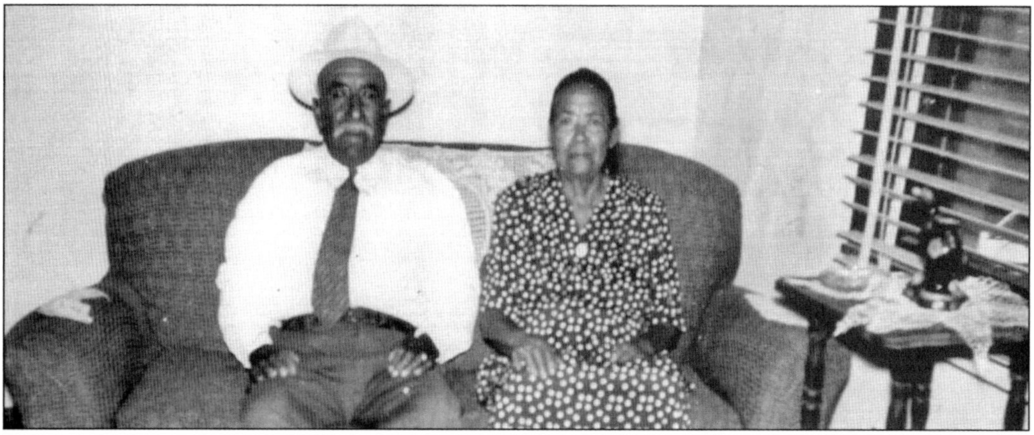

Jose Maria Arroyo and his wife, Marquitos, came to Tempe in the 1900s. Jose worked as a farm laborer, but on the side, he formed a music band, playing the bass fiddle. His music group was in great demand because music was one element that kept the community together. Music formed an integral part of religious activities such as baptisms, weddings, confirmations, and barrio festivities. Such celebrations included *tardeadas*, or afternoon gatherings of families and friends in someone's home where the backyard was sprinkled with water, swept bare, and hardened, thus turned into a dance floor. Then Jose Maria Arroyo and his band would play Mexican dance music such as *corridos*, *boleros*, *rancheras*, mambos, polkas, and also slower waltz pieces for older people in attendance. Children played their own games, running into and out of the crowd, and the older ones learned the dances.

Victoria Soto married John Floyd Gomez and managed a ranch by herself while she raised her children alone when Gomez went to Casa Grande to start his ranch. In time, Victoria and Gomez separated. Victoria supported her family by herself. She was the first Mexican American woman hired to work at the Hayden Flour Mill. She met Eugenio Gene Leon at the flour mill, and they later married. In 1950, they first lived in a tent, then moved into a frame wood house, and finally into an adobe house. That was the usual pattern for families upgrading their homes. Here is Victoria with her older daughter, Helen Gomez, on the left; in her arms, she holds baby Irene Gomez in 1937. When Victoria and her children lived at the Gomez Ranch at what today is Fifty-eighth Street and University Drive in 1939, Victoria had learned how to manage the ranch as taught to her by her aunt Maggie Jones Frank.

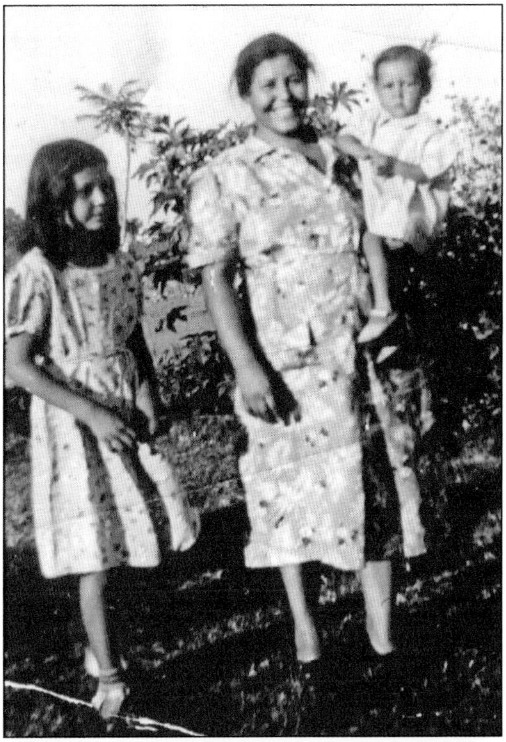

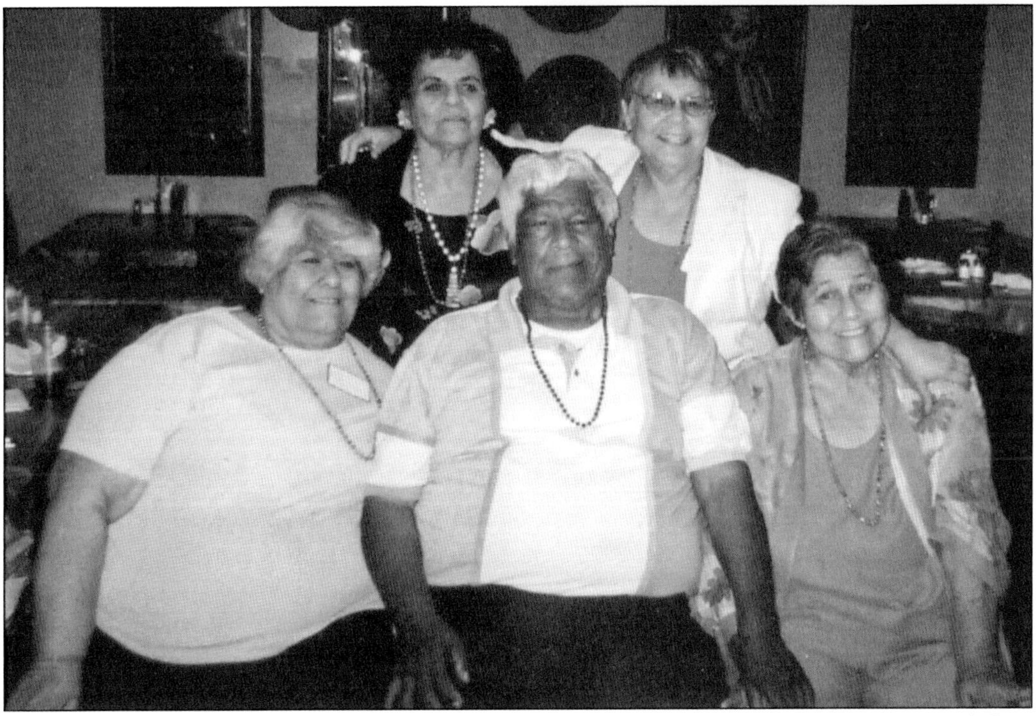

John Floyd Gomez Jr. celebrates his 65th birthday at Poncho's Restaurant in 2005. From left to right are (seated) Charlene Gomez Landreth, John Floyd, and Isabel Gomez; (standing) Helen Gomez Tramont and Irene Gomez Hormell. John Floyd Gomez Jr. was born in 1940.

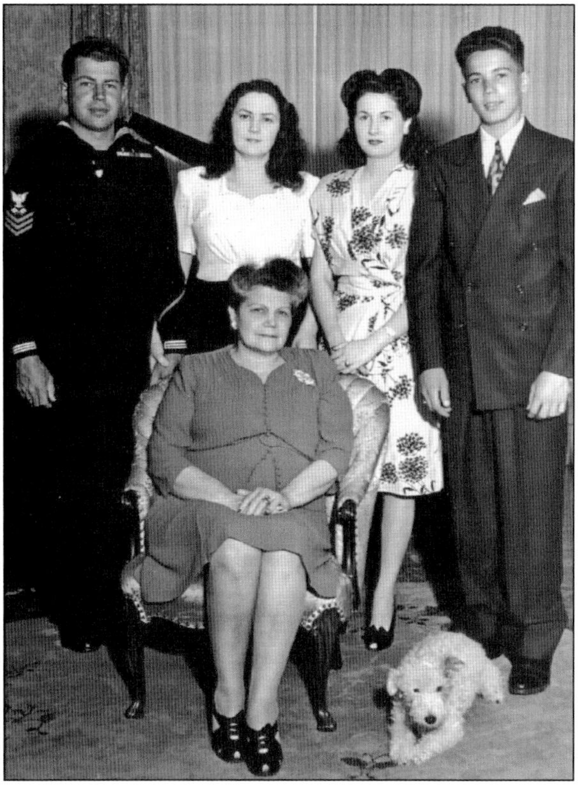

Laura F. Jones Curry (seated) is shown here with her family. Standing from left to right are her son-in-law John Arnold Richardson; her daughters Corrine and Monica; and her son Edward Curry. Laura was the youngest girl born to Alcaria Montoya Jones. Laura worked in California for the movie industry and had the responsibility to grade movies A, B, C, and so on in moral quality for showing to the public. Her husband, John Curry, performed as a stunt man in Hollywood. Laura and John lived in Brentwood, California.

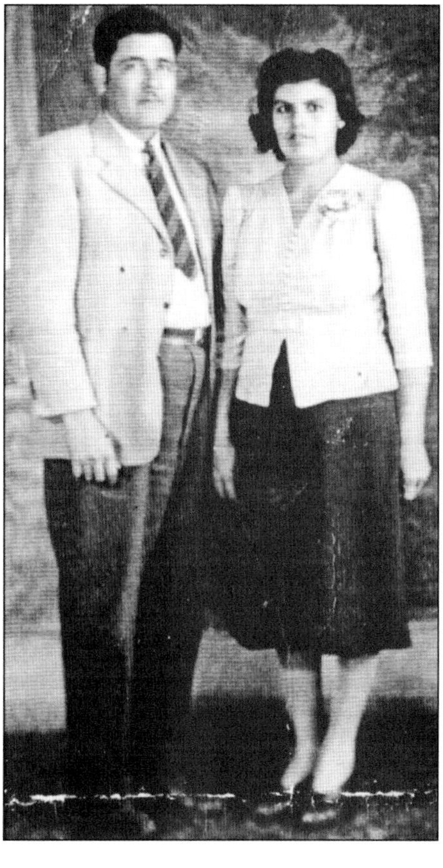

Victor Arroyo Sr. and his wife, Leonor Lopez, are shown here in a picture taken in 1937.

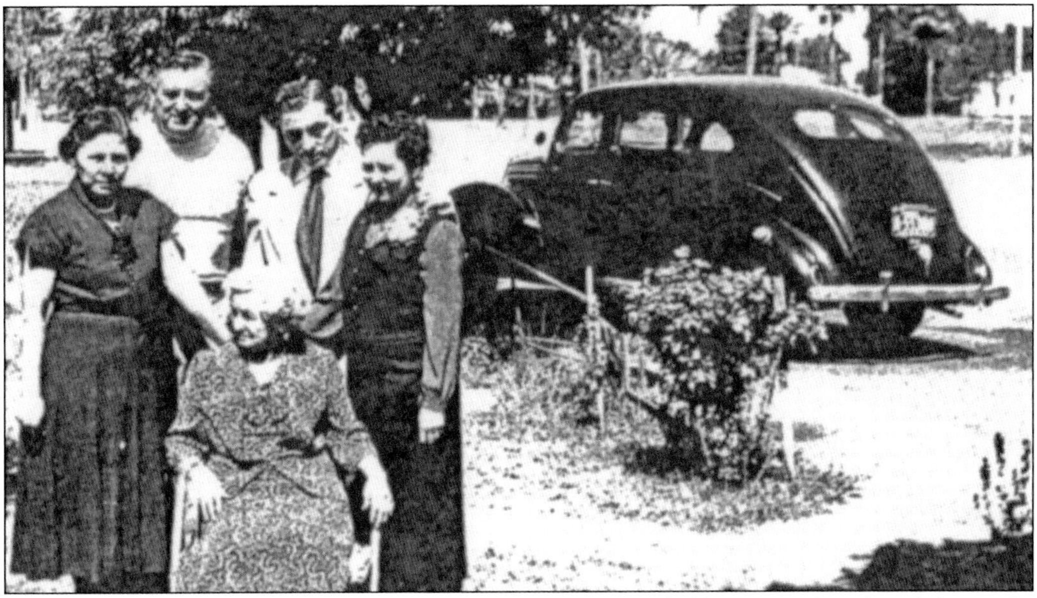

Guadalupe Acedo Varela ("Lupe") is surrounded by her adult children. Standing from left to right are Hilda V. Ruiz, Joe Varela, Echaldo Varela, and Sara V. Abril. Lupe served her family well as the "Dama de Casa," a housewife and mother in charge of the home. She was active in her church, the old Mount Carmel Mission, situated between the buttes, and later served the church on College Avenue and Eighth Street (before Eighth Street was renamed University Drive). Later she attended and helped where she could at the new Our Lady of Mount Carmel at 2121 South Rural Road in Tempe.

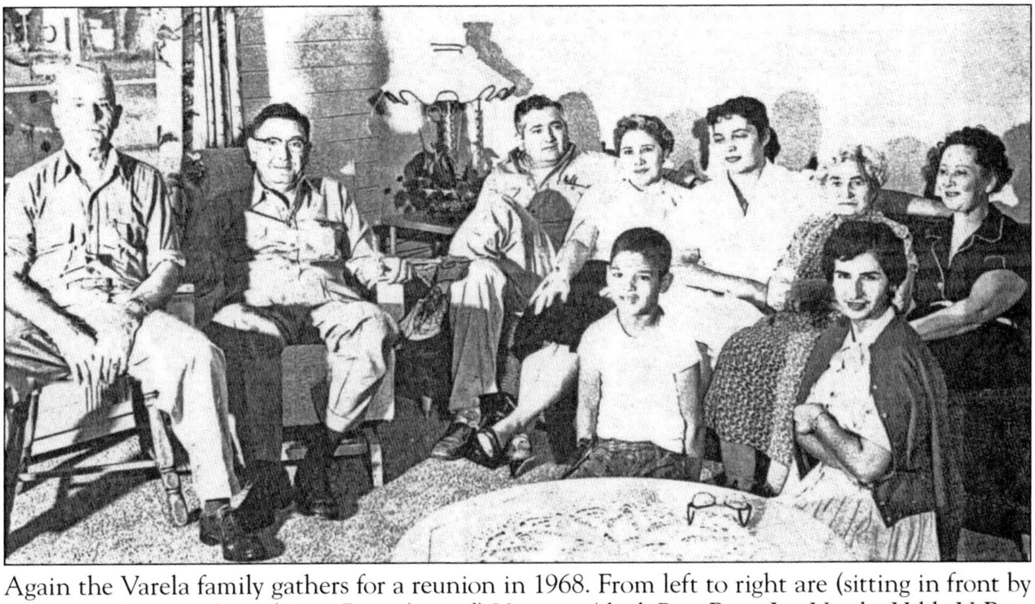

Again the Varela family gathers for a reunion in 1968. From left to right are (sitting in front by the table) Tim Varela and Vera Ruiz; (seated) Ventura Abril, Pete Ruiz, Joe Varela, Hilda V. Ruiz (Pete's wife), Carmela (Joe's wife), Lupe Varela, and Sarah V. Abril. Sarah and Ventura Abril's son, Ben Abril, who lives in California and is an artist, was commissioned by Cardinal Mahoney of Los Angeles to paint a picture of San Fernando Mission for the Holy Father, Pope John Paul II, given to him during his visit to the United States. The painting is housed in the Vatican.

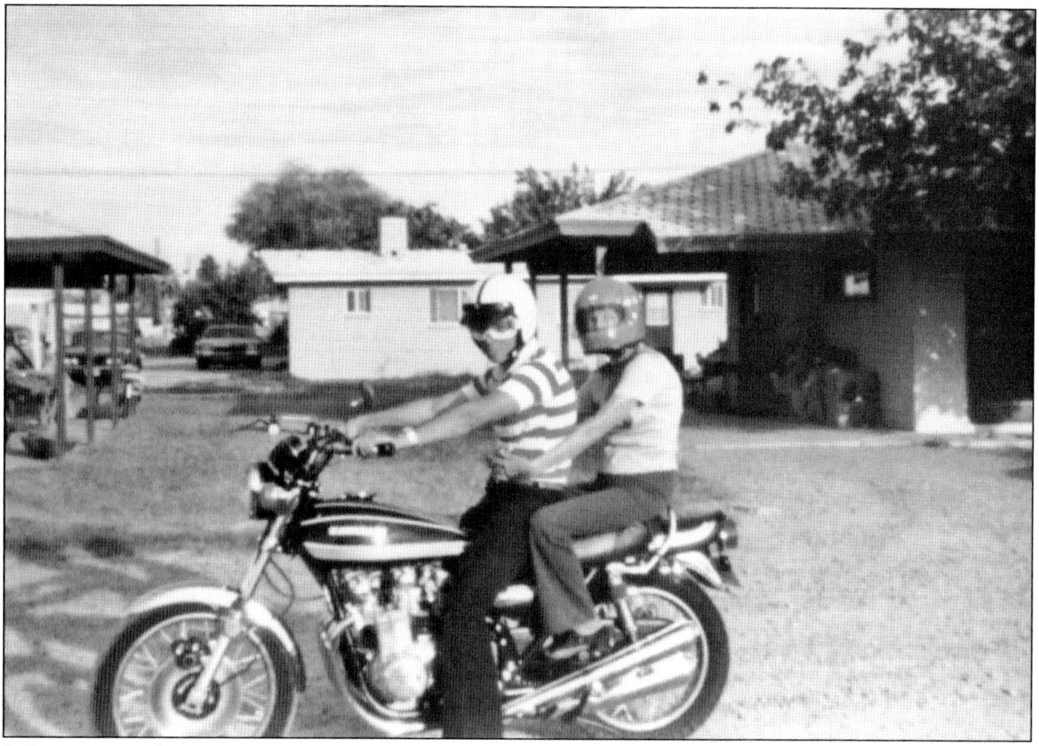

Juliana Gonzales Burgos proves to herself that one needs only do it to realize a goal of riding a motorcycle even after reaching one's golden age. With the help of John Soza Jr., Juliana takes her first motorcycle ride in the 1960s.

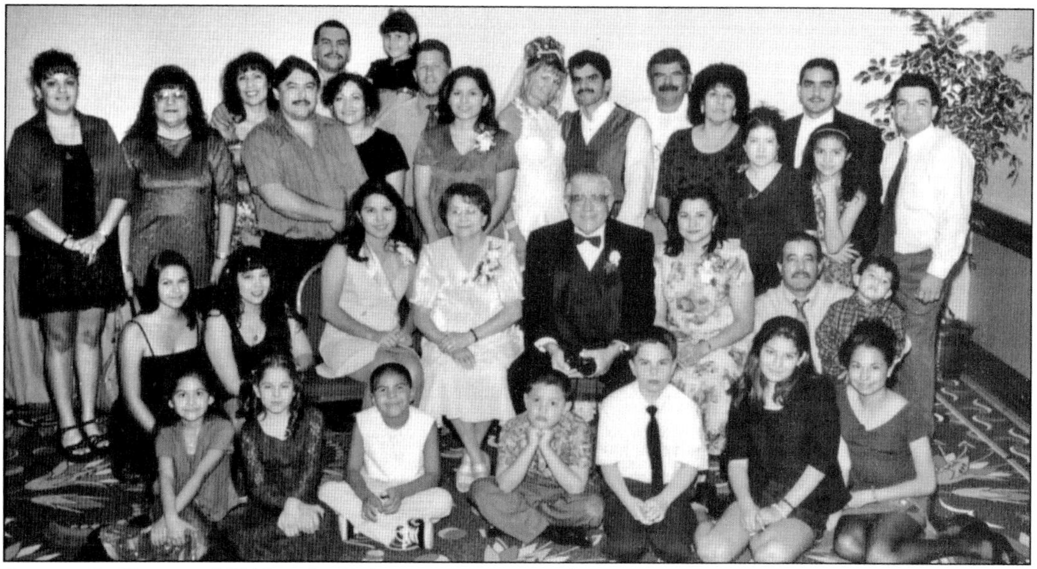

Santos C. Vega and Edilia G. "Lily" Vega get together for the wedding of their son Frank X. Vega to Debbie Wanczyk on October 15, 1999, at Our Lady of Mount Carmel Parish on Rural Road. Seated in the center are Edilia and Santos flanked by daughters Maria Victoria ("Vikki") on the left and Vivian on the right. The rest of the family includes sons, daughters, sons-in-law, daughters-in-law, and their children. (Author's collection.)

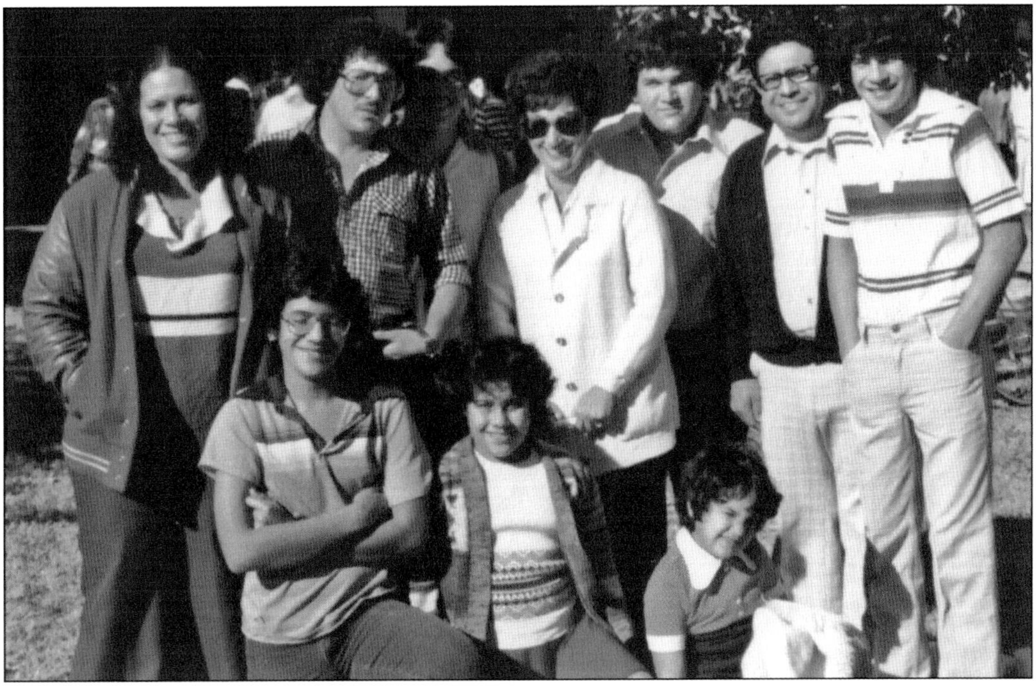

The Gilbert Montanez Sr. family is shown enjoying a day of recreation. From left to right are (first row) Paul; Annie; and Julie; (second row) Maria; Mark Gilbert Jr.; Rosalie, Gilbert Sr.'s wife; John; Gilbert Sr.; and Michael. (Gilbert Montanez Jr.)

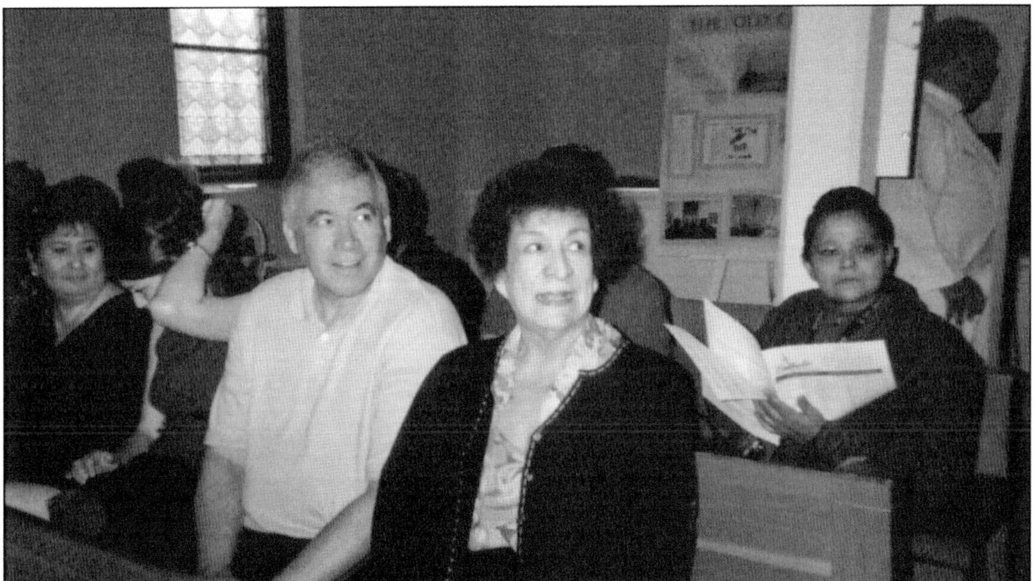

Robert Acosta and Lupe Ortega Acosta were leaders in forming a Hispanic Catholic group called Guadalupanas for prayer, worship, service, and community at Our Lady of Mount Carmel Parish (OLMC) on Rural Road in 1989. The Guadalupanas contributed funds to the OLMC Spring Festival by selling Mexican food. Members also performed apostolic works. This 2003 picture was taken at the old Our Lady of Mount Carmel Church located on College Avenue and University Drive.

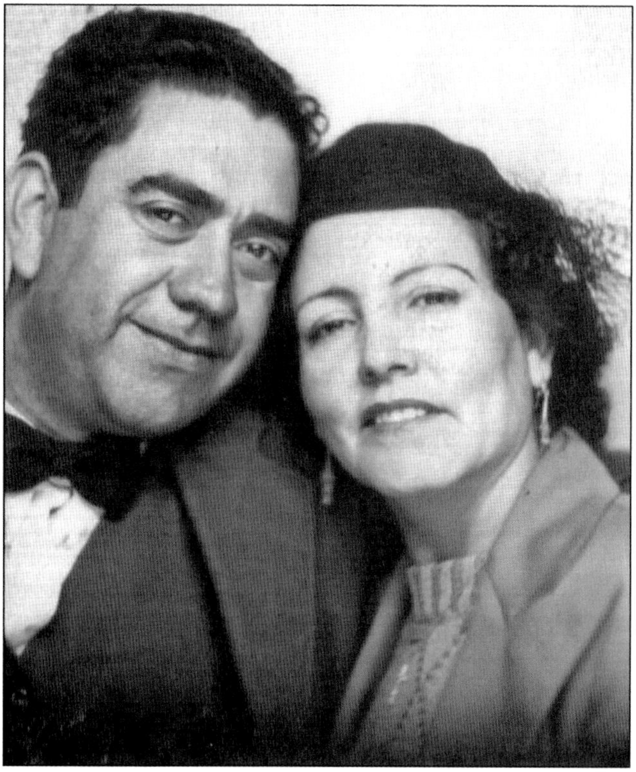

Otilio "Tily" Lopez and Angelita Soto pursued life careers first before getting married much later. Angelita completed her education and worked. Otilio was a musician and a band leader who formed his own band. He was a music composer and worked for Radio KALI as a radio announcer in California.

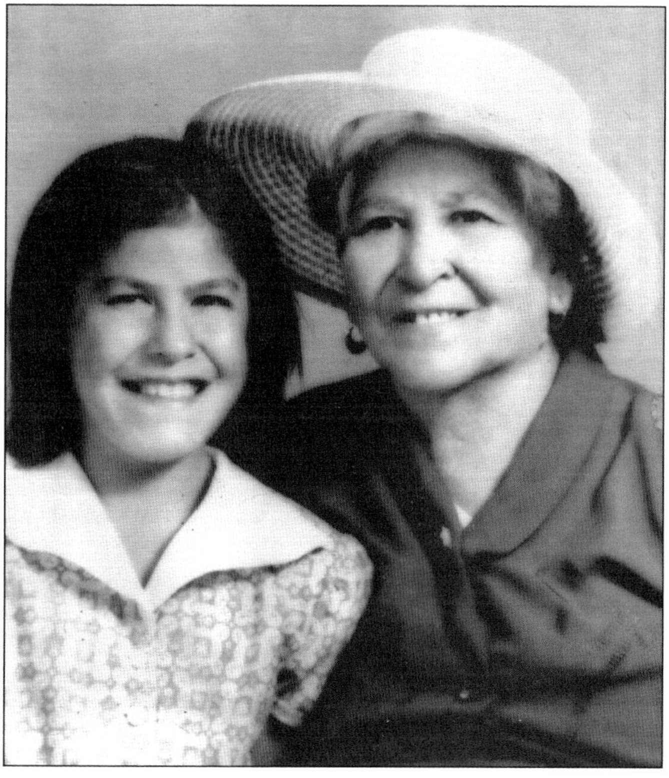

This picture, taken in 1951, shows Charlene Gomez with her grandmother Marina Ceballos Soto. Charlene is the daughter of Victoria Soto Gomez, the ranch woman and worker at the Hayden Flour Mill whose mother was Marina C. Soto, noted barrio peddler (*fayuquera*). Women played an important role in building neighborhoods and supporting the community through their families.

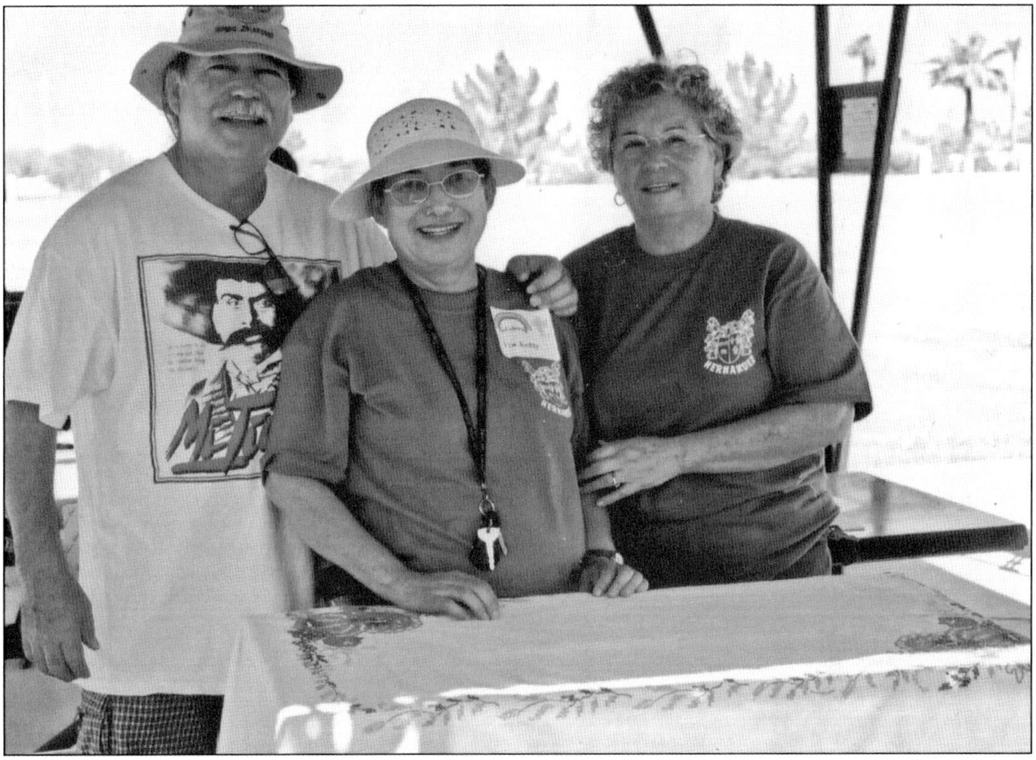

The Villagomez Hernandez family reunions bring out large numbers of participants in the different branches. The reunion held in October 2005 was no exception. In this picture are, from left to right, three participants, Johnny Hernandez, Rachel Hernandez Pollack, and Mary Hernandez, all siblings. (Author's collection.)

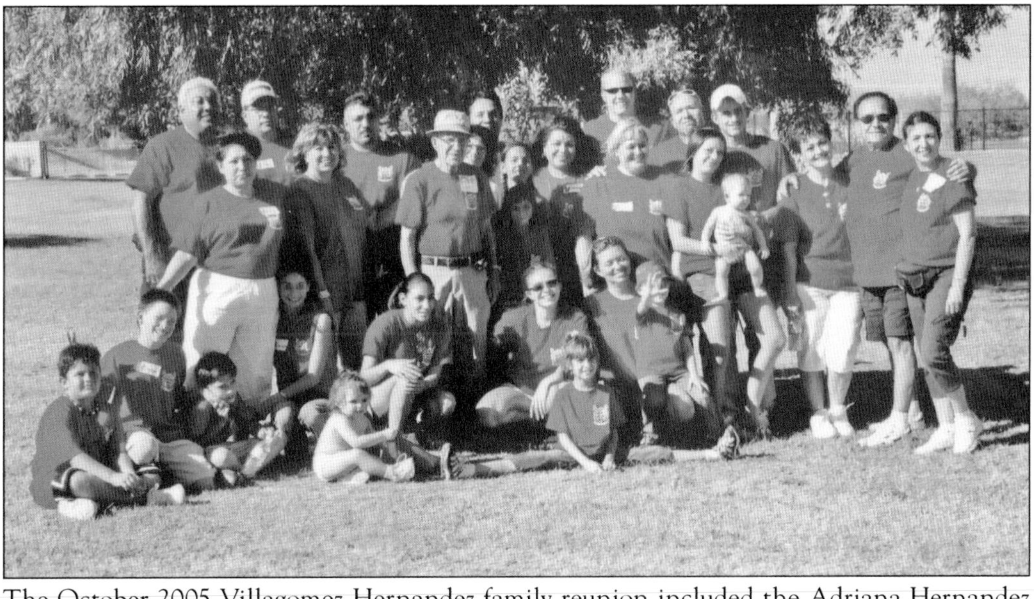

The October 2005 Villagomez Hernandez family reunion included the Adriana Hernandez group with Frank Lucero's branch of the family. Frank is standing in the center wearing a hat. (Author's collection.)

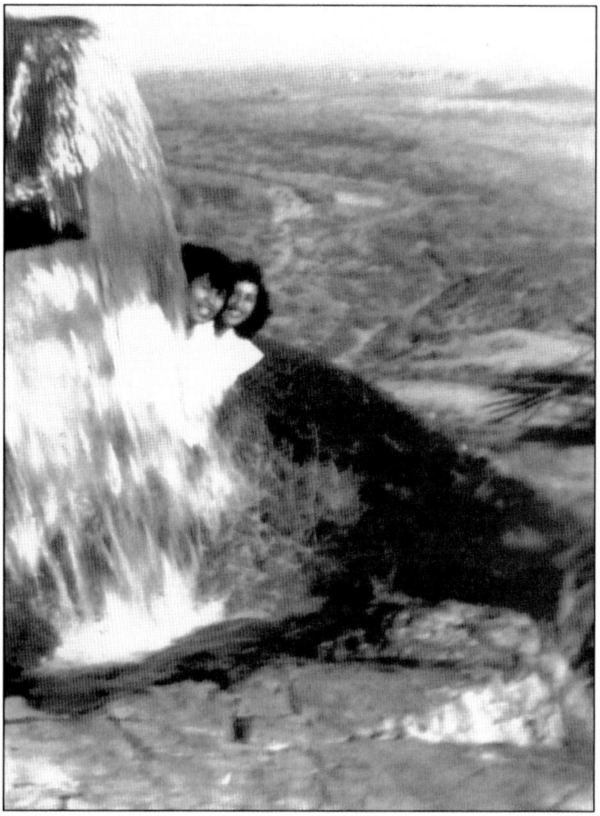

A favorite excursion for barrio teenagers was to climb the butte and cool off with water gushing up from a water well. On top of "A" Butte in the 1940s are Socorro Aguilar (left) and Michaela "Mickie" Guerrero.

In the barrios, one favorite pastime for teens was bicycle riding. This 1940s picture shows, from left to right, Mary Burgos, Terry Aguilar, and Michaela Guerrero. They are riding on Sixth and Center Streets in the barrio San Pablo. The butte can be seen in the background.

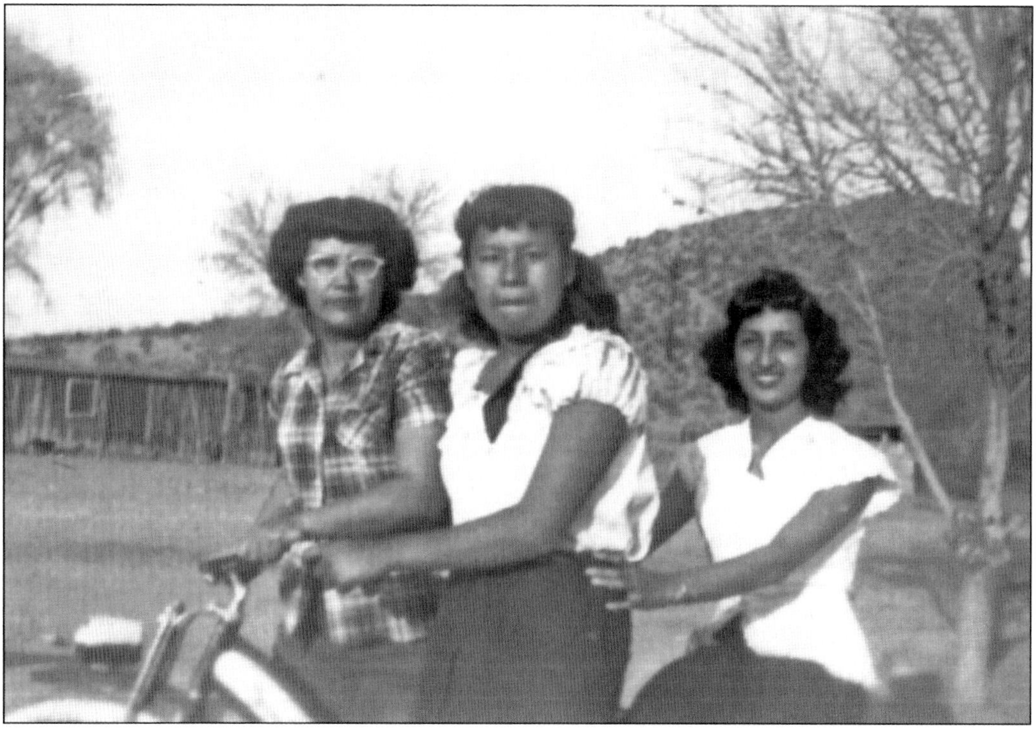

Drs. John H. Akers and Amy Douglas attended a ceremony in the Escalante Community Center in Escalante barrio for the distribution of the oral history booklet on Victory Acres and Escalante, which was completed in September 2004. (Author's collection.)

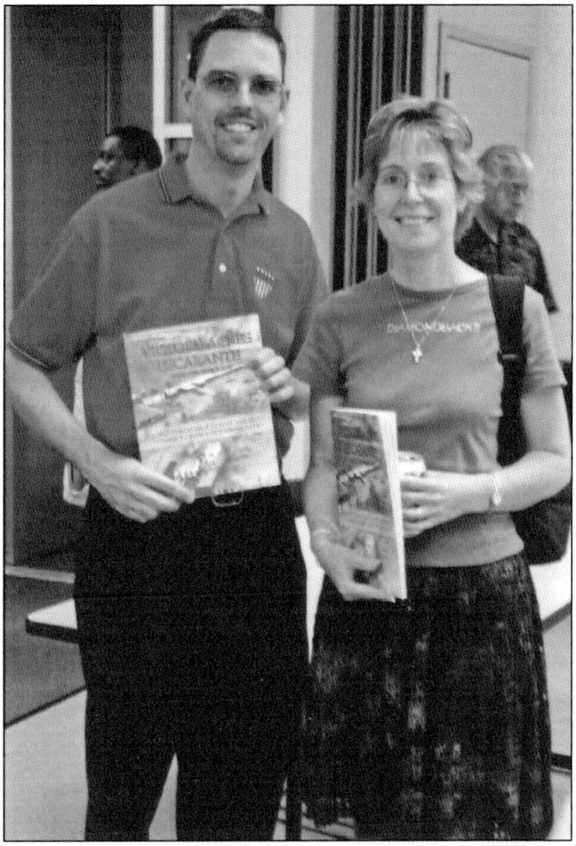

Prof. Elias Esquer (first row, second from left) is with the academic group he led on a study tour to Guanajuato, Mexico. The group picture shows attendees of the summer session sponsored through Maricopa Community College in Guanajuato, Mexico. The Guanajuato study program began in 1986, sponsored by three Mesa Community College professors: Elias Esquer, Jack Hannon, and Jose Torres. Standing on the right side are two academics from Guanajuato. (Elias and Cecilia D. Esquer.)

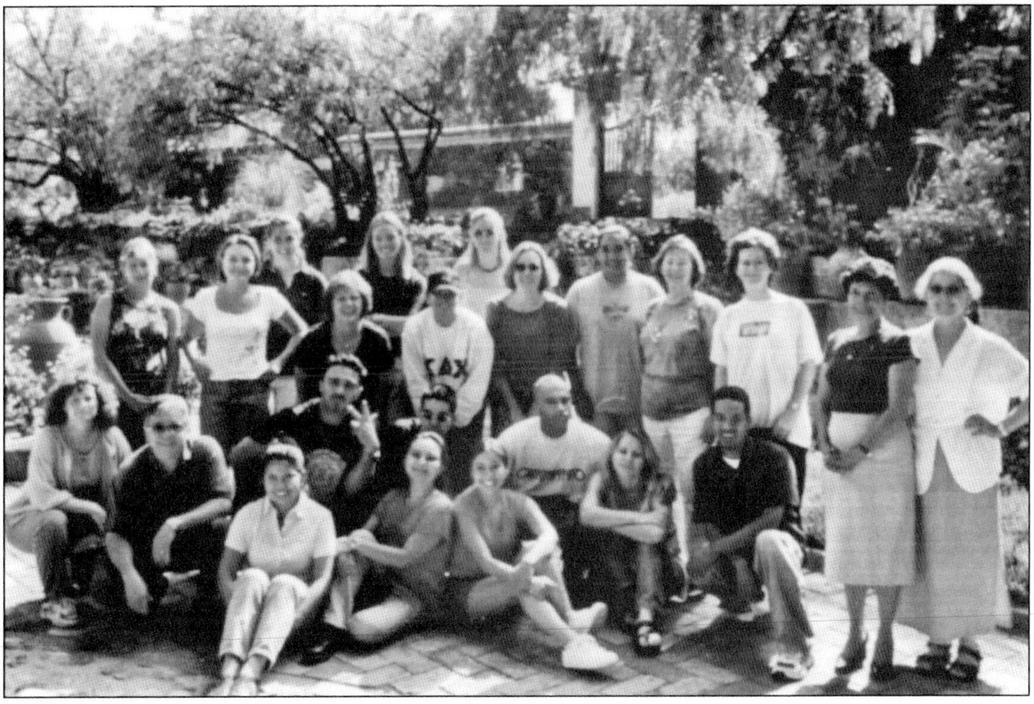

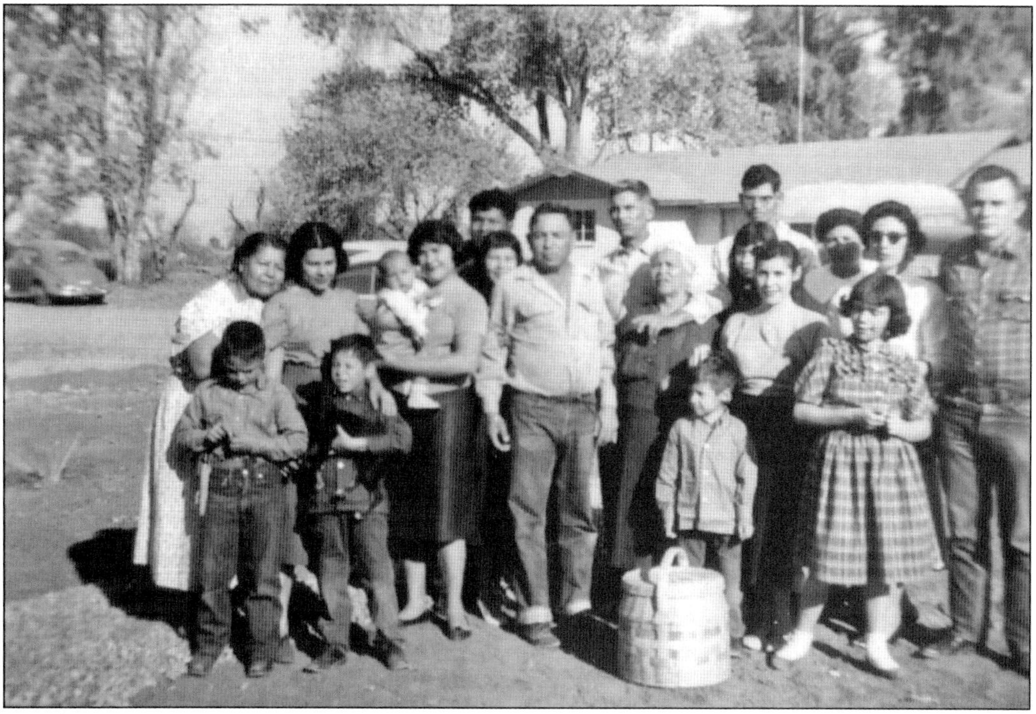

Another Tempe tradition is that of giving *despedidas*, or send-offs, for family members or friends who are leaving on a journey or moving away. A group of friends gathered to give Irene Gomez Hormell a send-off when she moved to Florida in 1959. This was a family reunion as well as a *despedida*. Gathered for the occasion are (first row) Steve Conklin, Louis Tramont, Victor Tramont, and Lorretta Conklin; (second row) Victoria Leon, Helen Tramont, Charlene Gomez with baby Stanley Hormell, Gene Leon, Marina Soto, and Isabel Gomez; (third row) Irene Hormell, Bridget Soto, Carmen Soto, Virginia Conklin, and Bill Conklin; (fourth row) Floyd Gomez Jr., Ignacio Soto, and Gabriel Soto.

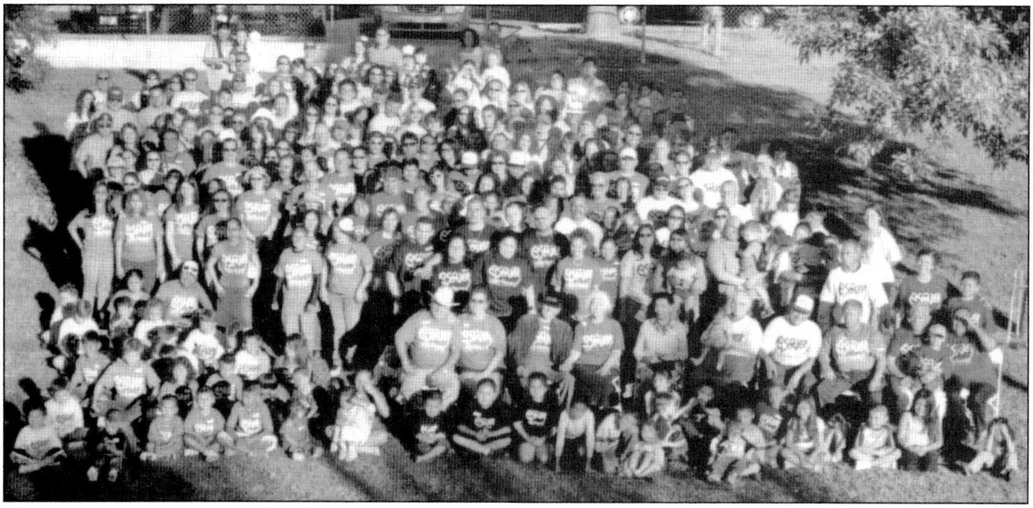

The Esquer family reunion was held in Kiwanis Park in Tempe, Arizona, in 2005. Family reunions are held by Mexican people as a family tradition to celebrate family unity, love, and support. (Elias and Cecilia D. Esquer.)

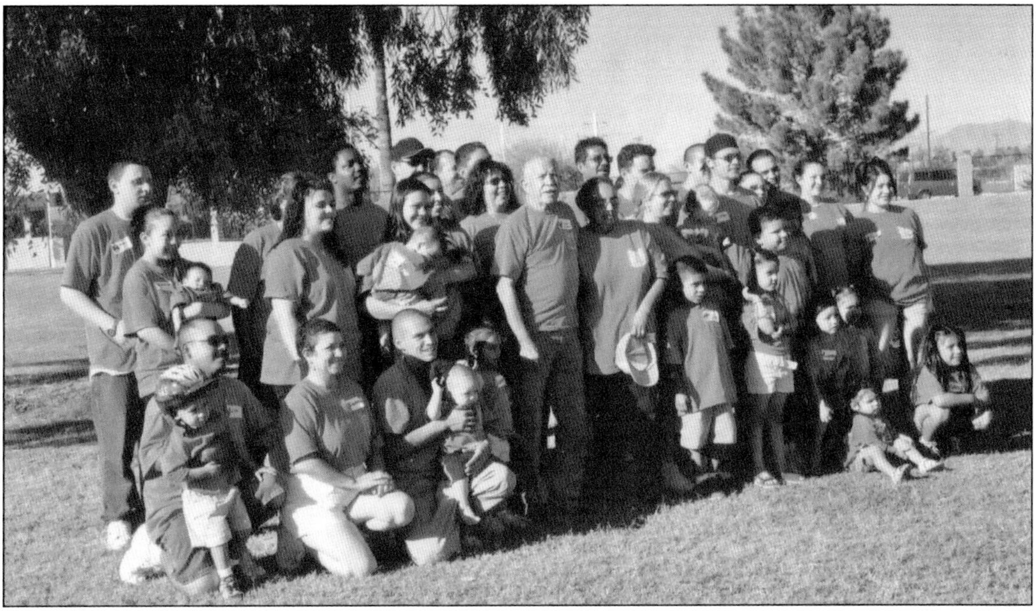

In October 2005 at the Villagomez Hernandez family reunion, the Ramon Esquer branch participated with other branches of this large family. Ramon Esquer and his wife, Rita Esquer, are standing in the center of the first row. (Author's collection.)

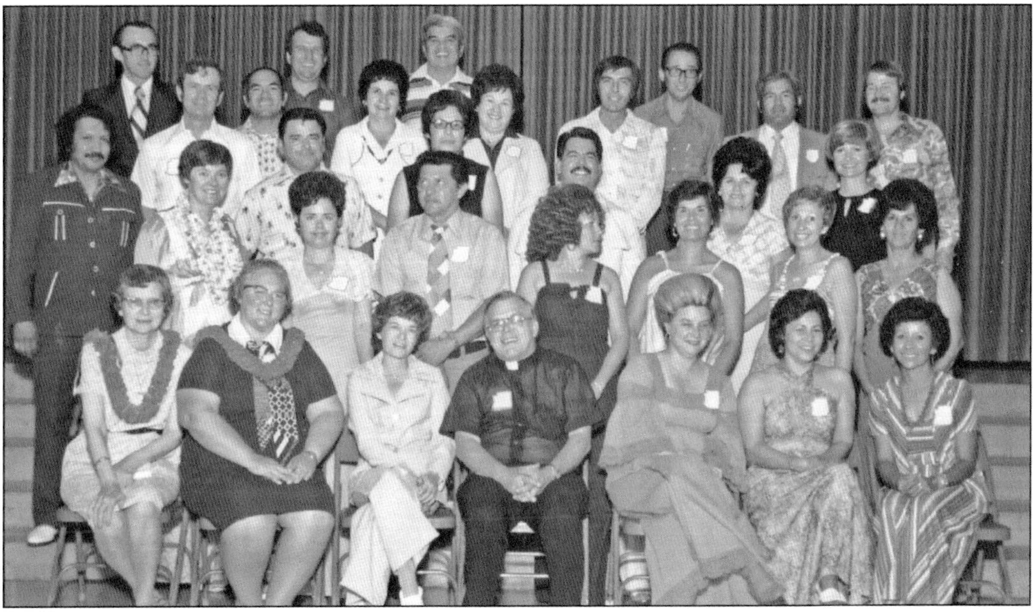

In addition to send-offs and family reunions, another tradition is celebrating graduations or class reunions. Here is the Our Lady of Mount Carmel Parish (OLMC) first class reunion, celebrated in 1976. This reunion group includes individuals from the first three graduating classes of the school (1950–1953). The graduates started their classes in the basement of the first Our Lady of Mount Carmel Church on College Avenue and Eighth Street (later named University Drive); here the class reunion met in the new OLMC located at 2121 South Rural Road. The guest priest was Rev. Francis Bectel. After Father Bectel served in the parish, Fr. John Curtis and Fr. Gilbert Padilla served as assistants to Rev. Daniel McCready, who served the parish for many years.

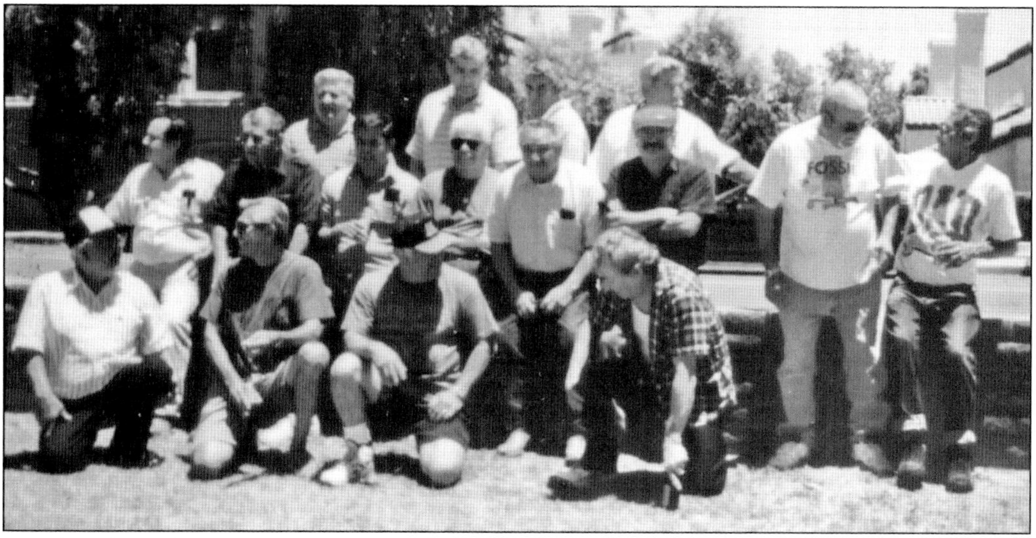

Another form of traditional heritage is group bonding. Here the Los Amigos de Tempe (Friends of Tempe), formed in 1986, gathered to bid one of their members, Henry "Jippy" Gamboa, "Adios Amigo" ("good-bye friend") during a farewell picnic. The friends include (third row) Frank Ruiz, Chris Varela, Rudy Arroyo, Robert Ruiz, and Henry Gamboa.

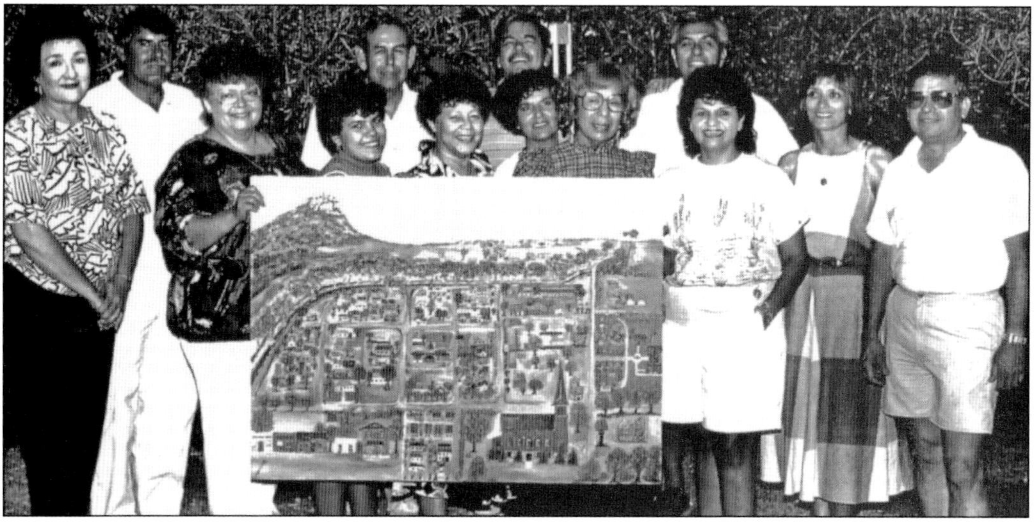

In 1986, Los Amigos de Tempe held up an art piece crafted by Joe Soto of a view of the barrio. The barrio view was changed dramatically by all the families that left their heartbeat and impressions of themselves throughout the years. Pictured are, from left to right, (first row) helpers of Los Amigos Clara Urbano, Vicki Gomez, Irene Gomez Hormell, Rachel Arroyo, Terri Gladney, Dolores Varela, Margaret Medina, and Elias Esquer; (second row) Ruth Ortega Garcia, Rudy Arroyo, Manuel Varela, Joe Soto, and Jess Valenzuela.

Three

CELEBRATIONS

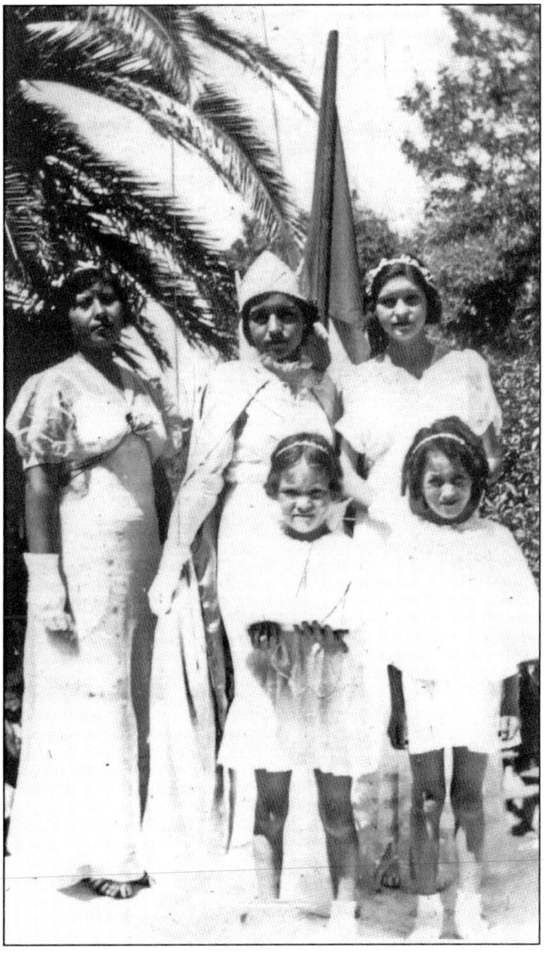

In this 1935 picture, Mary Sterling was 16 years old when she was voted first runner-up for the September 16 festival in Tempe, Arizona. Mary is standing at left in the back row. It is believed that the queen's last name was Moraga. The other people in the picture are unidentified. Fiestas Patrias (Patriotic Celebration) occurs annually every September 16 to commemorate Mexico's independence from Spain. Immigrants from Mexico, as part of their heritage, continued to celebrate the independence in their new country of residence in addition to celebrating American independence on the Fourth of July. (Barney S. Peralta.)

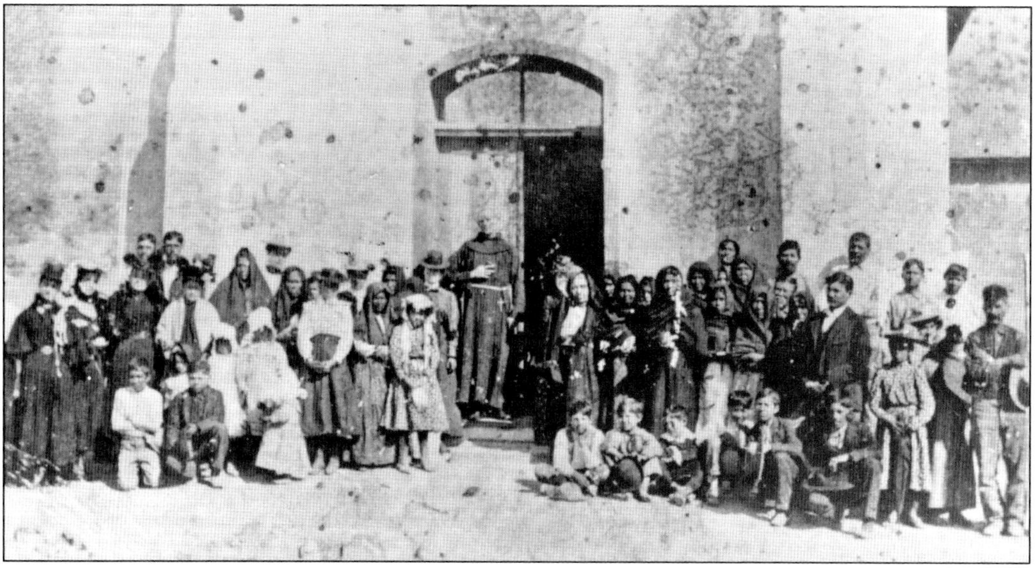

The first Catholic church structure was built at the foot of the Tempe Butte in San Pablo barrio by Mexican settlers skilled in making adobe brick and building structures with them. The church was named Nuestra Señora Del Carmen (Our Lady of Mount Carmel). Also a barrio cemetery used the area. A centennial commemoration was held on January 25, 2003. (ASU.)

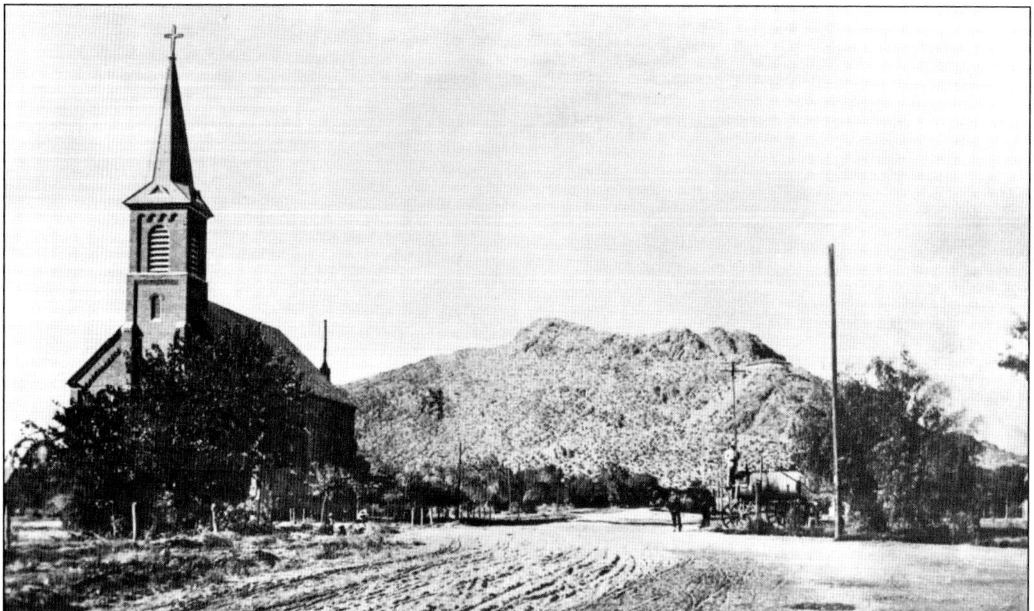

The Our Lady of Mount Carmel Church building was constructed anew on College Avenue and Eighth Street. The church sponsored an OLMC school in the early 1900s. Our Lady of Mount Carmel Church was, for a time, a mission church of St. Mary's in Phoenix and thus was called St. Mary's Mission Church. In this photograph, the church stands alone with plenty of fields all around it, and in the distance north of the church is Tempe Butte. Down the road going north can be seen Cresencio Varela managing the horse-drawn water wagon, sprinkling the dirt streets. (ASU.)

The first and only Mexican Methodist church in Tempe, named in Spanish "Iglesia Metodista de Tempe," was located on East Seventh Street in the area called Barrio Central near the intersection of College Avenue and University Drive. The church structure was constructed in 1920. This 1953 photograph by Bill Wood shows pastor Mardoqueo Garcia standing in the last row, third from left. (Elizabeth M. Rivera.)

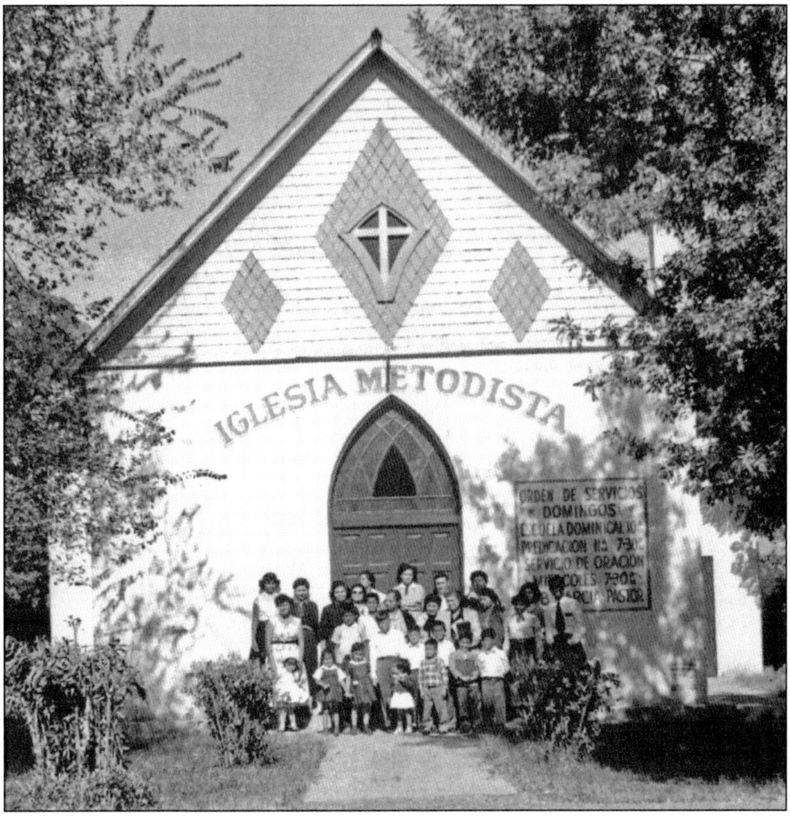

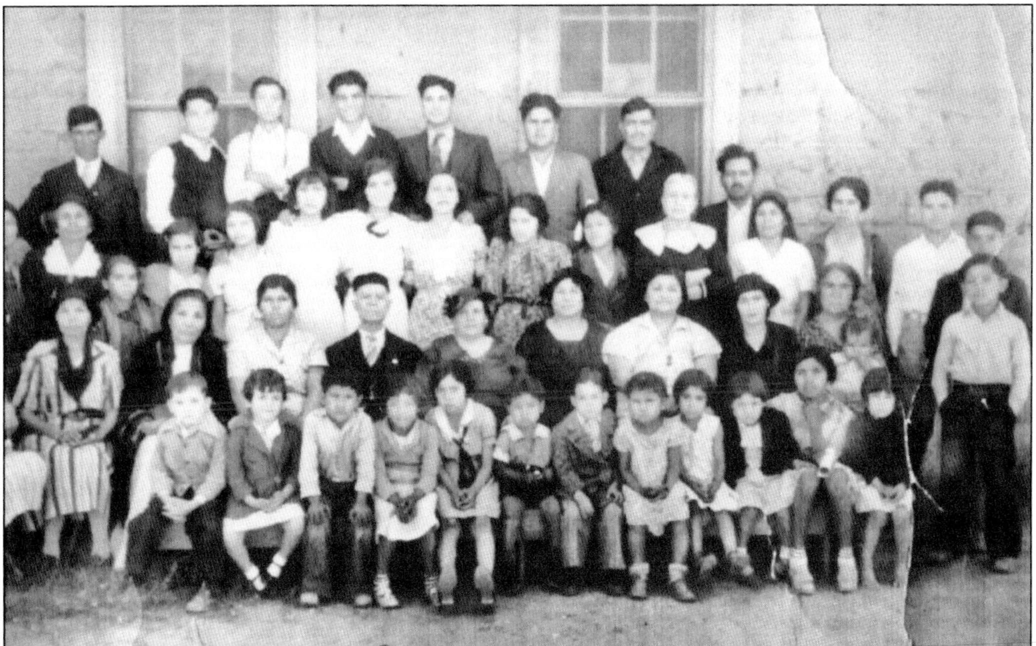

Pictured in the 1940s is a Mexican Methodist church congregation. The photograph was taken by Pastor Mardy Olivas. (Rev. Mardy Olivas.)

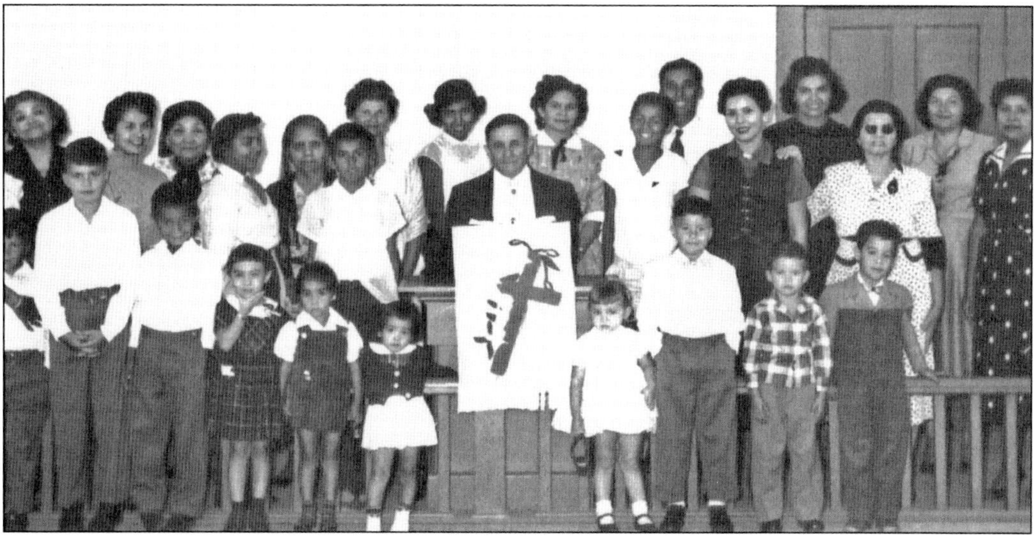

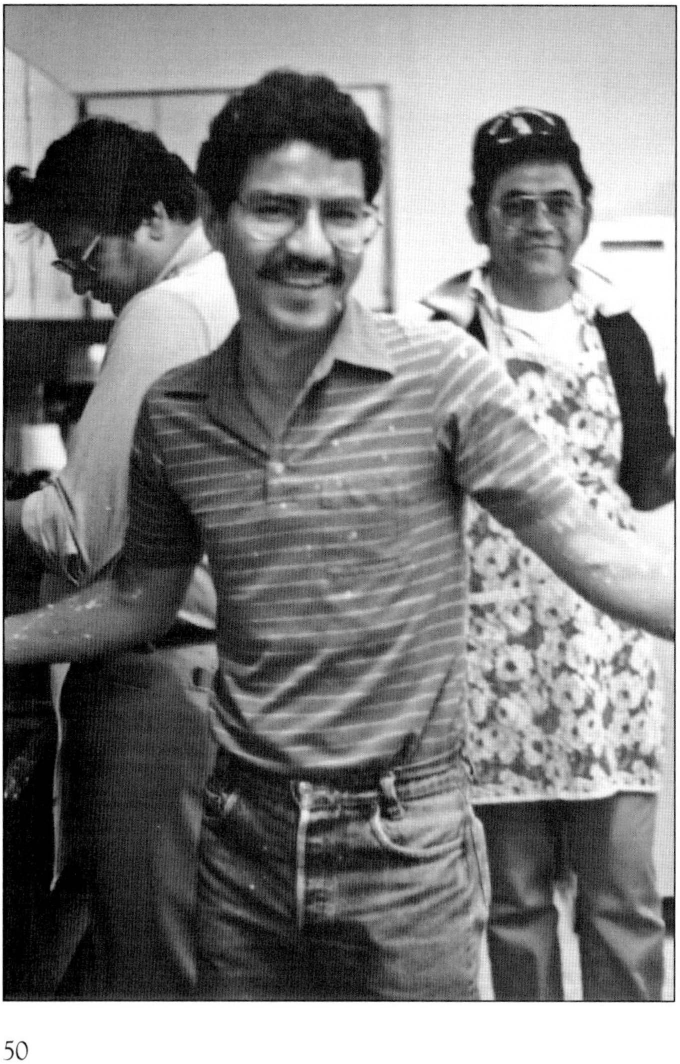

This Mexican Methodist Church of Tempe photograph was taken in November 1955. In the center behind the podium is Pastor Mardoqueo Garcia. All around him are members of his congregation. (Rev. Mardy Olivas.)

The Amistad Hispana Group gathered at the Escalante Community Center in the Escalante barrio of Tempe on December 7, 1985. Gilbert Daniels, a graduate of Florence High School who graduated from Arizona State University, participated in the heritage and culture program. The participants were learning the science and art of making tamales. In the background stands mentor Albert Marquez, wearing an apron. (Albert and Susana Marquez.)

Weddings in the Mexican culture have a long history, and the occasion carries with it many customs and traditions. The church setting and the attire of the brides and bridesmaids are always special. In this *c.* 1917 photograph are Flora Rosales Martinez and Juan Martinez (standing), witnessing and supporting the newly married couple of Angelita and Eliseo Jaime (seated). These were ranch-working people who resided on the ranches at the corner of what is today Baseline and Extension Roads, and they were probably born there. Flora was born in 1900; Juan was born around 1895; Angelita was born in 1902; Eliseo was born around 1895, and his place of birth was one of the ranches.

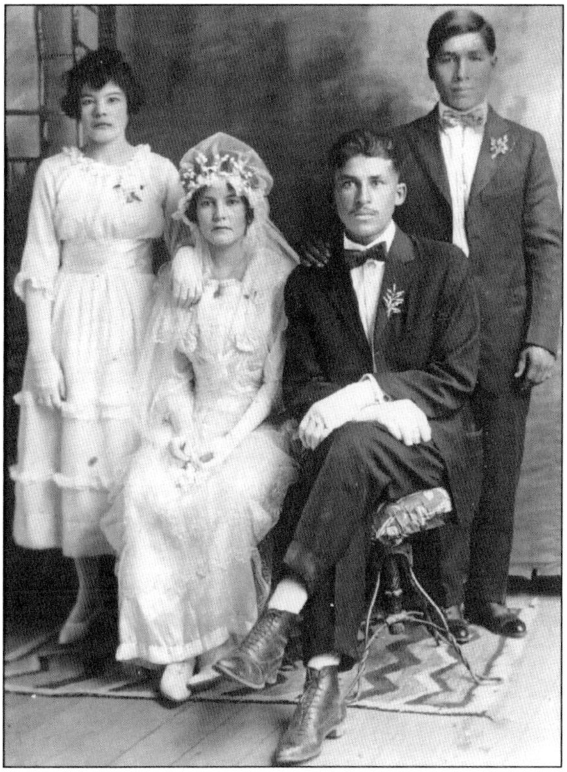

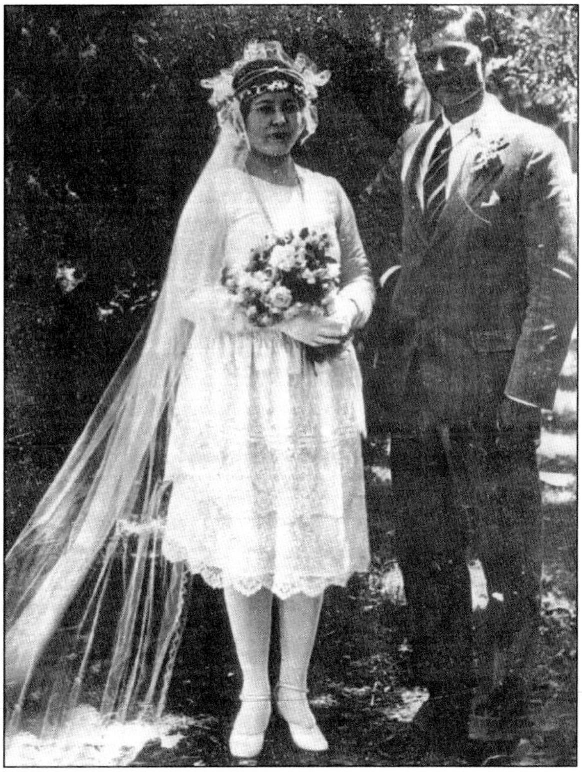

Many brides desire a June wedding. On June 24, 1928, Victoria C. Soto married John Floyd Jones Gomez. She had to learn to be a ranch woman. She was taught by John Floyd's aunt Maggie Frank; she especially needed skills when, in time, John Floyd departed to Casa Grande to start a cattle business.

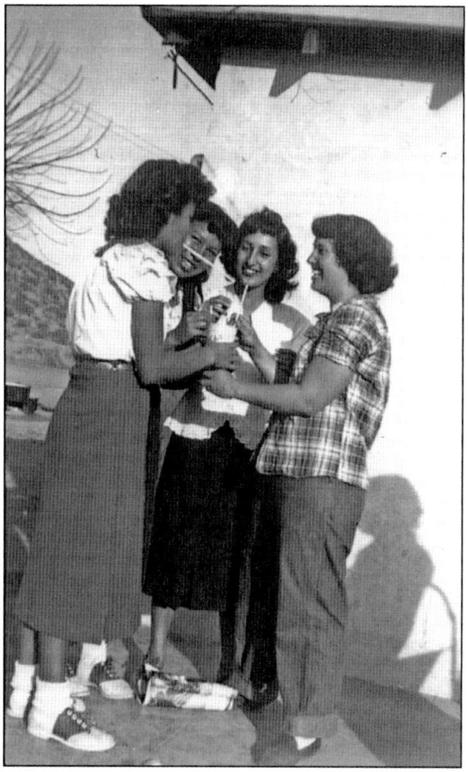

Celebrations include having fun, being happy to be alive, and spending time with friends. In the Tempe barrios, for Mexican teenagers, it was participating in a girls' outing. This group went to Upton's Ice Cream Shop on Mill Avenue, next door to the College Theatre (today the Harkins Valley Theatre), and pooled all the money in their pockets to purchase one large, cold, foamy ice-cream malt and four straws. Then the joyous treat began for, from left to right, Socorro Aguilar, Terri Aguilar, Michaela Guerrero, and Mary Burgos.

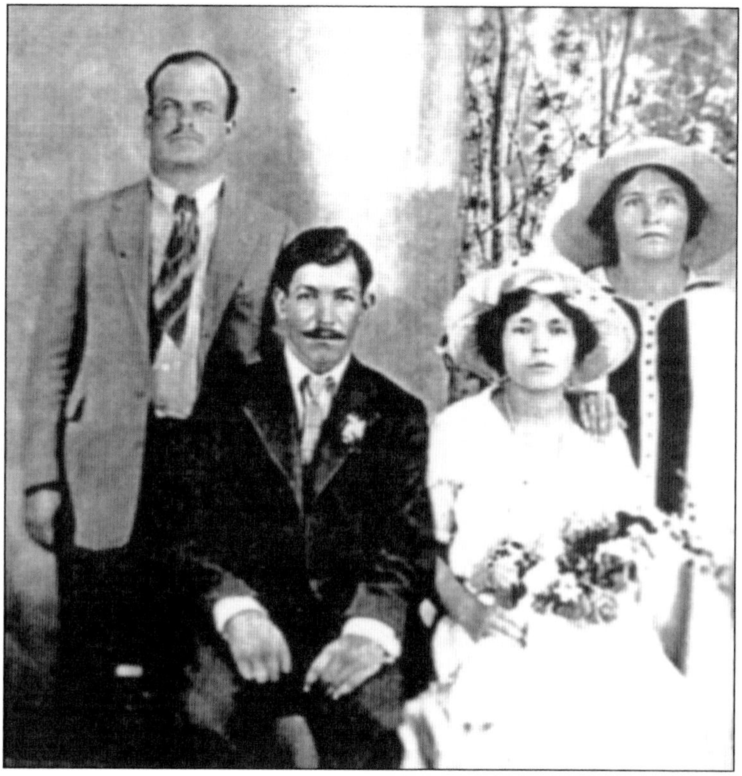

Pictured are (seated) Theodoro and Eutimia Hernandez, who were married in the mid-1920s, and (standing) Alfonso and Caretine Ungaray. (Rachel Hernandez Pollack.)

This wedding picture shows a bridegroom (left) and his bride (center) whose names are unknown. The wedding is estimated to have occurred in the 1920s. Identified in the picture is Victor Arroyo Sr. (seated left) and his sister Esperanza Arroyo (seated on the far right).

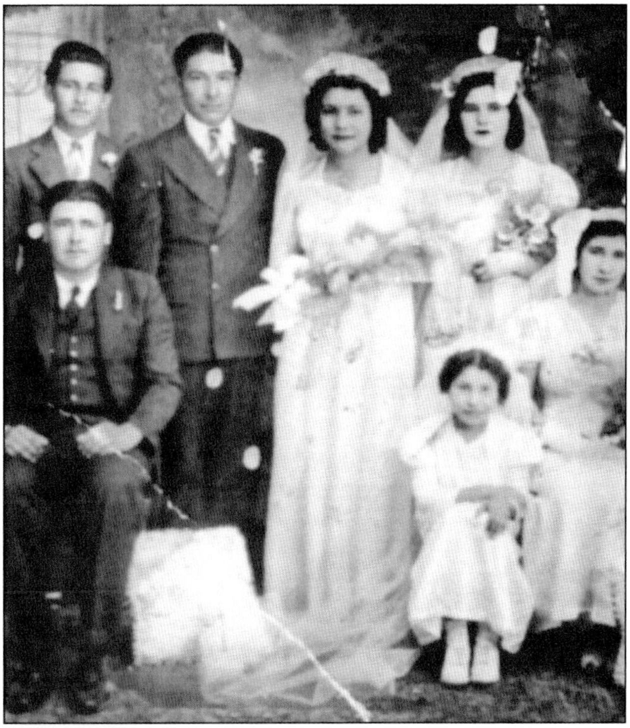

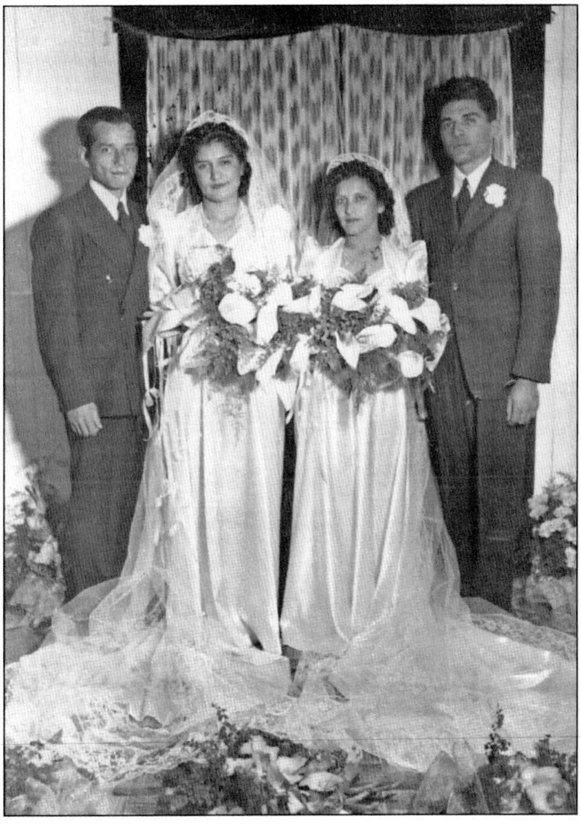

In this 1942 picture of Danny Rodriguez and his bride, Josephine, (the couple on the left), one can see that the style of attire differed from that of the 1920s (shown above) but has remained traditional.

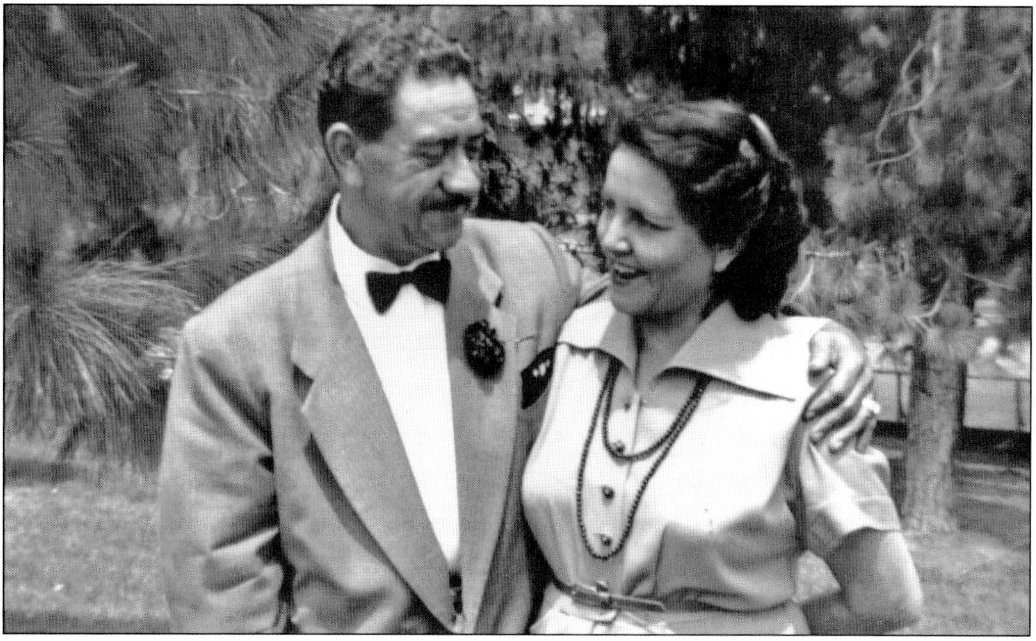

Otilio "Tily" Lopez, who had experienced repatriation in the 1930s, returned from Mexico, worked for the Southern Pacific (whose trains had carried him away during the country's repatriation), and made a name for himself as a leader of his own orchestra. He served the public media as a radio announcer for KALI and finally married Angelita Soto, a widow. Angelita for some years pursued her education and her career, and she did not want to marry Otilio so soon. He waited, and both continued the romance and happily married in 1959, the date of this photograph. Notice that the dress is less formal for weddings held outside the church setting.

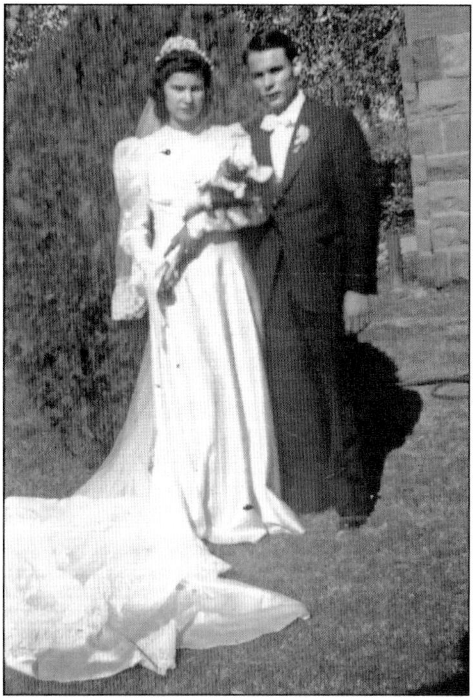

This picture shows Ramona Burgos and her husband, Juan Sosa. The interesting story involving this couple is that they were married in the 1940s, the time of this picture. World War II broke out, and Juan was drafted two weeks after his wedding. He served and returned with honor to continue his married life with Ramona. Ramona is the daughter of Juliana and Frank Burgos. Juan is the son of Perfecta Sotelo and Juan Sosa. The Sotelos came to Tempe in the early 1800s. Perfecta Sotelo had homesteaded a large section of land at that time.

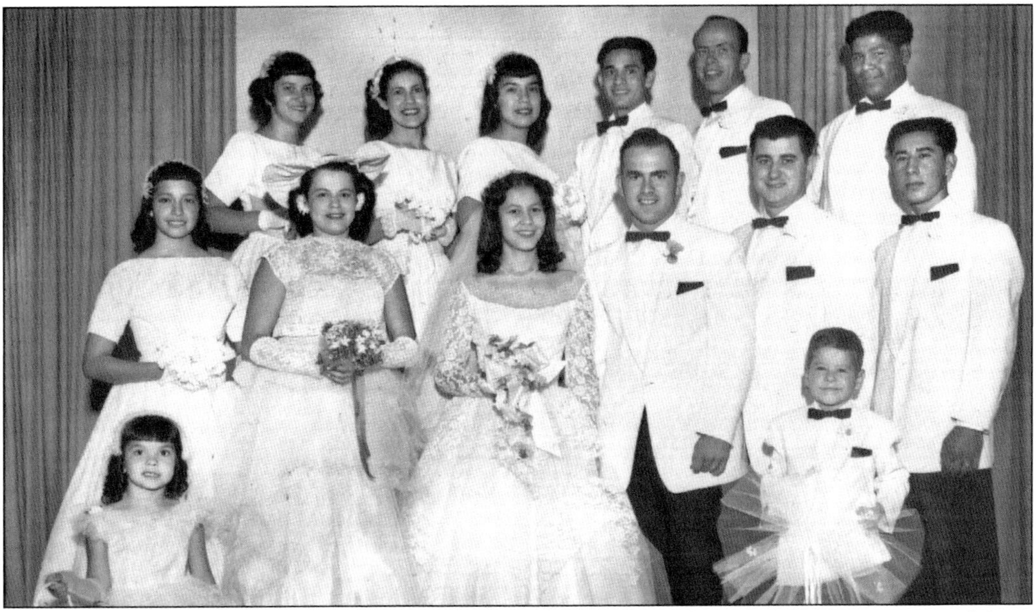

This is the wedding party of Maurice and Irene Gomez Hormell on May 11, 1957. Pictured from left to right are (first row) flower girl Rosalee Ballesteros and ring bearer Louis Tramont; (second row) bridesmaid Gloria Rubalcaba, matron of honor Helen Tramont, bride Irene Gomez Hormell, groom Maurice Bennett Hormell, Rocky Tramont, and Danny Peralta; (third row) bridesmaids Lucille Tramont, Isabel Gomez, and Camelita Jimenez, and ushers Danny Gamboa, Al Weigo, and Floyd Gomez Jr. Unlike at the other weddings pictured, these men wore white suit coats instead of black ones.

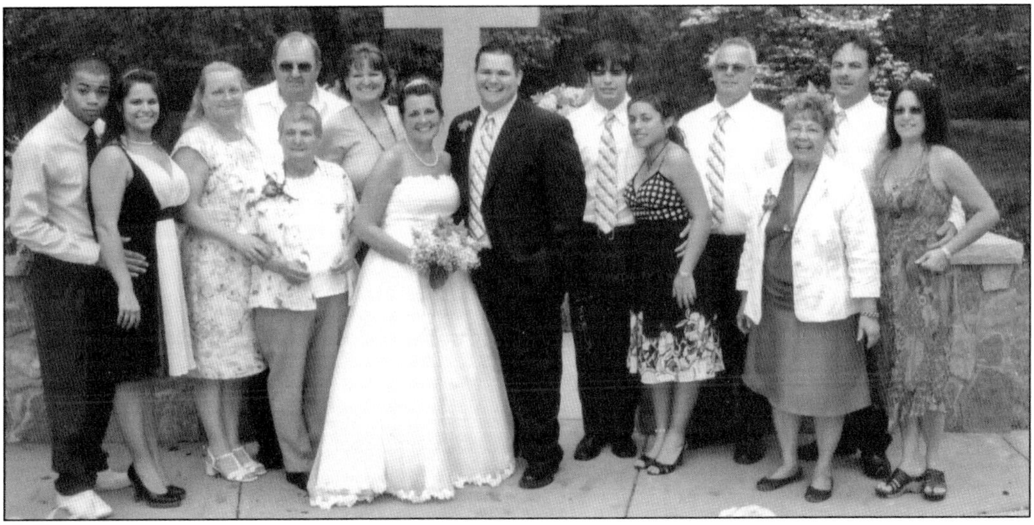

In future years, Irene Gomez Hormell would share in the happiness of her four sons' weddings, as well as grandson Stanley Brian Hormell's. This May 3, 2008, photograph shows Stanley's wedding to Amanda Lail in Hickory, North Carolina. Irene is standing in the first row, second from the right. Irene's great-grandmother Alcaria Montoya from Altar, Sonora, Mexico, immigrated north to Tempe and married Dr. Wilson Jones. One of their daughters, Kate Jones, married Jesus Aros Gomez. The Gomezes' son John Floyd Gomez was Irene's father. The footprints of heritage and immigration brought the family roots to Hickory, North Carolina.

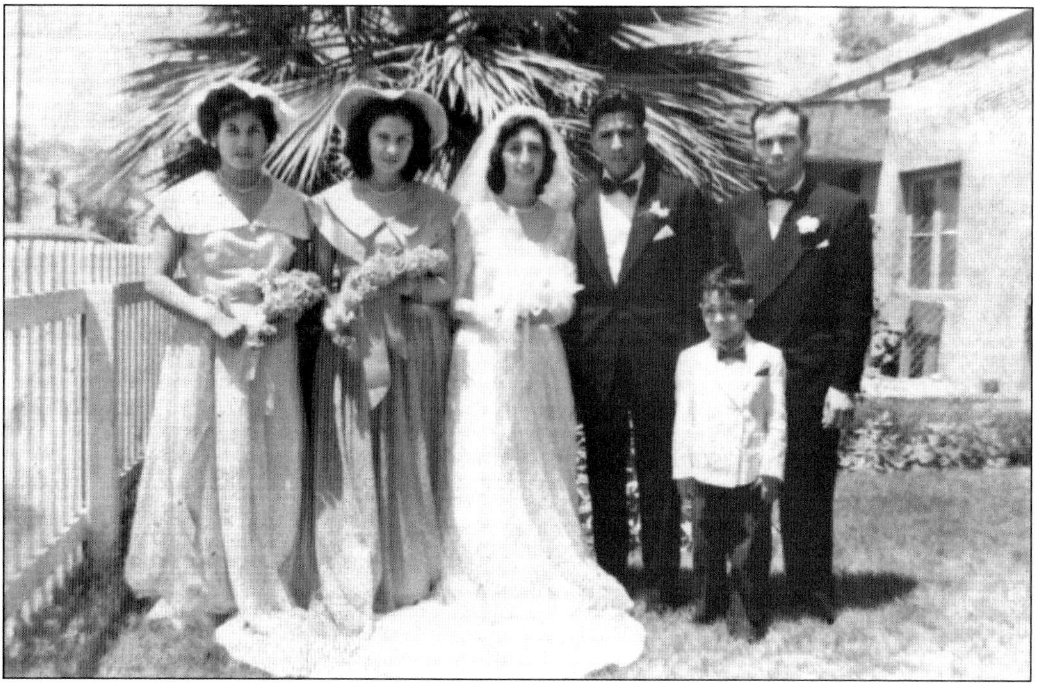

Michaela Gonzales Guerrero married Eleseo Escarcega in 1951. The men are wearing the usual black suit, with the exception of the ring bearer, who wears white. The style of dress of the bride and bridesmaids is also traditional. The taking of pictures, enjoying the occasion with a ride through town, a dance and dinner, and plenty of music demonstrate the strength of family values and customs.

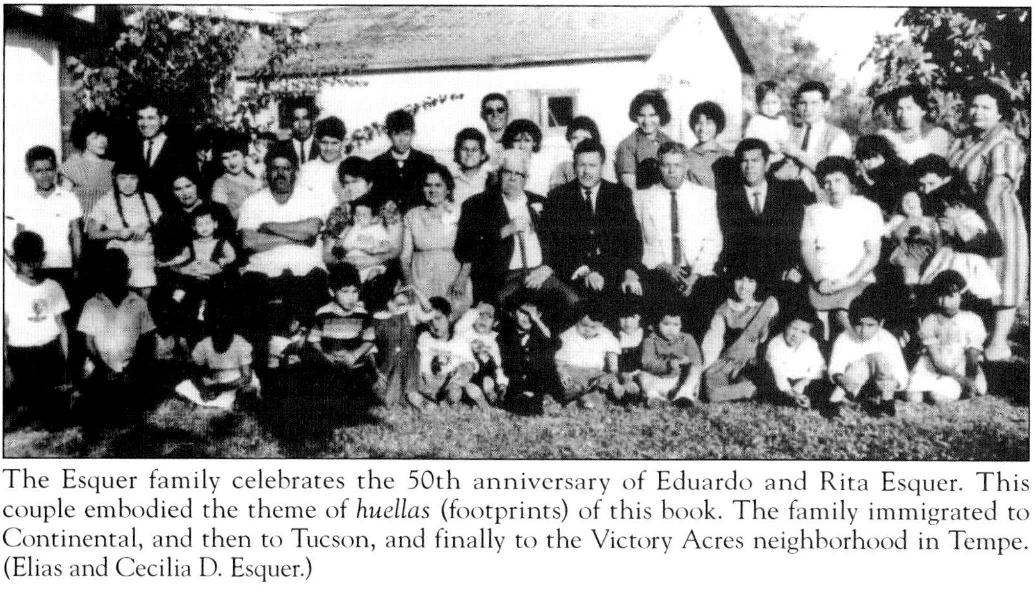

The Esquer family celebrates the 50th anniversary of Eduardo and Rita Esquer. This couple embodied the theme of *huellas* (footprints) of this book. The family immigrated to Continental, and then to Tucson, and finally to the Victory Acres neighborhood in Tempe. (Elias and Cecilia D. Esquer.)

Another tradition in Mexican culture is to honor one's mother and father, based in Holy Scripture. In this picture, Rachel Hernandez Pollack gives her mother, Eutimia Hernandez, her wedding bouquet because her mother granted Rachel the blessing of giving her away in marriage. (Rachel Hernandez Pollack.)

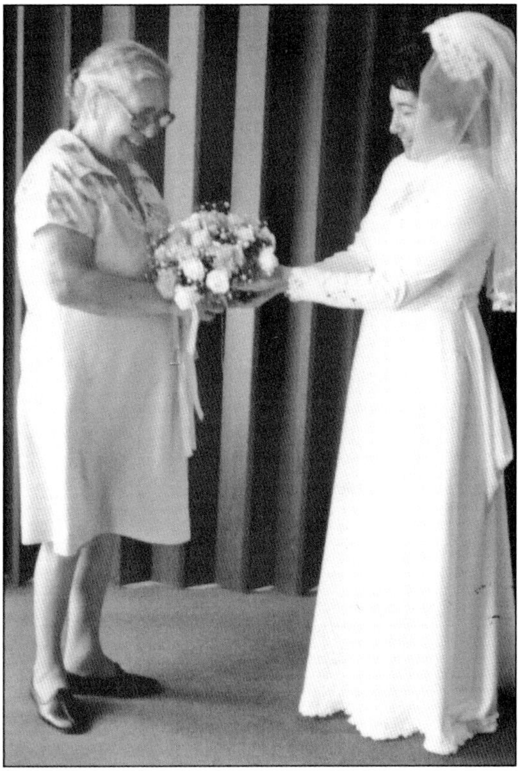

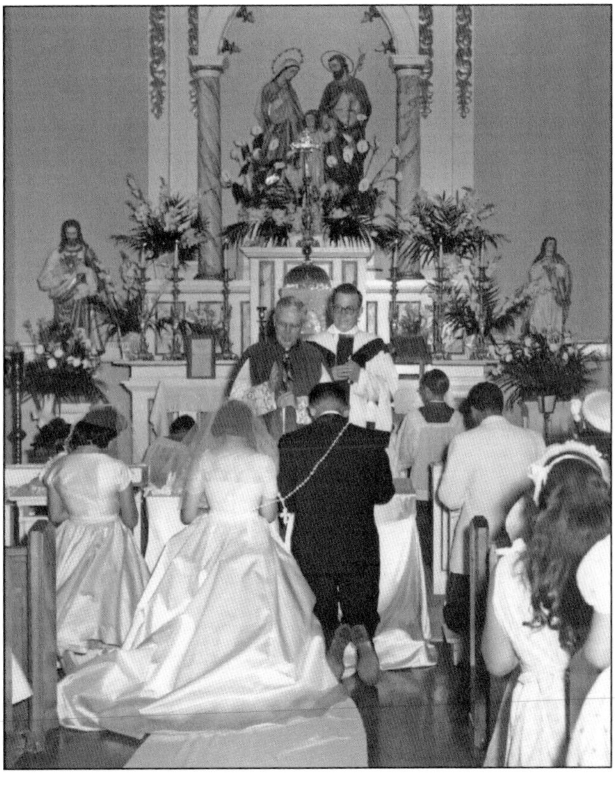

Susana and Albert Marquez celebrate their wedding in El Paso, Texas, in 1958. Monsignor ? Caffrey officiates and is assisted by Pastor Lol Pieza at Holy Family Church. Traditionally, a *lazo de compromise*, or bonding cord, is placed over the shoulders of the bride and groom, symbolically tying them together in a promise to love and cherish one another until death. (Albert and Susana Marquez.)

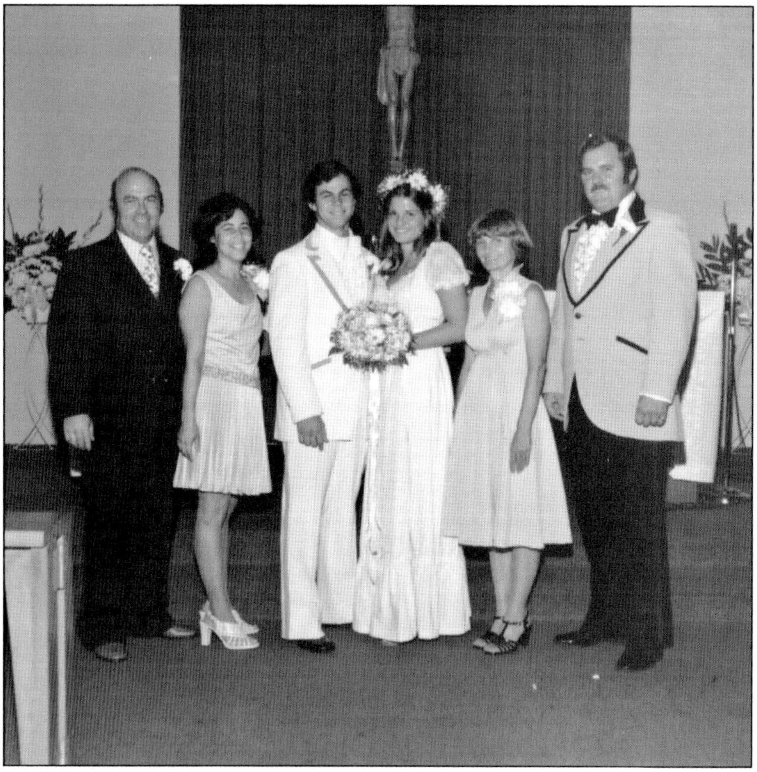

This August 1977 photograph shows the celebration of the wedding of Stanley Bennett Hormell and Tracey Clee. Stanley is the older son of Irene Gomez Hormell and Maurice Hormell. From left to right are Maurice Hormell, Irene Gomez Hormell, Stanley, Tracey, Nancy Clee, and Eric Clee.

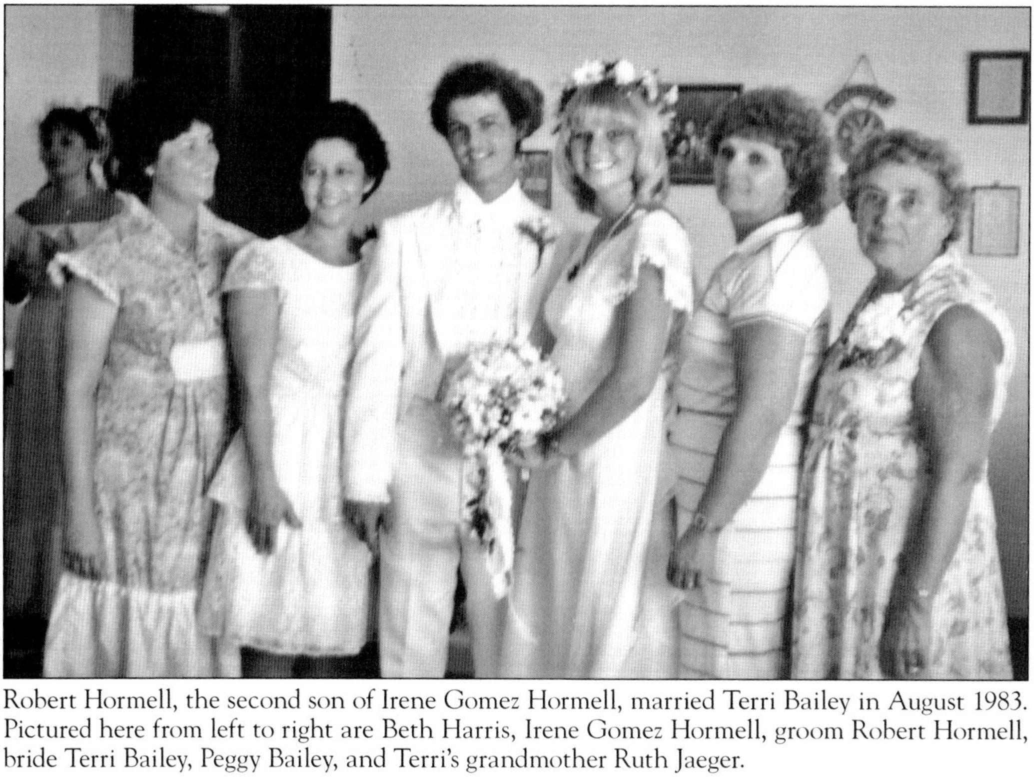

Robert Hormell, the second son of Irene Gomez Hormell, married Terri Bailey in August 1983. Pictured here from left to right are Beth Harris, Irene Gomez Hormell, groom Robert Hormell, bride Terri Bailey, Peggy Bailey, and Terri's grandmother Ruth Jaeger.

In this photograph, Victor Arroyo Jr. and Carmen Perez are all dressed up and ready to serve as an usher and a bridesmaid in Rudy and Rachel Arroyo's wedding on August 19, 1958.

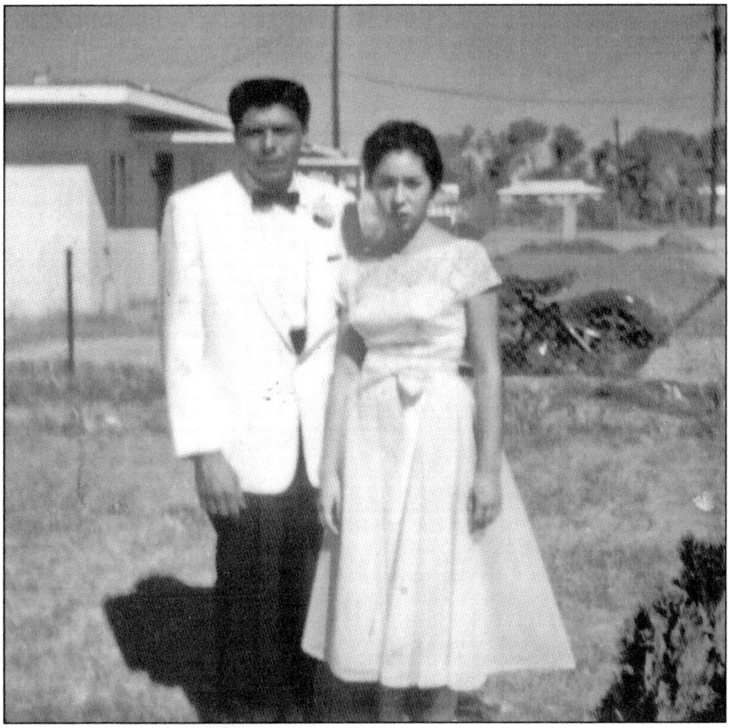

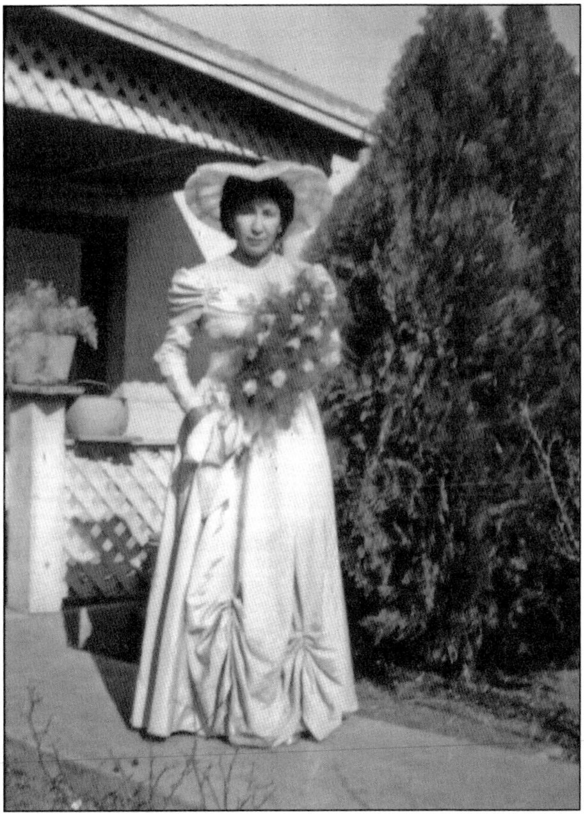

Esperanza Arroyo served as a bridesmaid in a friend's wedding in the 1940s.

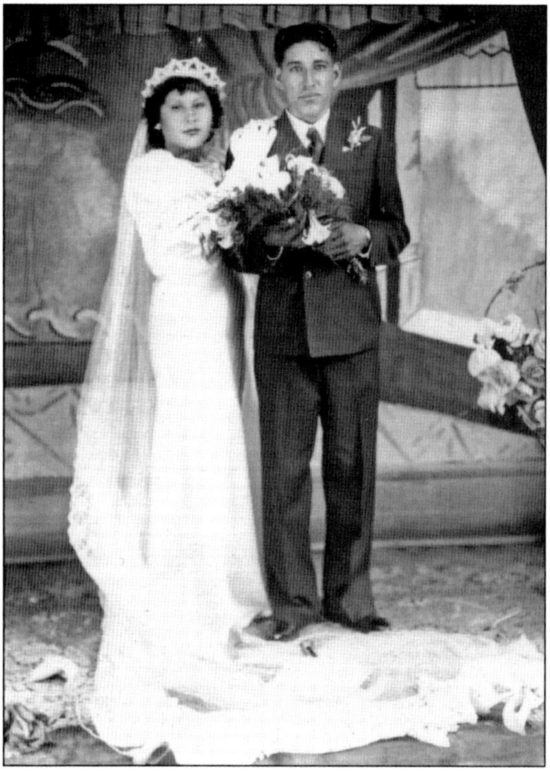

Mary Sterling and Reynaldo Peralta were married on October 9, 1937, at the original Our Lady of Mount Carmel Church, located on College Avenue and Eighth Street (now University Drive). They had their reception at the house of Enrique and Victoria Soza. The Sozas were their *padrinos*, commonly and more endearingly called *ninos* (godparents). Enrique was the son of Juan and Perfecta Sotelo Soza. (Barney S. Peralta.)

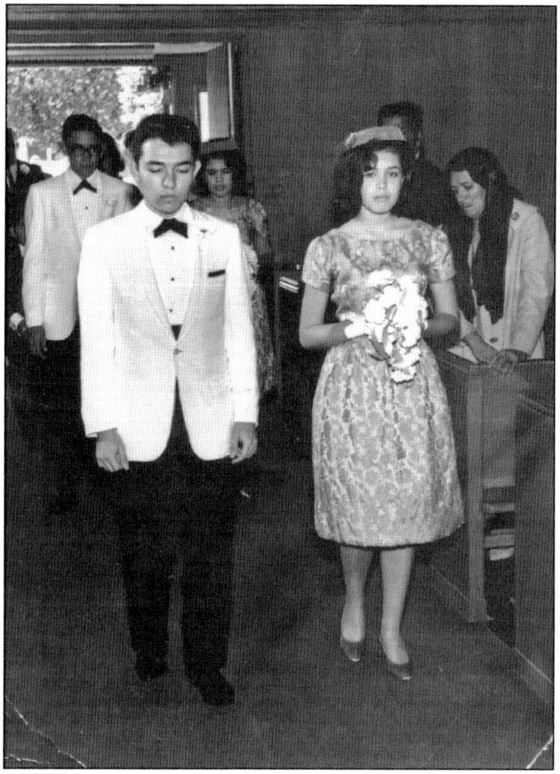

This wedding procession with Josie Solis (far right) and, from left to right, her cousins Gil Elias and Leo Enriquez, with Margie Berumen took place at St. Margaret's Church in the Victory Acres barrio in 1964. (Josephine O. Solis.)

Our Lady of Mount Carmel Church, fondly called the "Old Church," also had a basement school in the mid-1900s. Historically, the first Catholic church built by Mexican and Yaqui families at the foot of the butte was named Nuestra Señora del Carmen (Our Lady of Mount Carmel). In 1902, it became a mission served by St. Mary's in Phoenix. The church, begun by the San Pablo community, was completed in 1903; it was dedicated in January 1904. The late Bishop Daniel J. Gercke decreed a new parish, Our Lady of Mount Carmel, to serve Tempe in 1957. Our Lady of Mount Carmel was on Eighth Street and College Avenue until 1968, when a new Mount Carmel church was completed; the Old Church passed into the care of the Newman Center. The Old Church was placed on the National Register of Historic Places in January 1978, and in March 1980, the Old Church was reopened and rededicated. In this 2002 photograph, Josephine R. "Josie" Vega and Santos C. Vega stand in front of the Old Church. (Author's collection.)

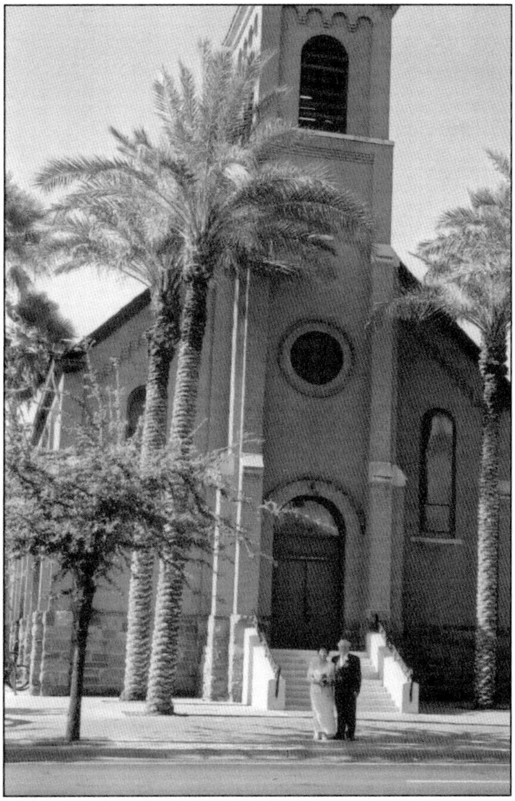

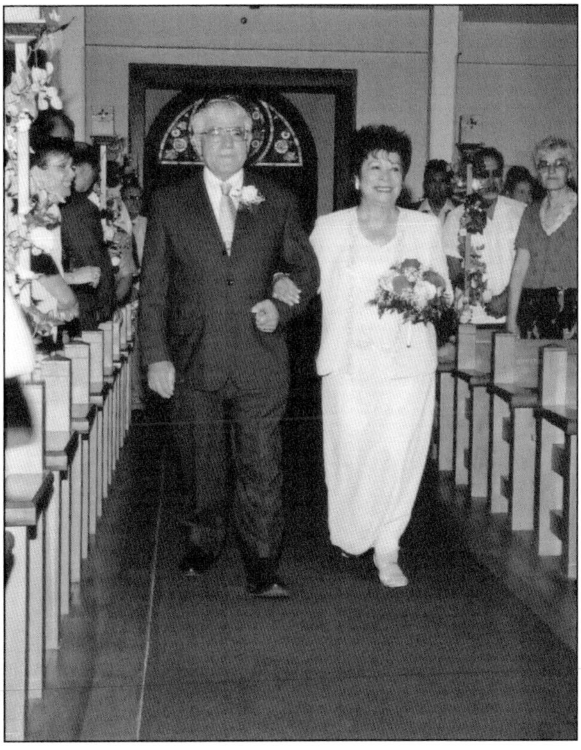

Josie Ramirez and Santos C. Vega renewed their marriage vows at the Our Lady of Mount Carmel Church on June 13, 2002.

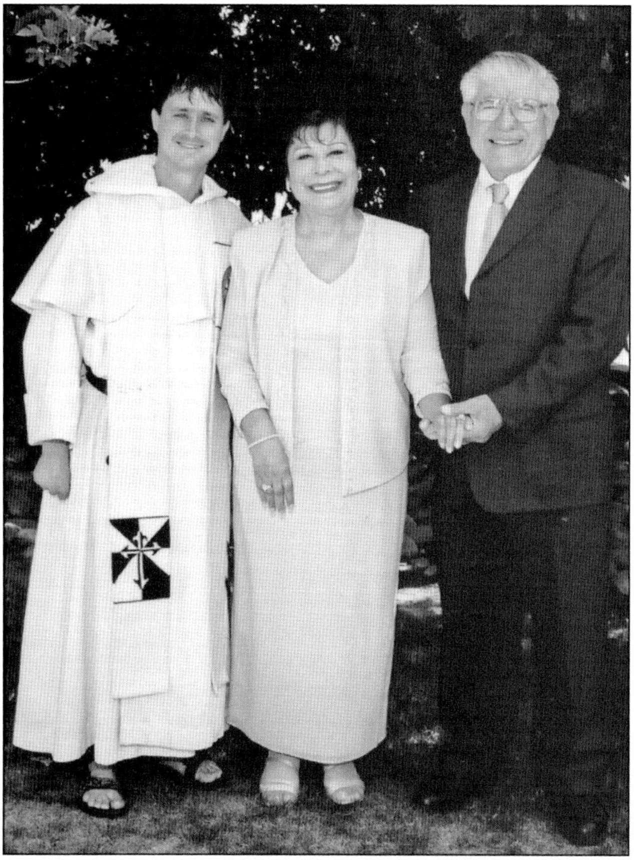

Rev. Fred Lucci, O.P., officiated at a renewal of vows of Josie O. Ramirez and Santos C. Vega in the Old Church at the Newman Center on June 13, 2002. Rev. Fr. Cassian T. Lewinski, O.P., had married Josie and Santos in the small chapel at the Newman Center on April 8, 2002, but the couple had previously planned a wedding in the Old Church. (Author's collection.)

The families of Josie R. Vega and Santos C. Vega were reunited on June 13, 2002, in celebration of Josie and Santos's wedding in Tempe. They enjoyed a dinner and dance at the Holiday Inn, formerly located on the corner of Apache Boulevard and Rural Road. Another Mexican tradition is that marriage unites different families into one. (Author's collection.)

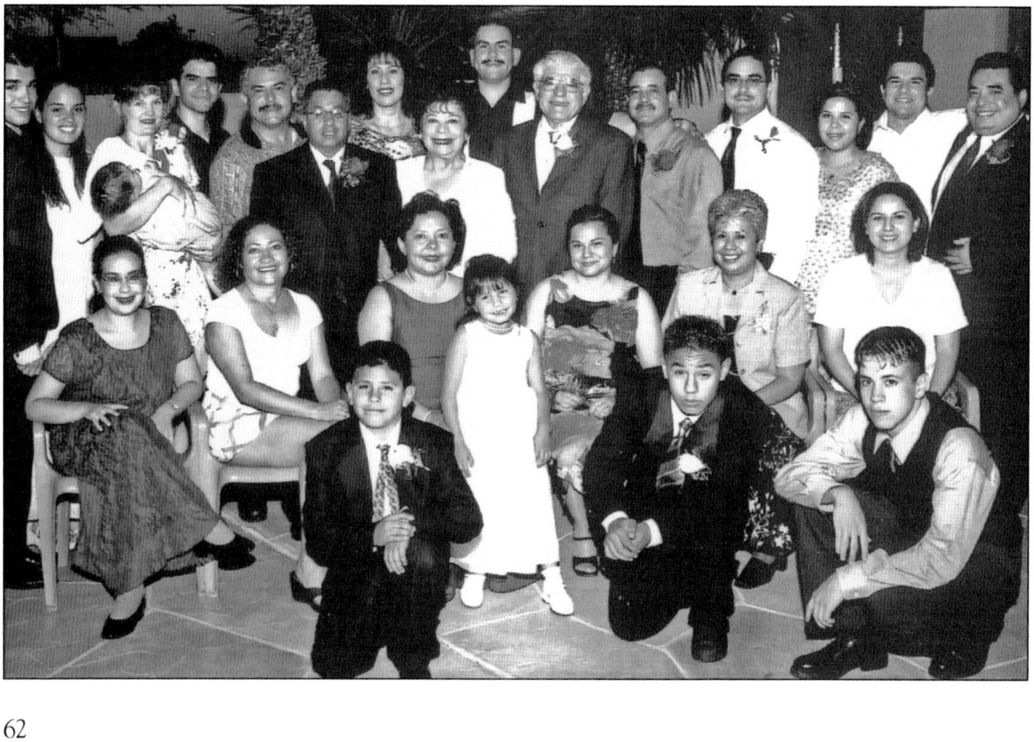

Four

Work, Military Service, and Organizations

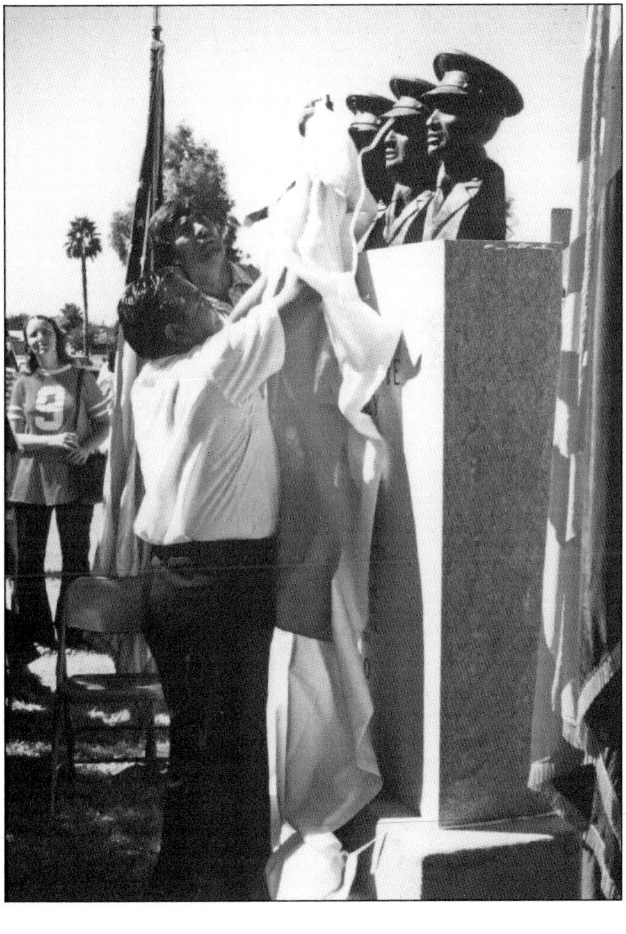

Escalante Park and Center was dedicated in honor of the Escalante brothers—George, Cipriano, and Gabriel—who gave up their lives fighting for the United States in World War II. The Escalante family, c. 1890 settlers in Tempe, had family members who served in several wars. (ASU.)

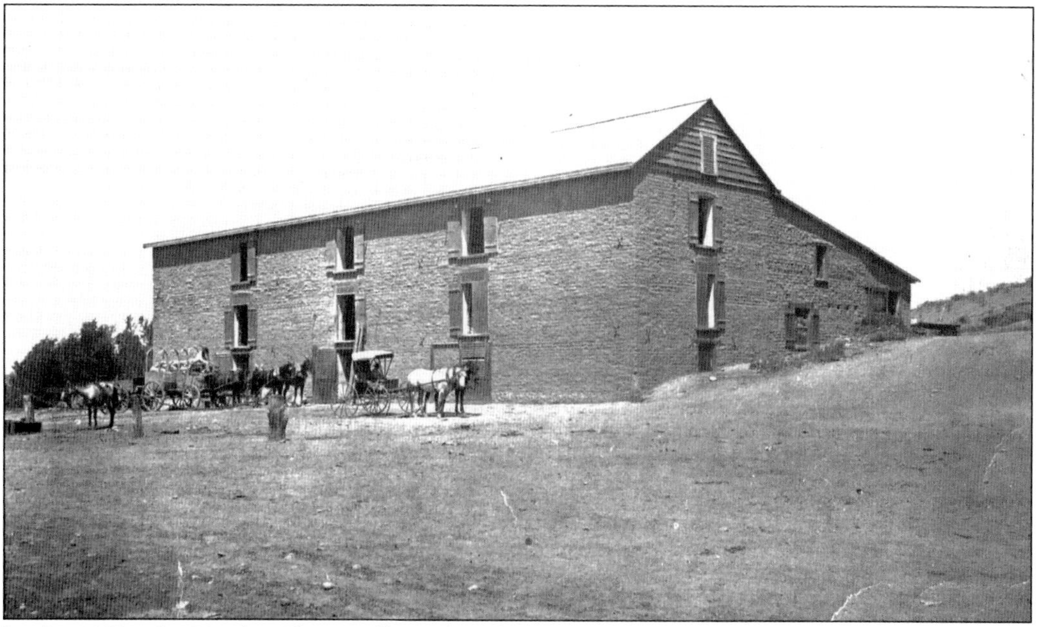

In the 1870s, the Hayden Flour Mill employed Mexican residents of San Pablo in its operation, processing flour for sale and distribution. (ASU.)

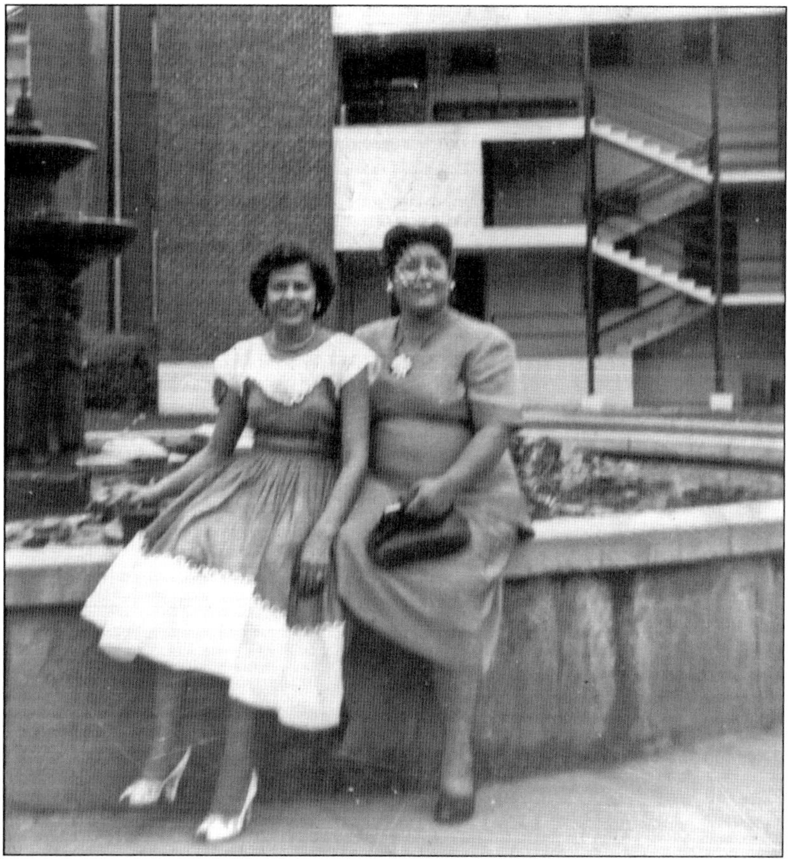

Victoria Soto Gomez sits with her daughter Helen around 1947 at the water pond on the Arizona State University campus. Many Tempe residents would seek out a place to have their picture taken on the campus. Later, when Victoria's marriage to John Floyd Gomez ended, she became the first Mexican American woman to work at the Hayden Flour Mill in Tempe. In time, she met Gene R. Leon while both worked at the mill.

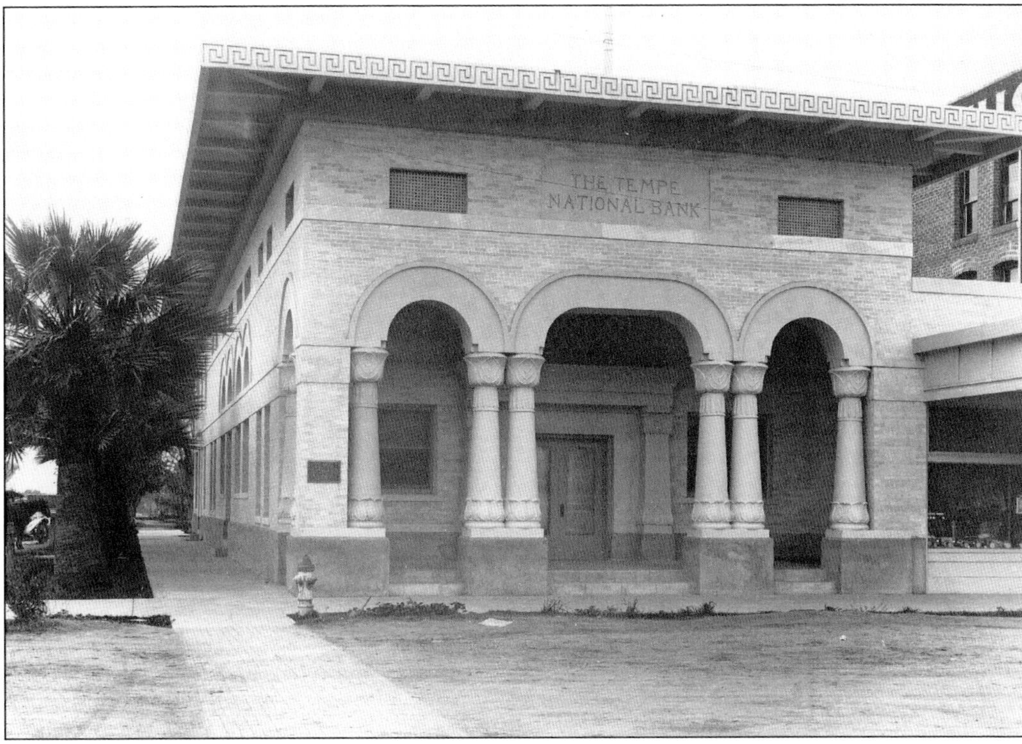

The Tempe National Bank, shown in 1919, served Tempe residents for all their banking needs. The banking industry changed over the years, banks had new names, and new banks came to town to do business. But the Tempe National Bank building continued to be a popular architectural construction and still stands in downtown Tempe. (AHF.)

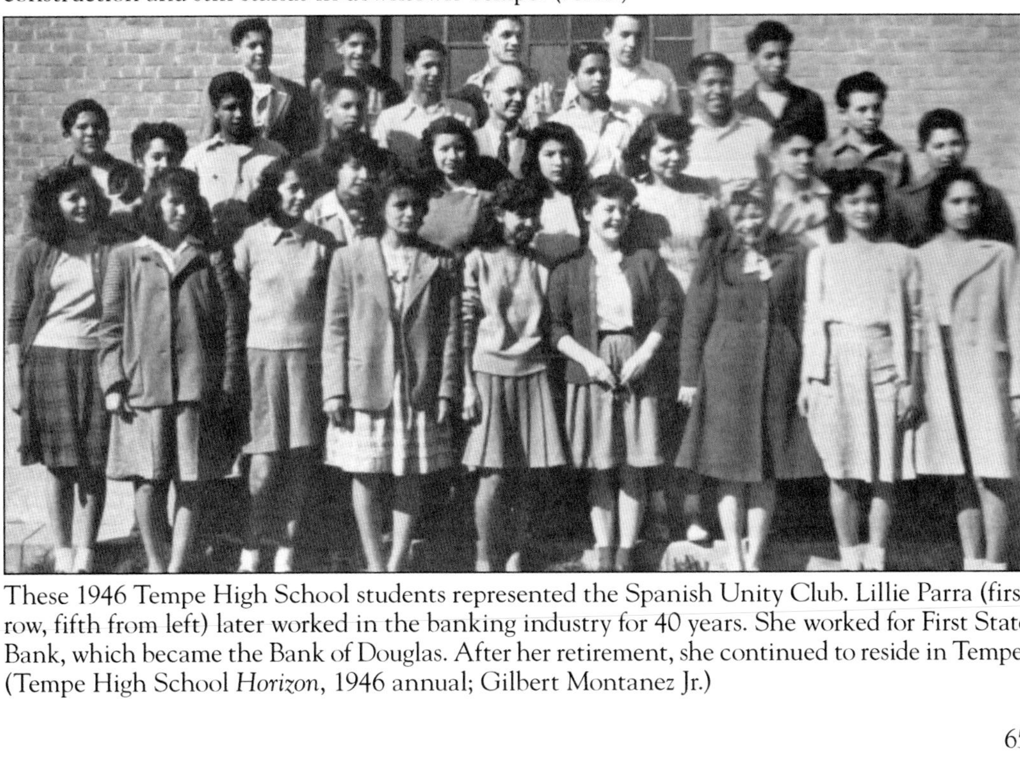

These 1946 Tempe High School students represented the Spanish Unity Club. Lillie Parra (first row, fifth from left) later worked in the banking industry for 40 years. She worked for First State Bank, which became the Bank of Douglas. After her retirement, she continued to reside in Tempe. (Tempe High School *Horizon*, 1946 annual; Gilbert Montanez Jr.)

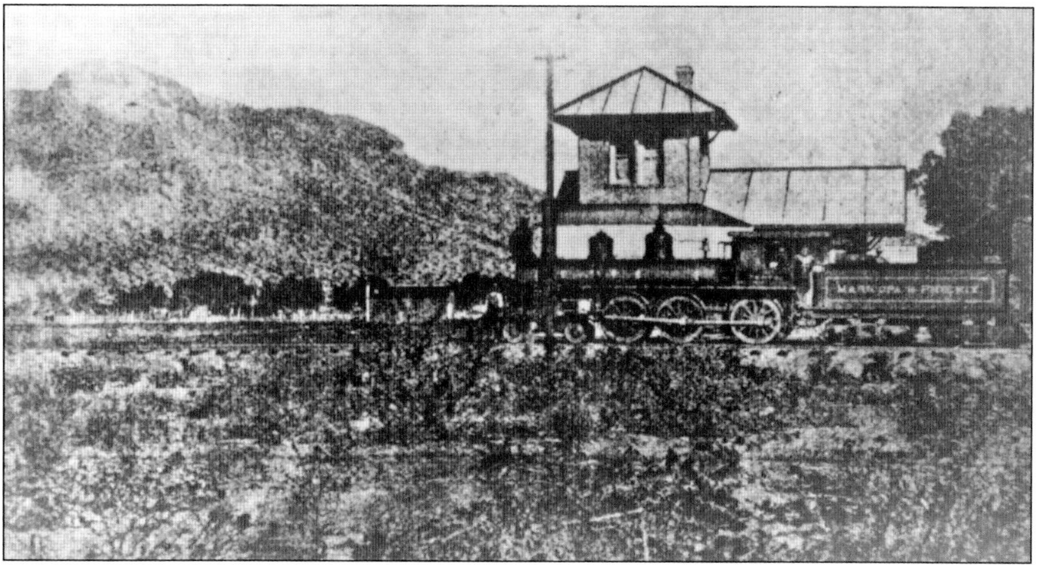

The eastern train station is pictured in Tempe in 1906. Immigrant Mexican labor had helped build the railroads that connected the West Coast with the East Coast and helped join the country in the development of its economy. The produce of mines, agriculture, and ranching flowed over the train rails to markets in the eastern part of the country. In the late 1800s, the railroad provided transportation for immigrants from the Midwest, South, and East. Arizona, along with Tempe, grew in population and industry. Mexican laborers continued to work for the railroads for many years in Tempe and elsewhere. (ASU.)

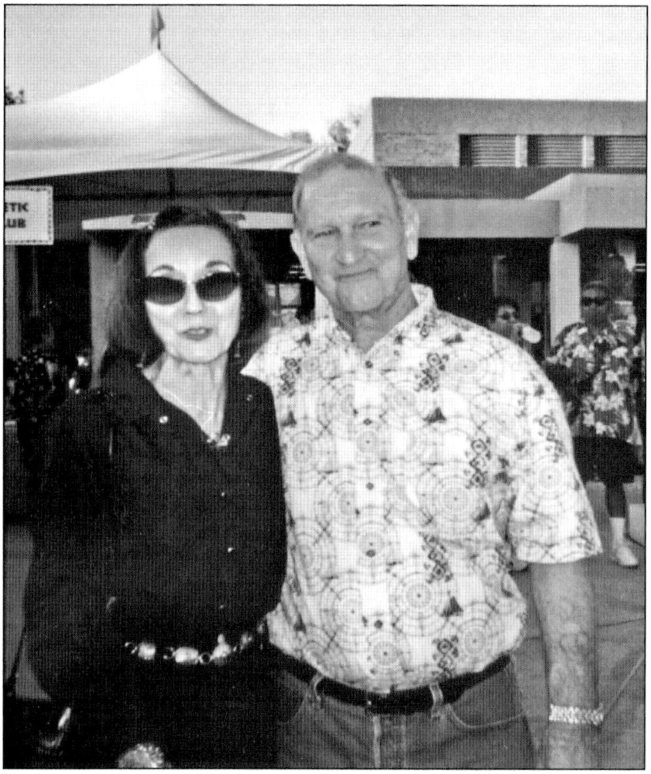

In addition to the railroad as a mode of transportation, the airplane, in time, became popular and started to overtake the trains for all types of transportation. Armida Guaderrama served as the first Mexican American airplane stewardess with United Air Lines. Armida is pictured here with an unidentified friend when she attended the Tempe Tardeada Fiesta in 2003.

The ranching industry began in the early 1700s in the Southwest to provide beef for hungry miners who had congregated near the areas containing desired minerals, and this gave impetus to the first mining communities in the mountains. Ranching thrived in the desert valleys, but after water was controlled by the canal systems to provide field irrigation, ranching lands made room for agricultural endeavors. Pictured here is the Pump Ditch Tempe Canal. Mexican labor helped dig the canal systems in the valley using mules to pull heavy wood dredges that scooped out the dirt while men dug with picks and shovels. (AHF.)

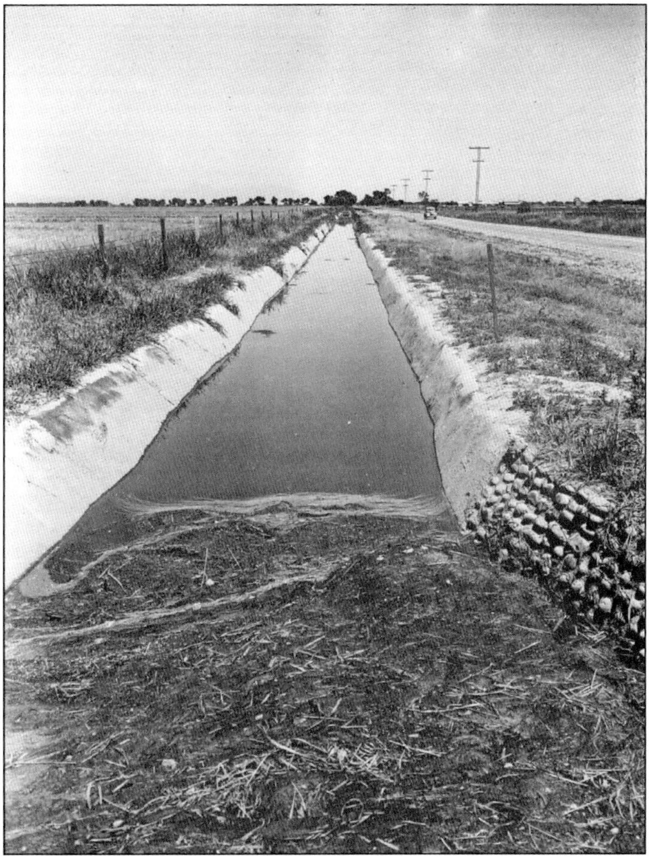

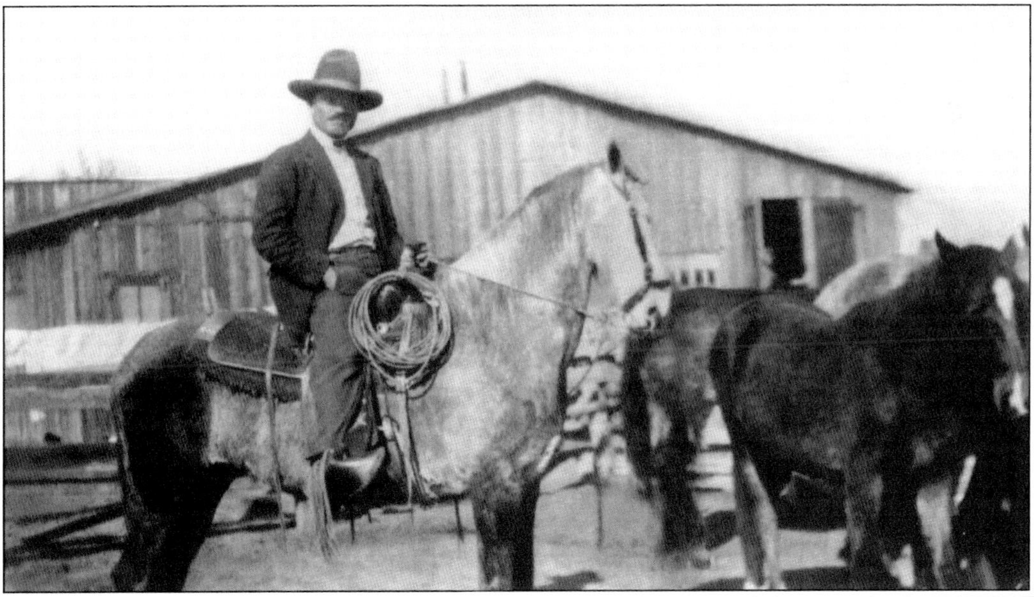

Juan Jimenez was fondly nicknamed "Juan Caballos" (John Horses) because he bought and sold horses. In this picture, taken in 1922 or 1927, Juan rides his horse as he tends to the business of ranching.

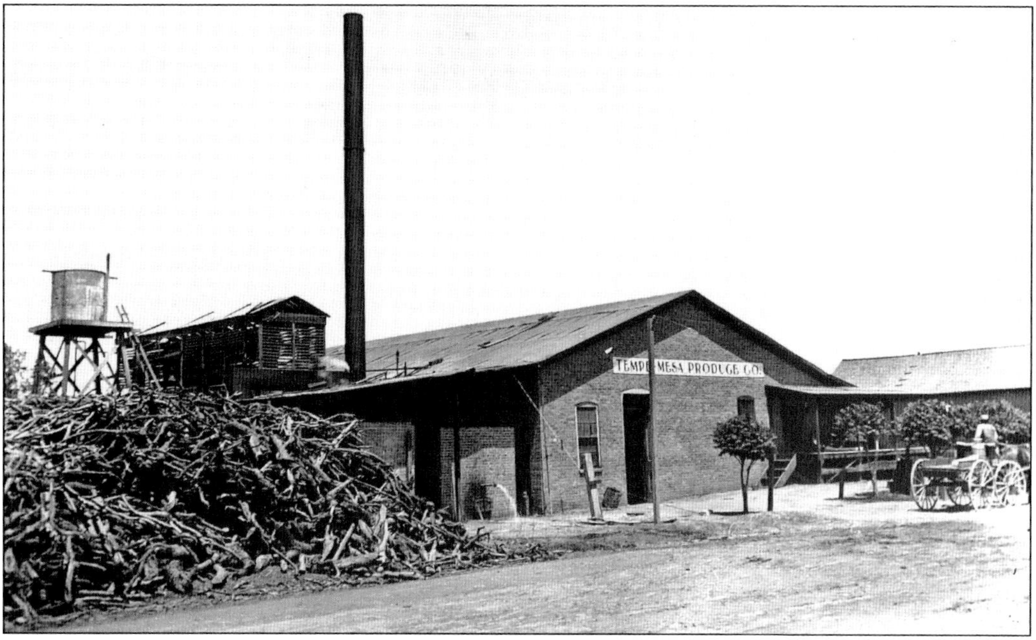

This is a late-1800s photograph of the creamery and the ice plant. The processing of dairy goods provided a variety of employment opportunities for Mexican settlers of San Pablo and other Mexican barrios. Dairy products were a result of cattle ranching in the Tempe area. (AHF.)

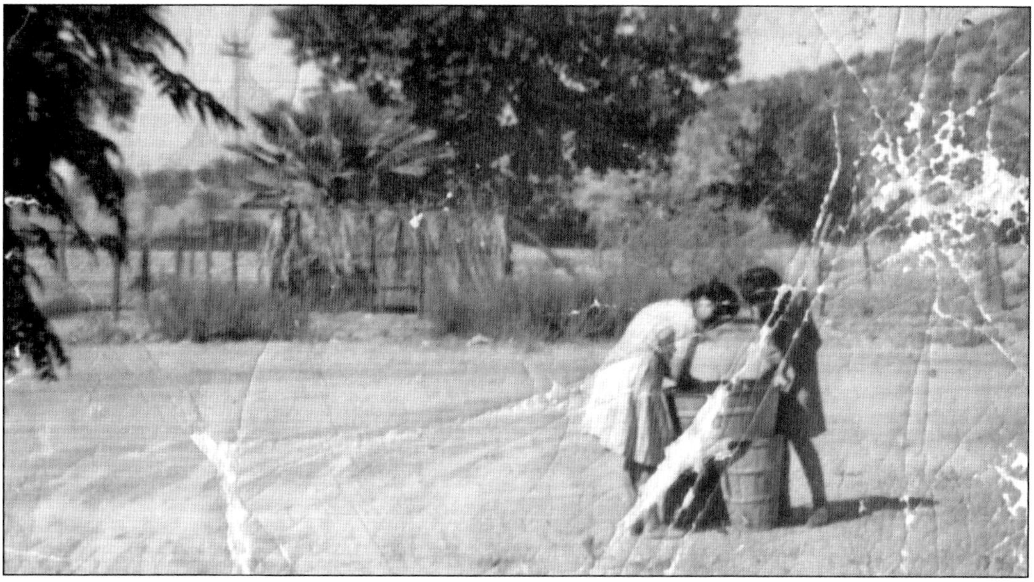

Two young girls, Maria (left) and Ramona Burgos, who lived in the barrio Central on Sixth and Center Streets, are washing clothes in 1939 using a scrub board in a tub of water. Women's work was never done in the barrios, with washing, making tortillas at 5:00 a.m. using an iron wood stove, and cooking supper for the men who returned at sunset from their work in the ranches, in the fields, or at the Hayden Flour Mill or at the creamery. The Tempe Butte can be seen in the background. One can imagine the brown waters flowing in the San Pablo canal on its way to quench the thirst of plants, cotton, vegetables, hay, and other crops. There were plenty of trees, mesquite wood fences, and hot days and *chubascos* (summer storms) in July and August.

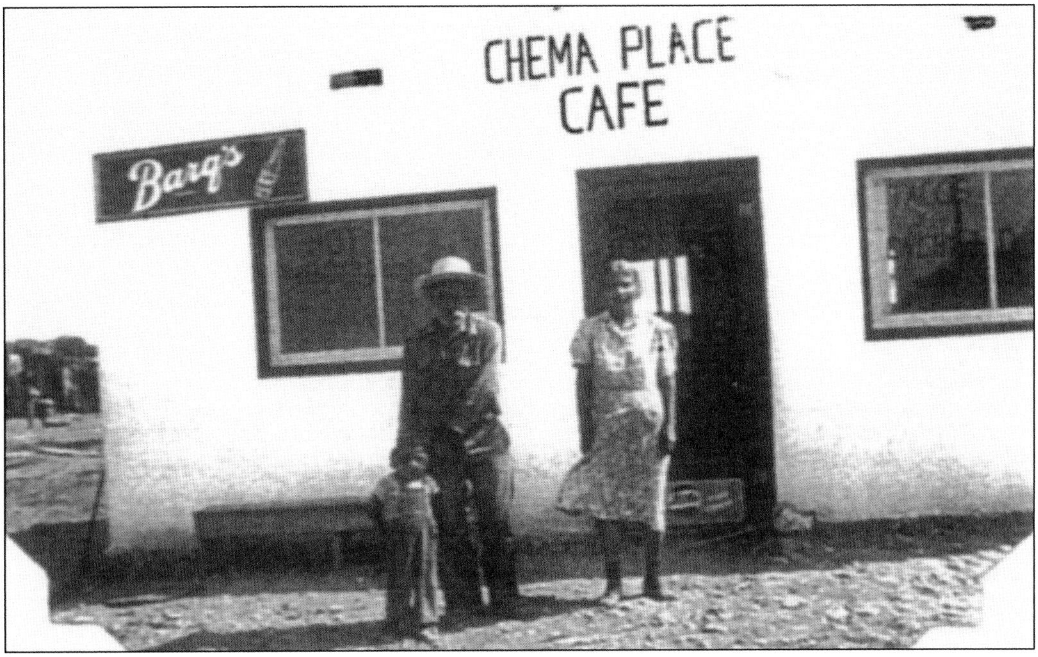

There were early barrio entrepreneurs of many kinds. At Chema Place Café, Jose Maria Villagomez and his wife, Maria Villagomez, offered good Mexican food to hungry customers in the Victory Acres neighborhood, or, as it is commonly called "La Victoria." This photograph was taken in the 1940s. The boy standing beside Jose Maria is thought to be Johnny Gonzalez. (Rachel Hernandez Pollack.)

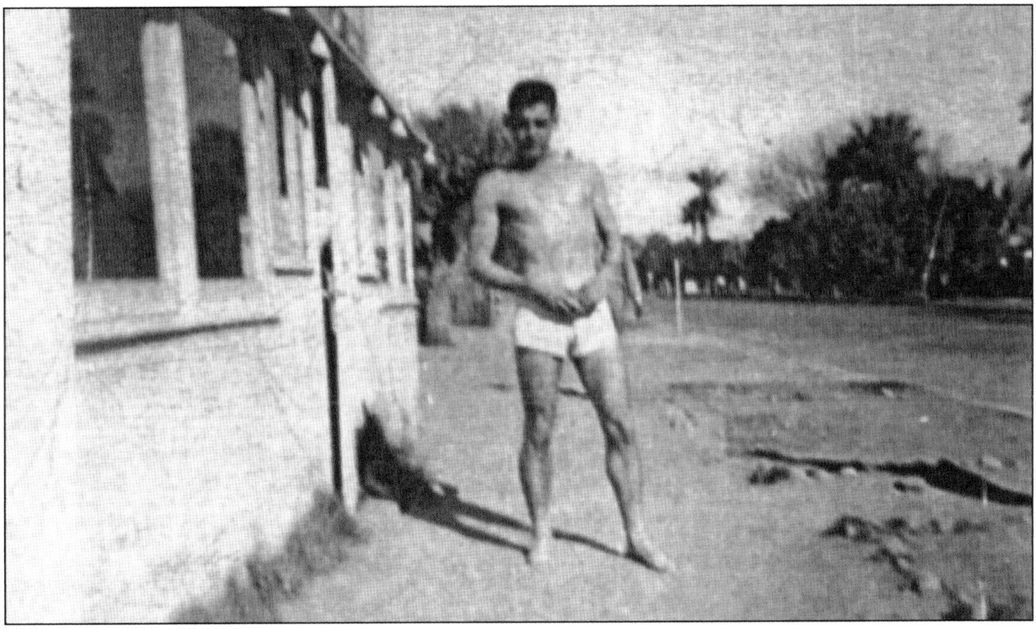

Across from Arizona State University on 358 East Eighth Street (later named University Drive) hungry students could find food and refreshments at Vicky's Place. Here track runner Truett McCollough stops to buy body nutrients. Notice that young Truett appears to be barefoot and running on unpaved street.

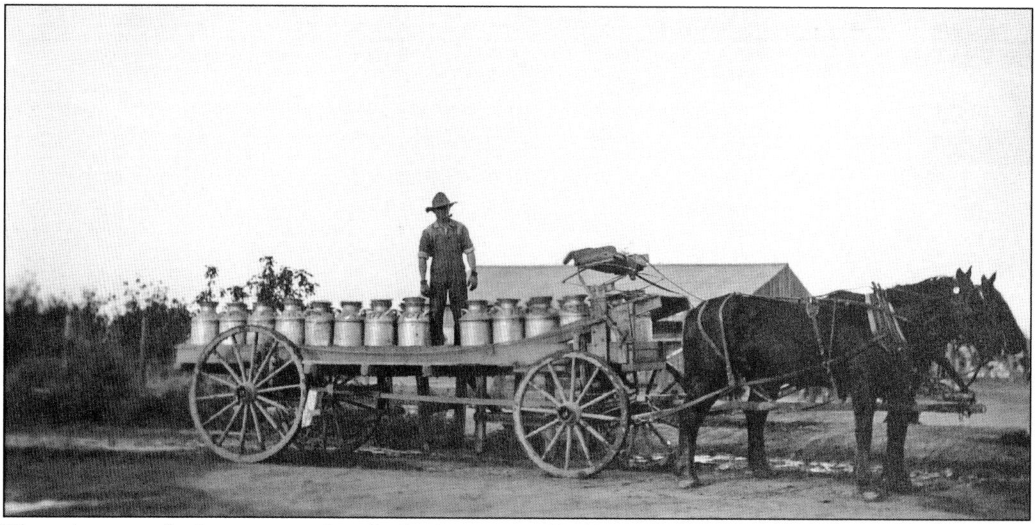

This photograph shows a wooden flatbed wagon pulled by a team of horses. The wagon is loaded with milk containers the man used to collect the milk from the dairy. The large containers of milk would then be delivered to the creamery, where the milk would be processed into dairy goods for sale to retailers. (AHF.)

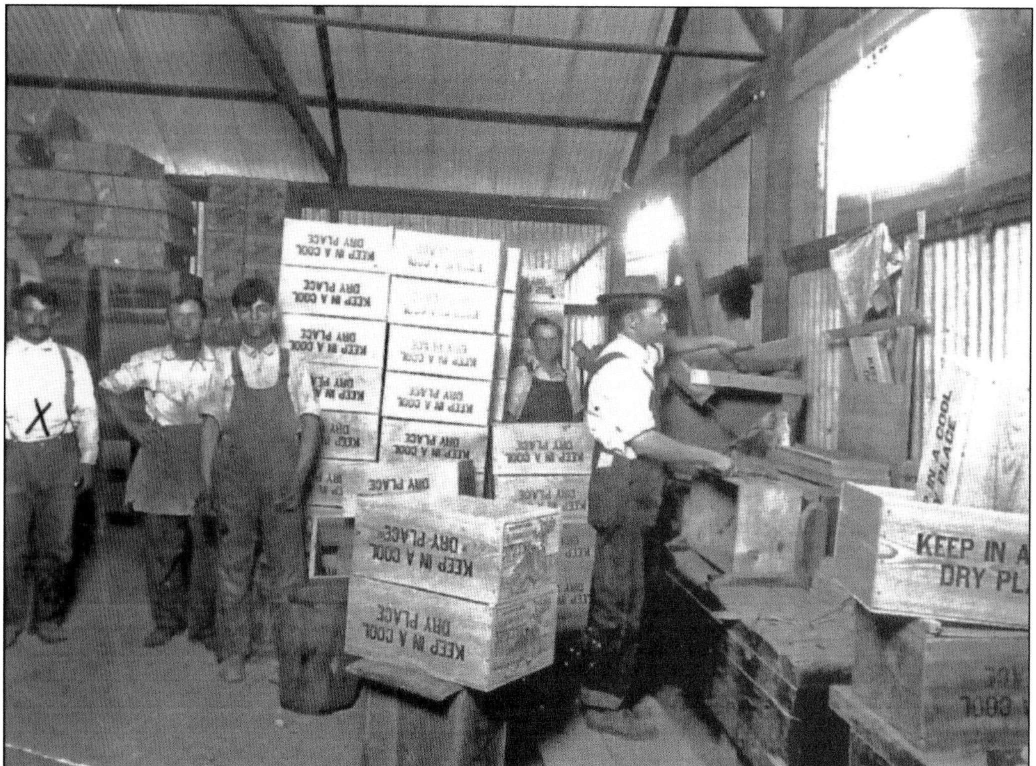

Jose Maria Rodriguez is identified by an "X" in this picture, taken inside the creamery located on Eighth Street in Tempe. The box labels read, "Keep in a cool dry place." Perhaps ice was hauled in from the ice plant as well with the large containers of milk. (Elizabeth Rodriguez Montanez de Rivera.)

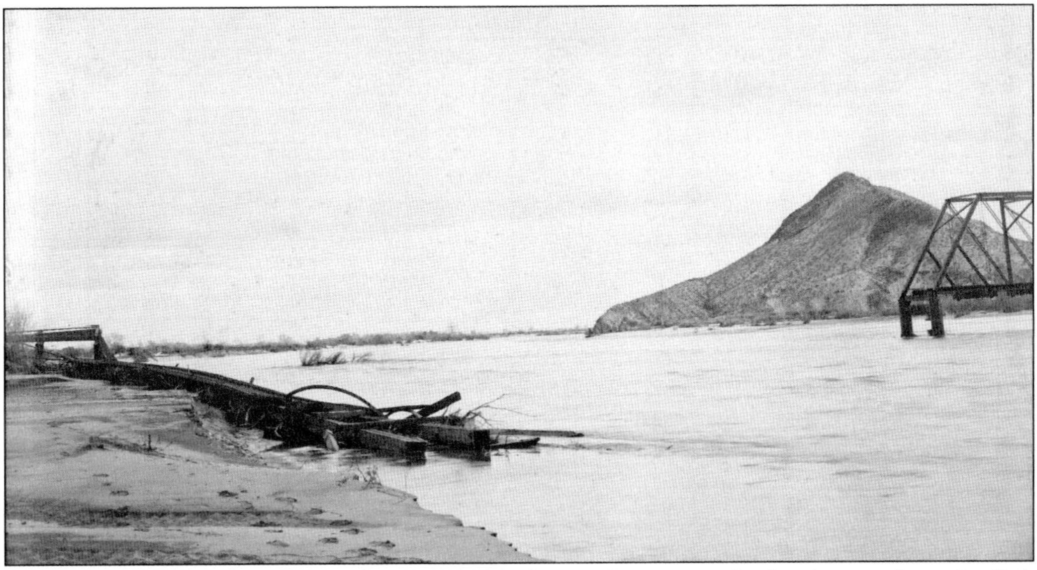

The railroad bridge in Tempe is shown in 1890 after its destruction by floodwaters from the Salt River. In the background is the back or north side of the butte; on the south side of the butte would be San Pablo and Tempe. Floods by the Salt River, the Gila River in the Pima Reservation several miles south of Tempe, and the San Pedro River in the Hayden area (southeast of Tempe by 60 miles) have from time to time provoked concerns even up to the 1950s. The Santa Cruz River, running south from Mexico through Tucson and connecting with the Gila southwest of Tempe, has presented problems with flooding south of Phoenix. The destruction of bridges and other structures created opportunities for Mexicans living in Tempe barrios to find work. There have been several bridges built over a century connecting Tempe with other communities. Early on, Tempe had the Carriage Bridge, the Quarry Road, a new bridge providing passage to Phoenix, and then a new bridge with the road connecting Tempe to Scottsdale. Bridges have played an important role for Tempe transportation since after Hayden's Ferry ended service. (AHF.)

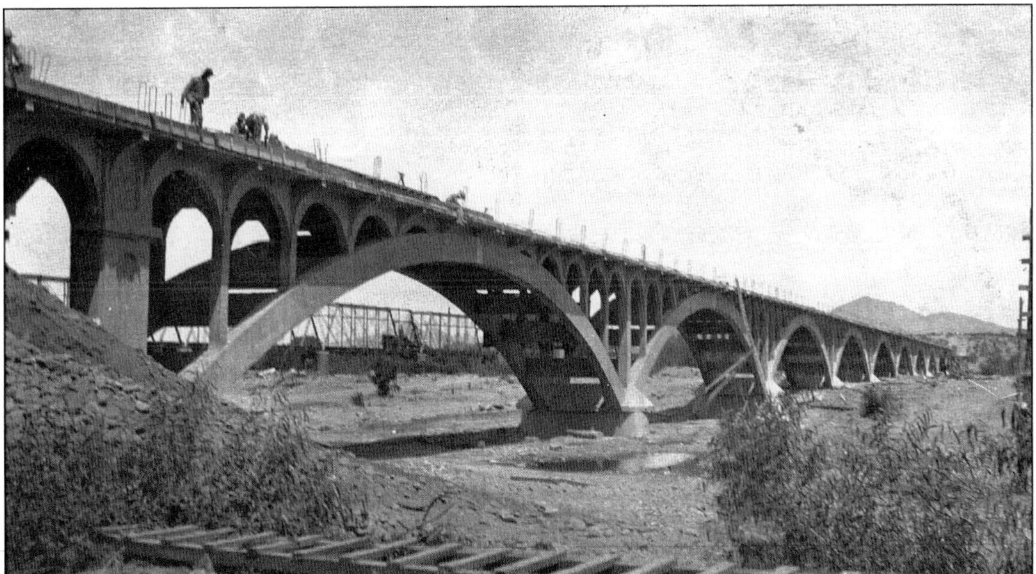

The Tempe Bridge in 1920 was under construction. (AHF.)

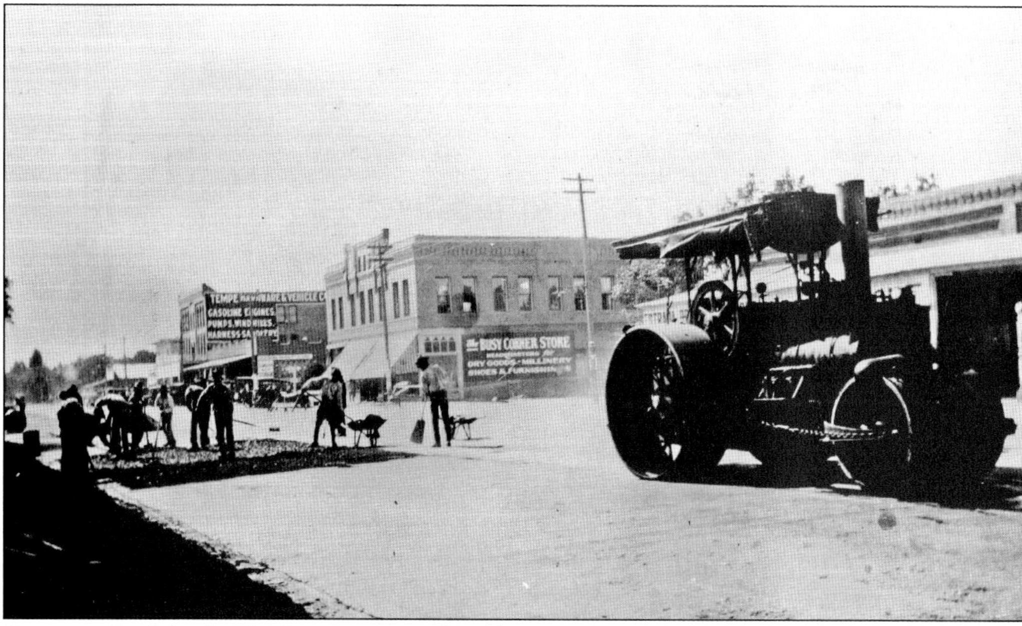

On page 19 of this book, the story was told of how Cresencio Varela in 1905 worked for the city by watering down the unpaved dirt streets of Tempe. In this picture, workers are busy paving Mill Avenue in 1919. The most modern heavy-duty equipment is being used, but the workmen are still using wheelbarrows and shovels. These pieces of equipment have continued to be tools of the trade. In the background are two new brick buildings. (AHF.)

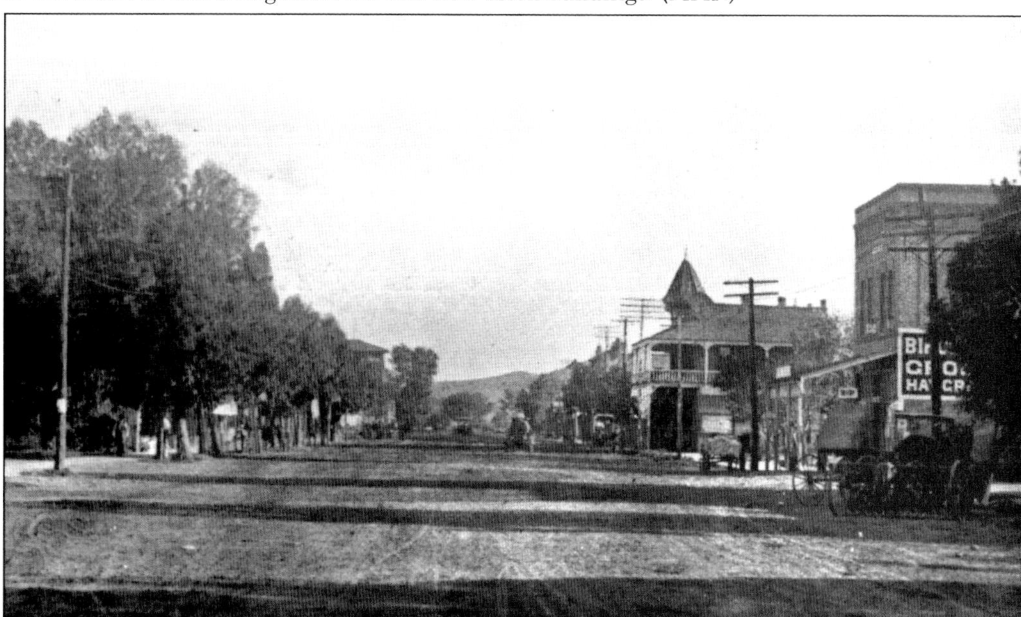

Mill Avenue is still dirt in this northward-looking picture, so it may be prior to 1919. In the 1930s, for the first time, many Arizona communities had cement sidewalks constructed on their main streets with help from federal government programs like the Work Progress Administration (WPA). Mexican workers, through employment in the WPA, made Rock Park near Tempe Beach and constructed the baseball field. (AHF.)

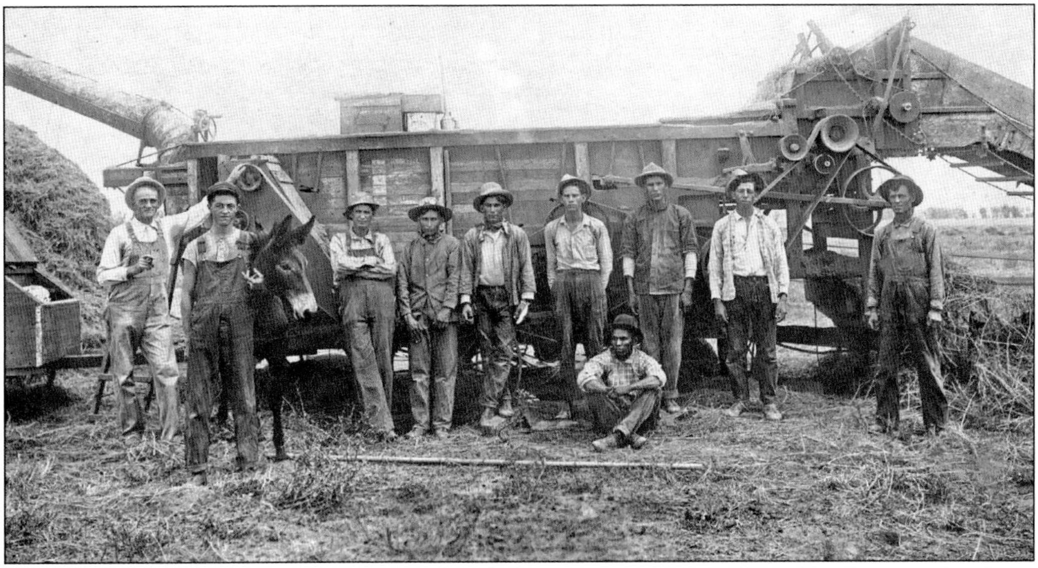

Ranching and farming activities provided work for many men out in the fields. Here is a threshing crew. The availability of laborers in a time when the country needed to build up its industries helped the country develop into an economic power. (AHF.)

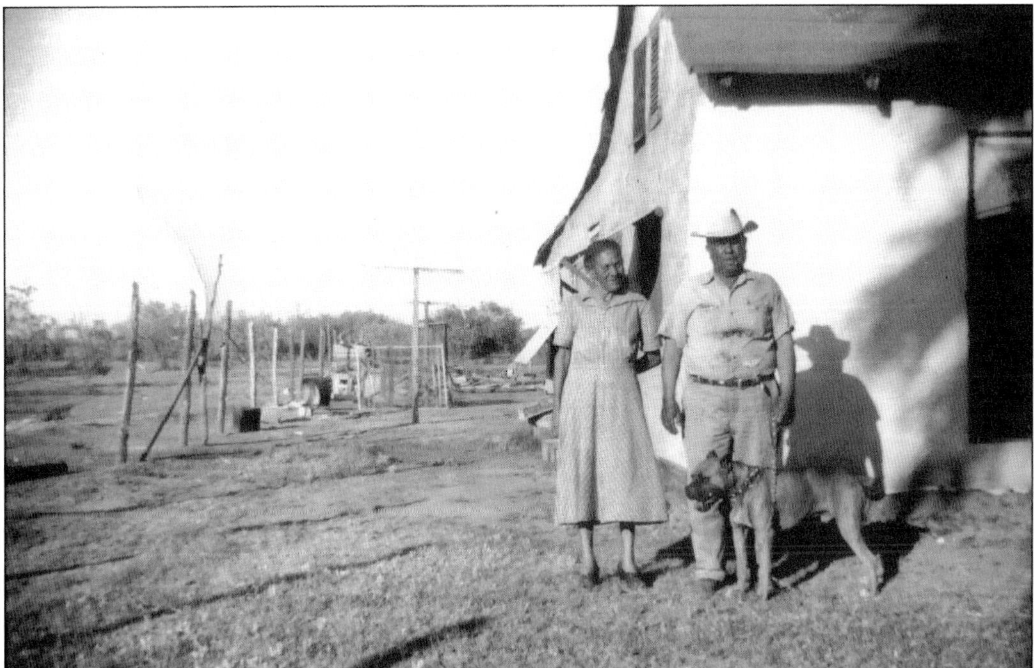

In Mickey Mouse barrio, Teresa and Manuel Solarez stand beside their house in the early afternoon (as shown by the shadows pointing east). The yards in the barrios were bare dirt and enclosed by mesquite-pole fences. The houses were either adobe block or wooden-frame structures. But both types were usually covered with white plaster. Most homes had chickens for meat and eggs, maybe a goat for milk, and maybe a horse, if they could afford the extra costs of feeding one. Families kept dogs for protection; in this picture can be seen a brown Great Dane that served as a loyal pet and guardian of the property.

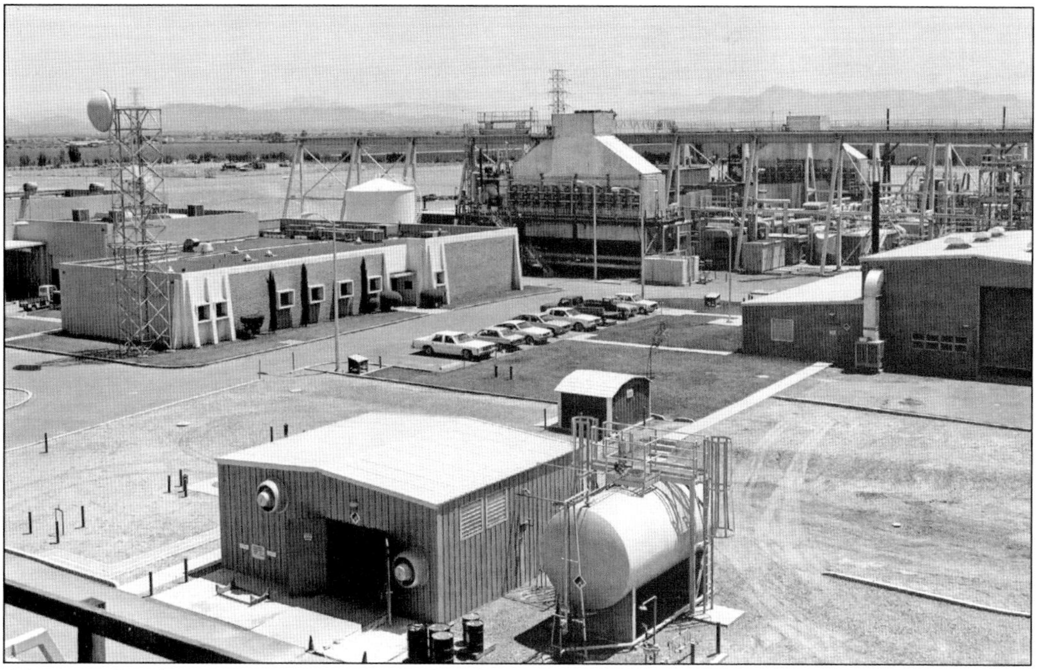

Along with other service institutions that have helped build Tempe is the Salt River Project Company (SRP). Here is a picture of the SRP Power Plant west and north of Tempe. (AHF.)

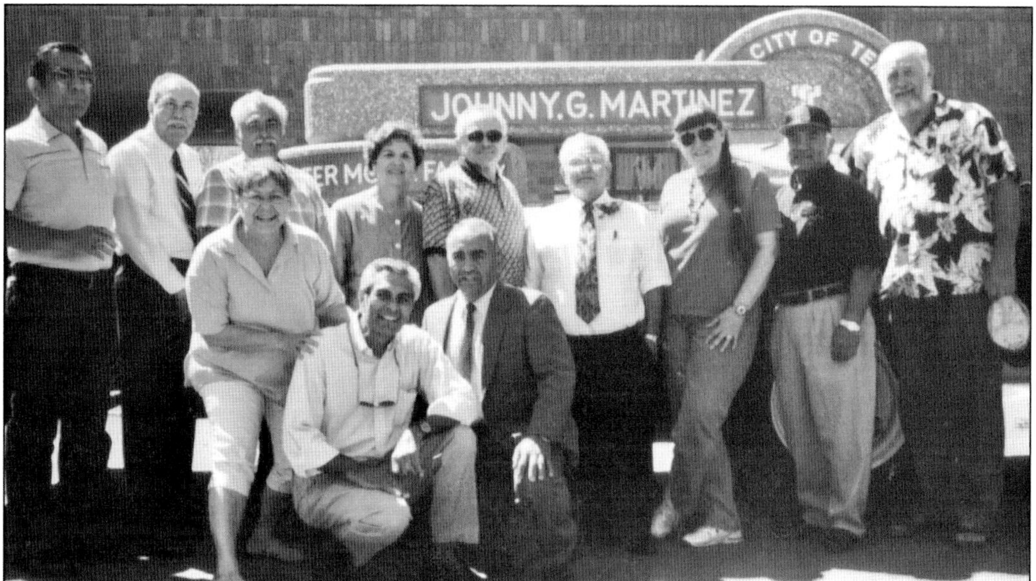

A group of friends congratulate Johnny Martinez, who worked for the city water treatment facility for many years; before his retirement, the city government approved the naming of the water treatment facility the City of Tempe Johnny G. Martinez Water Maintenance Facility. His friends were present on this occasion; from left to right are (first row) Irene Gomez Hormell, Jesse Valenzuela, and Richard Martinez (Johnny's brother); (second row) Armando Verdugo, Joe Ortega, Manuel Vital, Rachel Arroyo, Arnold Ruiz, Johnny Martinez (in white shirt and tie), Sue Westervelt Enright, Bobby Martinez (Johnny's brother), and Dennis Cahill.

Gil V. Montanez was serving as the acting postmaster when Arizona senator Carl Hayden recommended to the Post Office Department that Montanez be permanently appointed as the Tempe postmaster. The Senate confirmed the appointment in August 1966. U.S. president L. B. Johnson officially appointed him as postmaster. In his office, Montanez always kept a painting of a little boy carrying a sack of cotton. This reminded him of his youth when he picked cotton to help his parents earn money. Many young Mexican boys and girls started working in a various array of jobs, such as newspaper carriers, shoe shine boys, picking cotton alongside their parents, washing and ironing jobs, cooking, baby care, and selling from door to door. The one thing that defines Mexican people in their barrios is always being involved in hard work. Montanez rose up the ladder in his line of work to become Tempe postmaster and was also voted by his peers as Arizona Postmaster of the Year in 1980. (Gil Montanez Jr.)

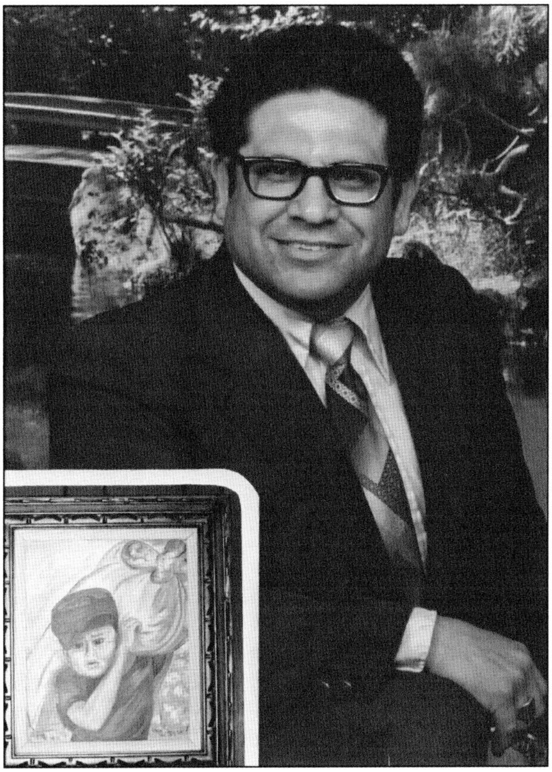

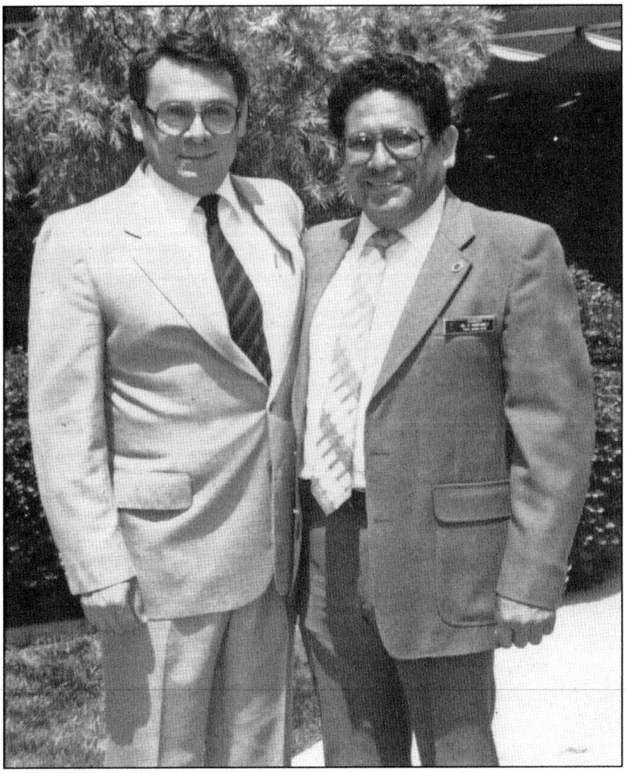

Joseph R. Caraveo, regional postmaster general, (left) and Gil V. Montanez, Tempe postmaster, support themselves by doing the most-needed work of the U.S. Post Office. (Gil Montanez Jr.)

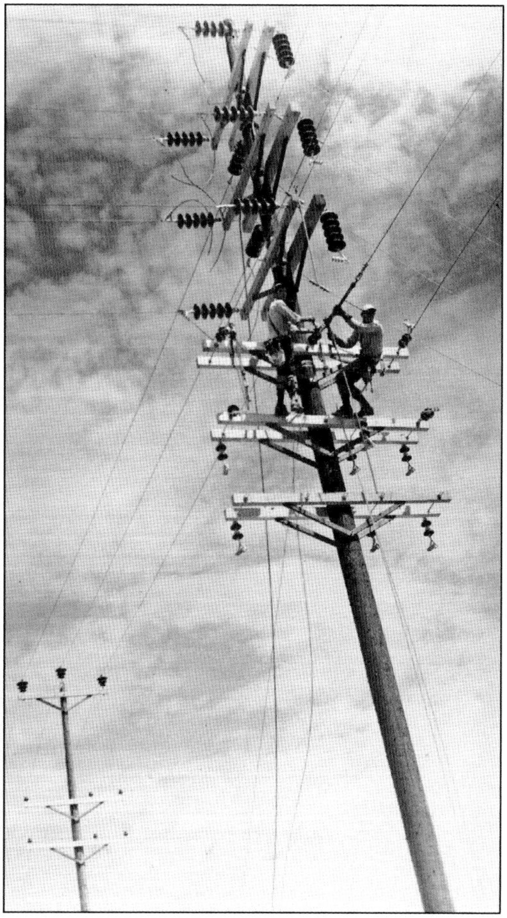

Electricity is an energy that keeps every community economically solvent. In Mexican barrios, the radio served as the link with the outside world in the 1930s and even in modern times, now in addition to television. It provided announcements about jobs, second-goods sales, store bargains, weather reports, school news, community meetings, entertainment, and much more that is local and more meaningful for the barrio. Working on the high tension wire is crucial for the community and demands safety considerations at all times. (AHF.)

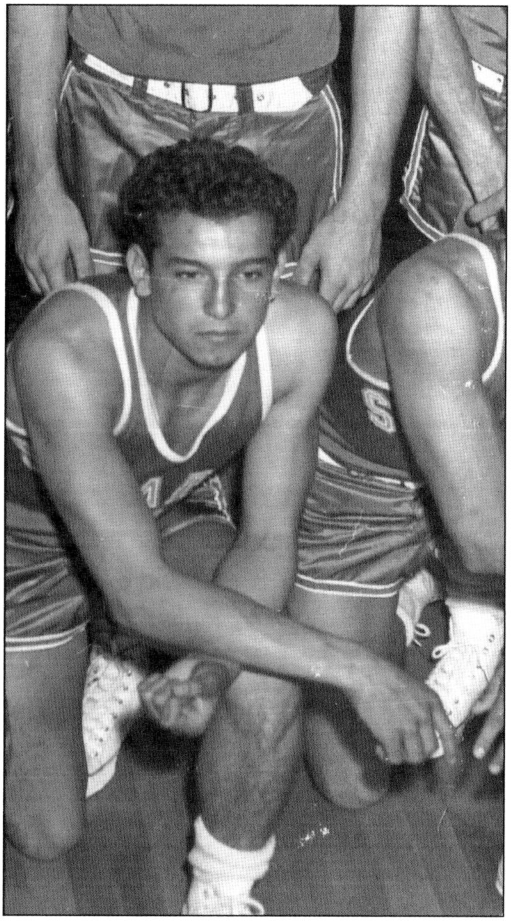

Jose Guaderrama played basketball for Tempe High School in 1953. After graduation, Jose was employed by the Arizona Public Service at the entry level. Work is an important tradition of the Mexican heritage and culture; this sustained Jose as he worked hard and long. Eventually, his ideas, hard work, and contributions helped him reach the supervisor level. That achievement would be applauded in its own merits, but it becomes most appreciated since he did not know English until learning it in grade school.

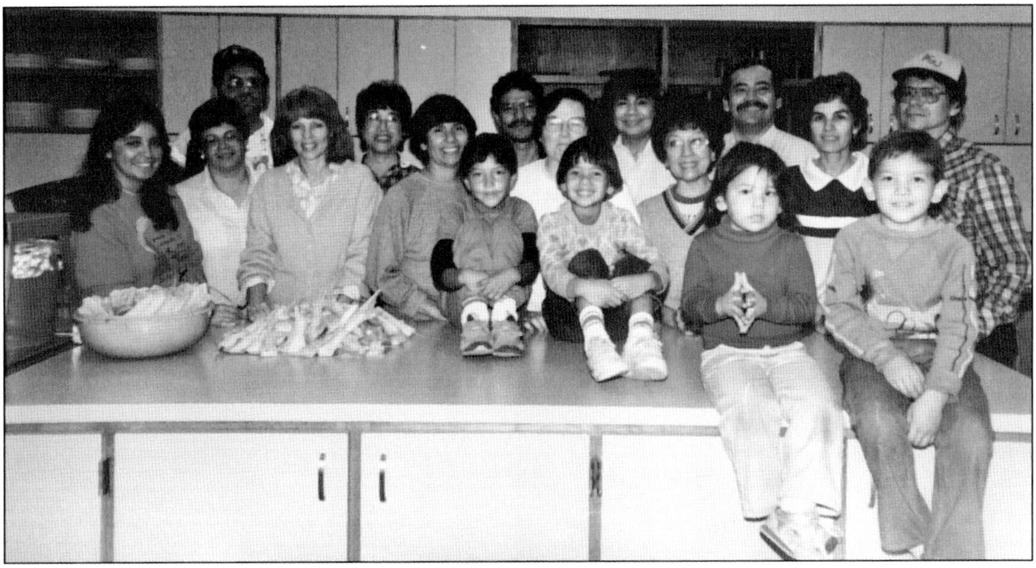

Amistad Hispana, a Tempe cultural organization, sponsored a tamale-making session at the Escalante Community Center. In the background is Albert Marquez (last row, far left), monitor of the occasion, along with his wife, Susana R. Marquez (second row, center, wearing a white dress). Assisting are Virginia Pesqueira and Ed Delci, community educators (second row, far right). Most of the children sitting on the counter have since graduated from Arizona State University; Albert holds a degree in electrical engineering and worked for a state company for 20 years until retirement; Virginia earned a doctorate in education, and Ed earned a master's degree and had served in Latin America with the U.S. Peace Corps. Tamales are a Native American food that has become American. Mexican Americans have a tradition of making tamales for special occasions like Christmas. (Albert and Susana Marquez.)

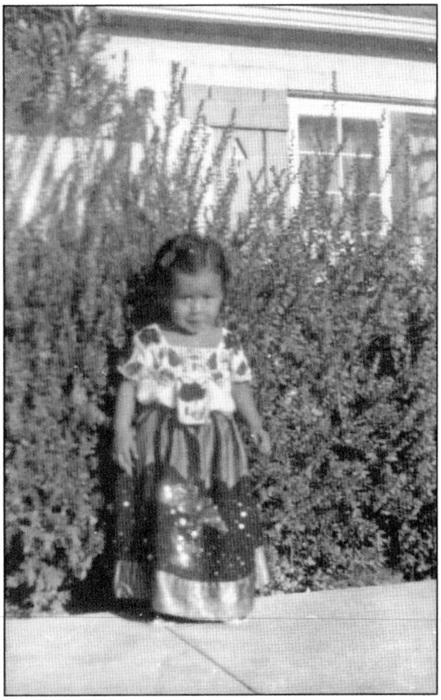

In San Pablo barrio lived a little girl, Norma Carbajal Jiemez, whose parents believed in the wonders of music and dance. The girl started early learning the music of the Jarabe Tapatio and its dance. Here she wears the correct dress for this dance, a China poblana, the Mexican regional dance dress. China is a type of cloth used with this style of dress that is particular to Guadalajara, Mexico. (Norma C. Pinate.)

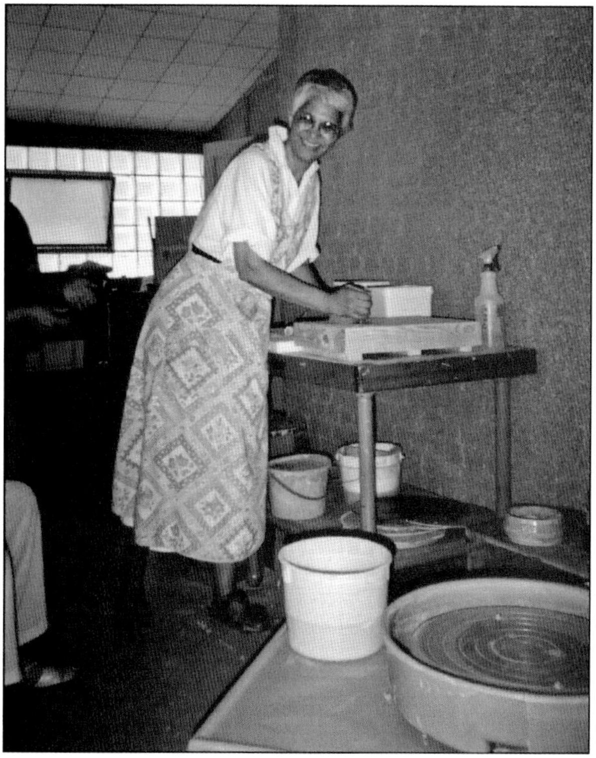

Sr. Ramona Varela creates a piece of art with pottery clay. In this way, items can be sold to help provide income for her Benedictine Order. She was the fourth child of Joe and Carmela Varela. Joe is the son of Cresencio and Guadalupe Acedo Varela.

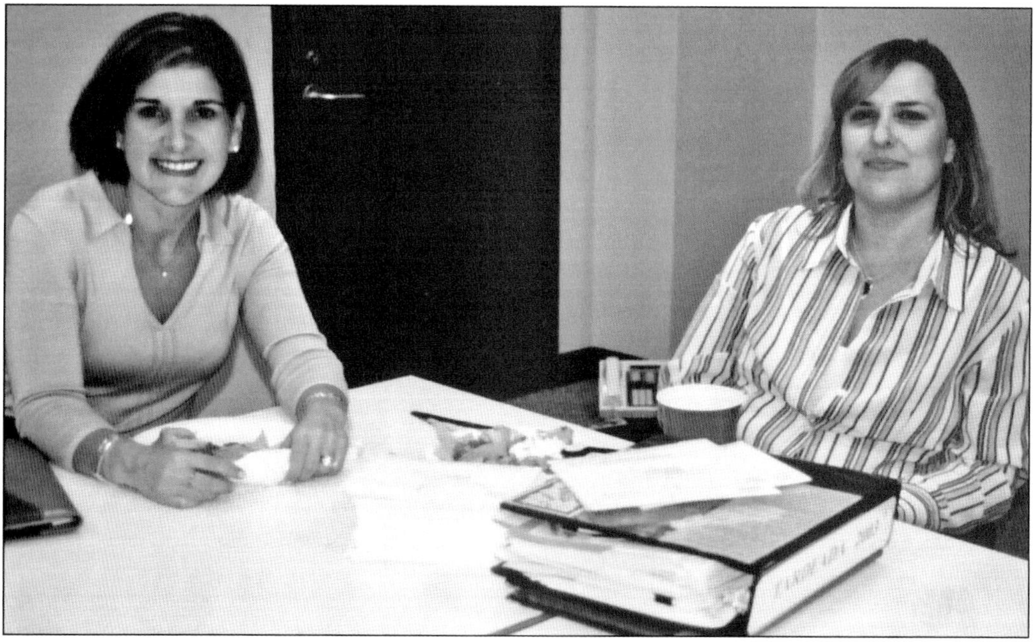

The City of Tempe has a Diversity Department, and Rosa Inchausti (left), manager, and Ginny Belousek are the two staff members that comprise the department. Between them, they initiate, monitor, and support many diversity projects. Among these projects is the Tardeada, an annual festival held during Hispanic Heritage Month from September 15 to October 15 of each year. (Author's collection.)

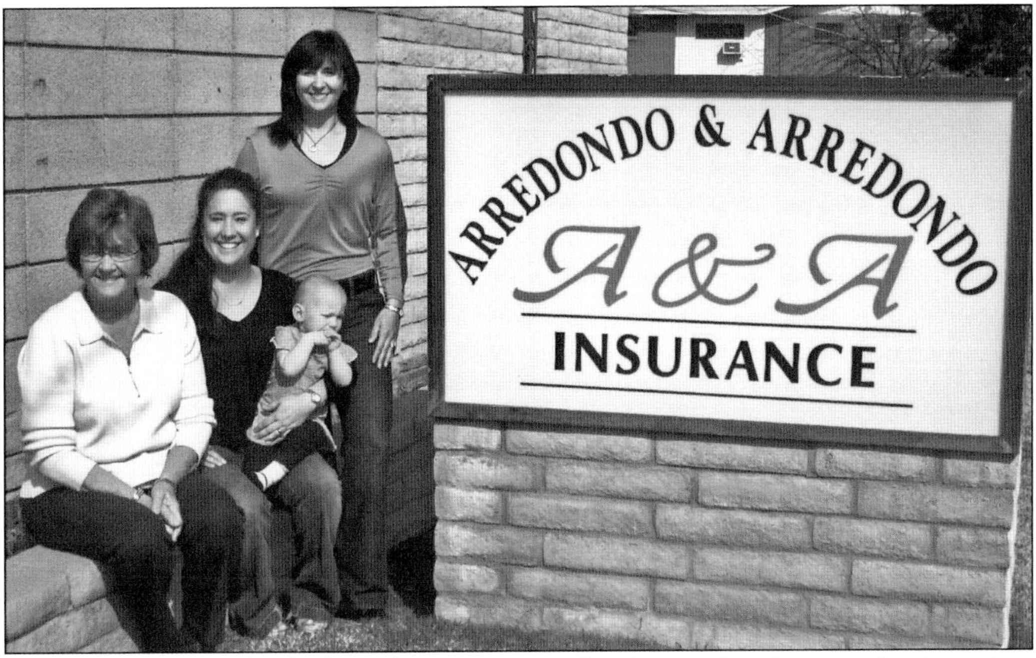

Arredondo and Arredondo (A&A) Insurance is a family-owned-and-operated independent insurance agency in central Tempe. Joe and Karen Arredondo founded the agency in 1988. From left to right in the photograph are Karen and her two daughters Robin Arredondo-Savage and Jaime Arredondo-Brunk. Robin is holding Jaime's daughter Suzanne Arredondo-Brunk. Both of Karen's daughters work with Karen in the agency. All employees of the family business have attended local schools, graduated from Arizona State University, live in local neighborhoods with strong ties to the community, and contribute their time and skills by serving with various boards, commissions, and organizations in Tempe. (Joe and Karen Arredondo.)

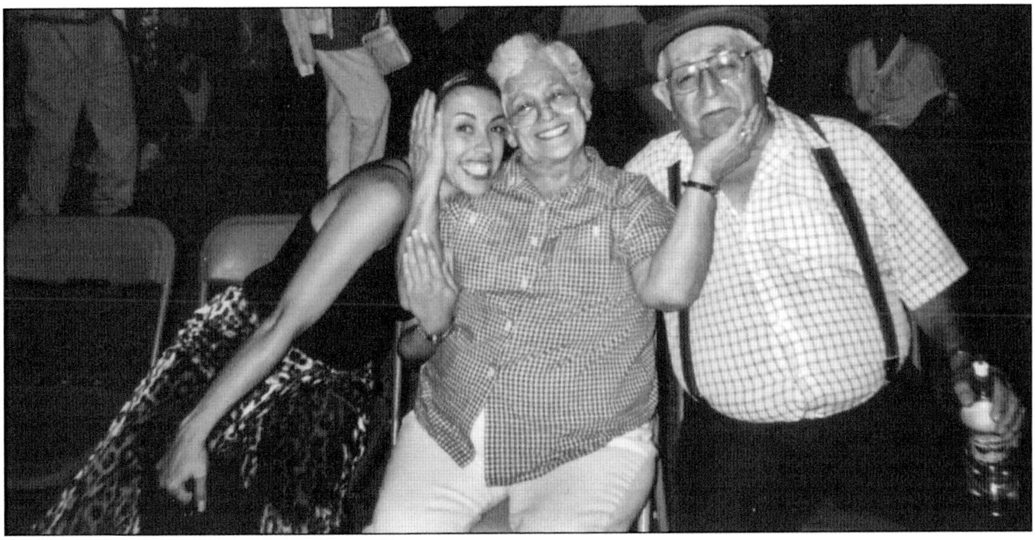

Ralph Chavarria Jr. is fondly known as "Chapito" by his family, friends, and fans. He is a popular musician and composer who, for many years, has entertained Tempeneños at fiestas, community dances, and private celebrations. In this picture, Chapito celebrates at the Tempe Tardeada of 2006 with his wife, Connie, and daughter Barbara.

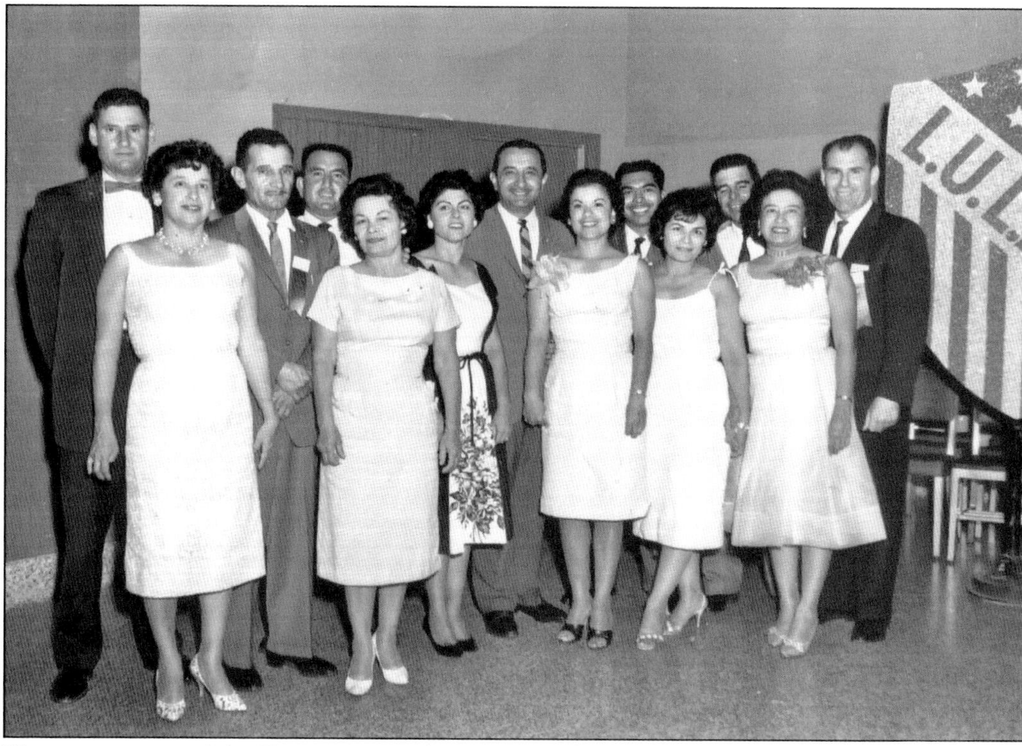

This is a picture of the Tempe Council No. 361 of the national organization of the League of United Latin American Citizens (LULAC). The council, for many years, supported community and national projects of benefit to society. (Narcisa M. Espinoza.)

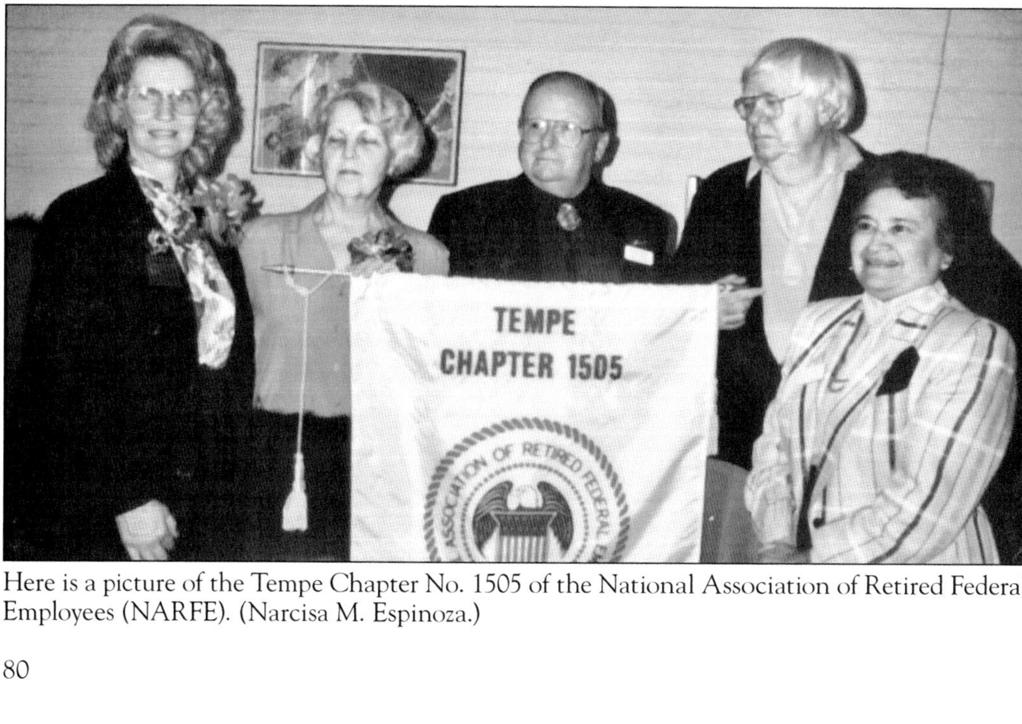

Here is a picture of the Tempe Chapter No. 1505 of the National Association of Retired Federal Employees (NARFE). (Narcisa M. Espinoza.)

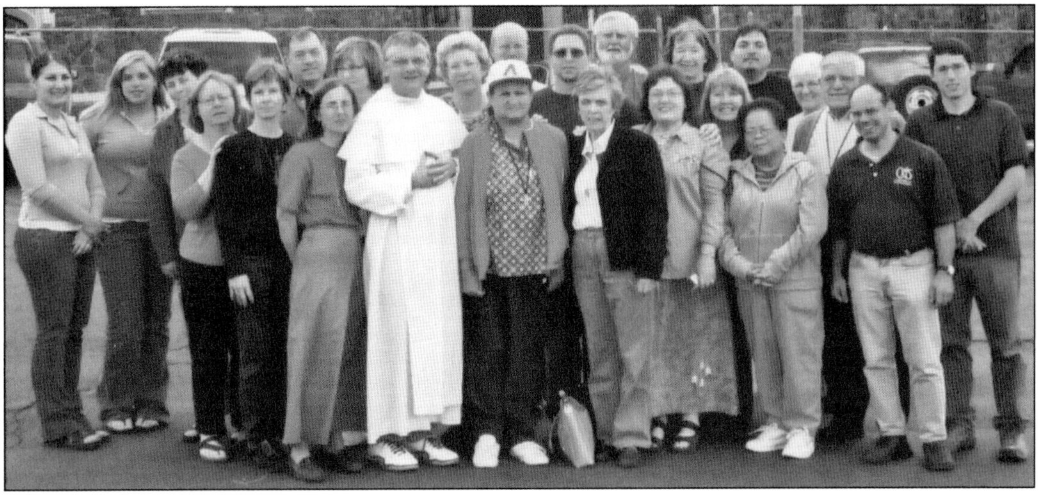

The Order of Preachers Laity, a religious order for laypersons, is part of the Dominican family of priests, religious sisters, and laypersons. In this picture, the St. Mary Magdalene chapter, situated at the All Saints Newman Center in Tempe, completed a weekend retreat in Flagstaff. Rev. Fr. Nathan Castle (first row, center) of the Newman Center conducted several sessions at the retreat. (Author's collection.)

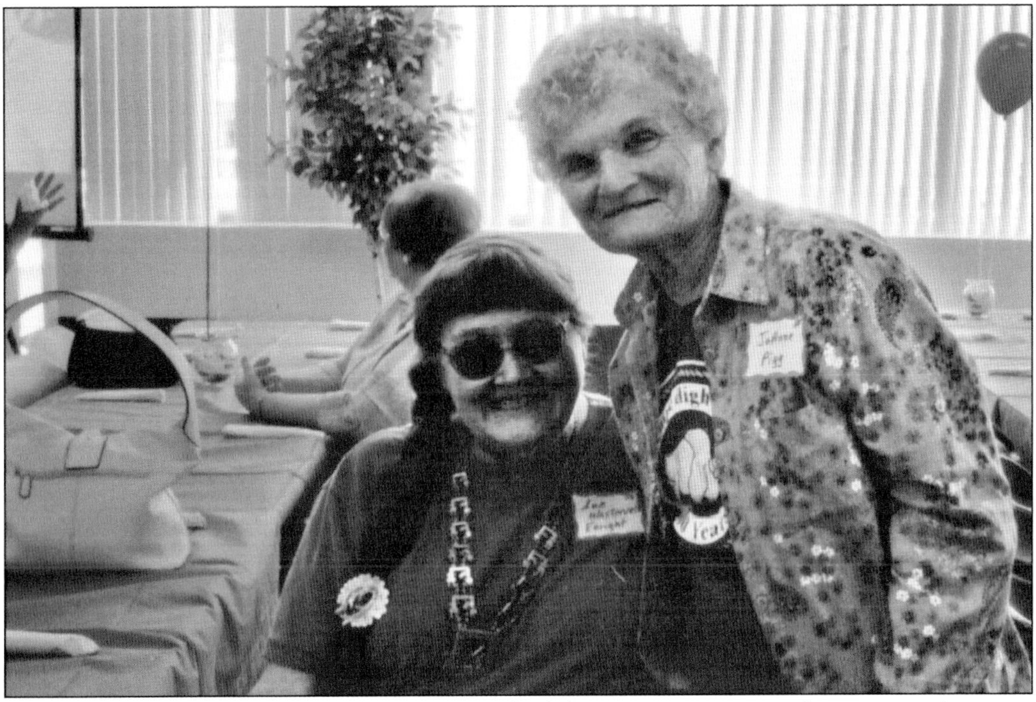

Sue Westervelt Enright (left) and JoAnn Pigg (right) enjoy conversation during some free time when attending the Tempe reunion at the Old High School. Enright serves as a librarian at St. Daniels Catholic School in North Tempe. Her brother is Dr. Vincent Sheridan, Ph.D., principal of Our Lady of Mount Carmel School. JoAnn Pigg retired from teaching school in New Mexico. JoAnn's mother, Alice Pigg, taught school for many years at the Rural School Elementary. Mexican children attended the Rural School Elementary, and many attend Our Lady of Mount Carmel School.

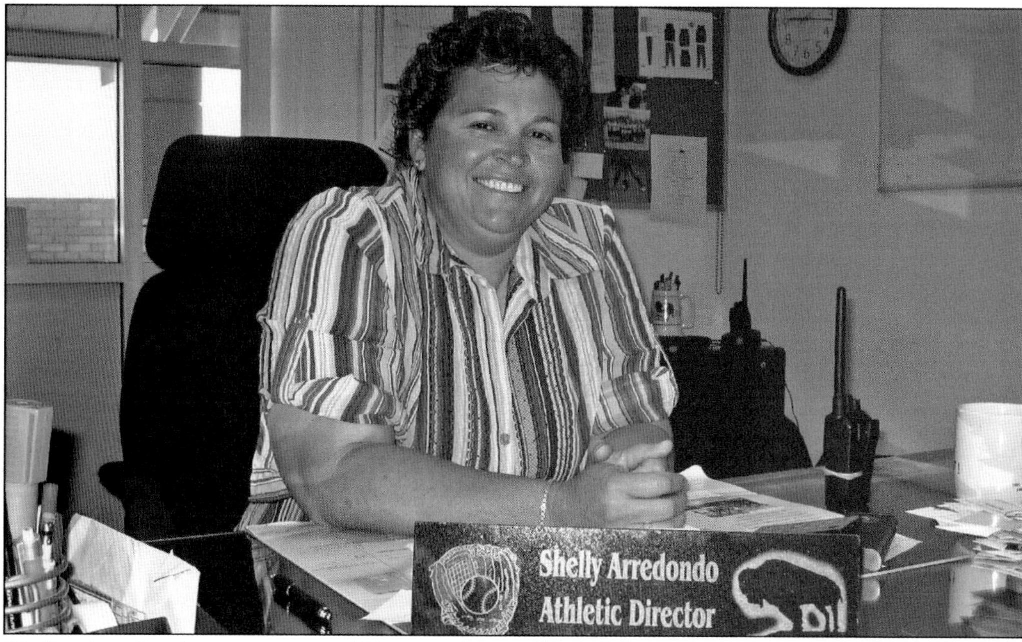

Shelly Arredondo is a native of Tempe who graduated from the Tempe Union High School District. She graduated from Arizona State University and then received her master's degree in administration and leadership education from Northern Arizona University. Shelly has been a successful educator at Tempe High School for more than 10 years. She served as an athletic coach in basketball and badminton, and led the Tempe High School Buffalo softball team to a state runner-up title in 2006. Her family consists of two daughters: Jacie, who teaches fifth grade in the Tempe Elementary School District, and K'Lee, a sophomore at the University of Arizona. K'Lee Arredondo played softball for the University of Arizona Wildcats, which won the national softball championship in 2007. Shelly currently serves as assistant principal of athletics at Tempe Union High School. (Joe and Karen Arredondo.)

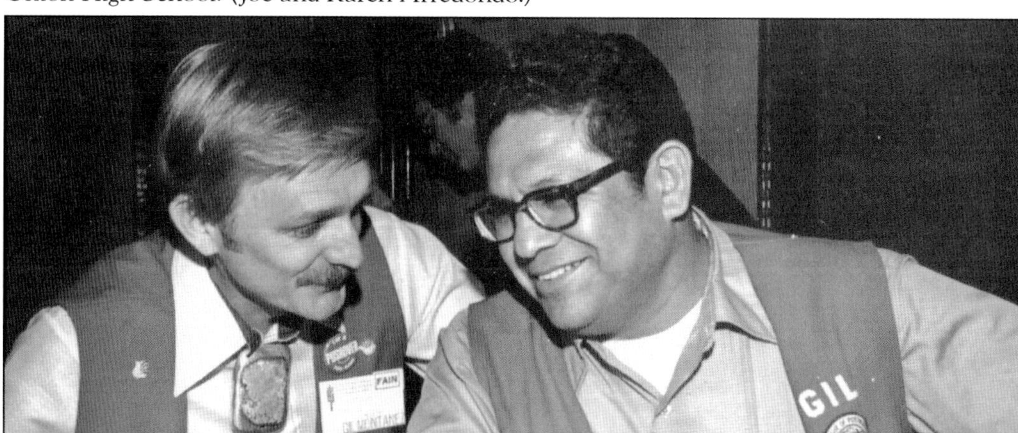

Pictured are Ron Swisher (left), the Mesa, Arizona, postmaster at the time, and Gilbert V. Montanez. Montanez, the Tempe postmaster and a co-member of the National League of Postmasters (NLP), helped organize the Arizona NLP branch and served as host postmaster at the national convention in Phoenix in 1976. He was instrumental in helping to organize other state branches of the NLP. (Gilbert Montanez Jr.)

In 1963, Rosa Keeme opened her first Mexican restaurant on Fifth and Beck Streets in Tempe. Her customers tasted her food and returned for more. Her business grew, and in 1991, she opened her second Rosita's on Dobson and Guadalupe Roads in Mesa. In 1987, she moved her original Rosita's to University Drive and Hardy Street, where her restaurant continues to serve delicious food. The advertising brochures and menus tell a story of her courageous struggles to survive, from her family eluding the dangers of a Mexican revolution, to her working in the agricultural fields in earlier years, to founding her food establishments. This is her picture from a brochure, as beautiful as ever and smiling with life. (Elias and Cecilia D. Esquer.)

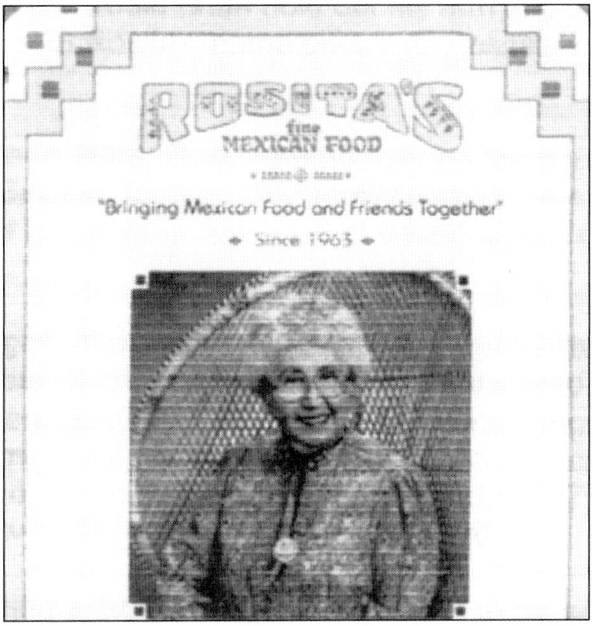

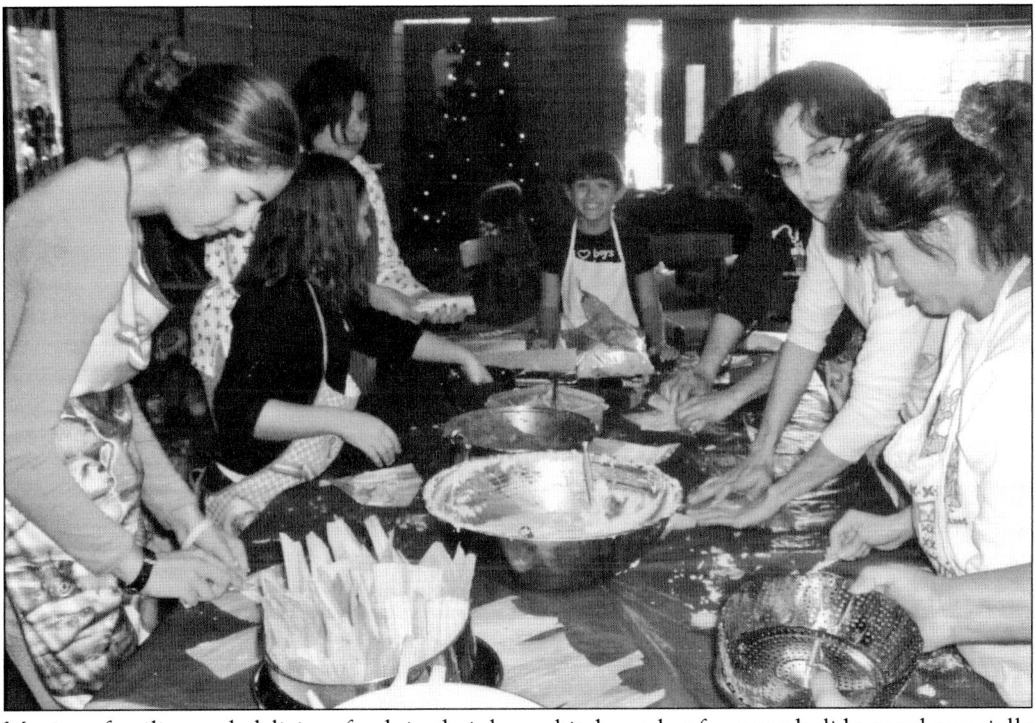

Mexican families cook delicious foods in their home kitchens, but for many holidays and especially for Christmas, the families have the tradition of coming together to make tamales, and sometimes men also join in the festivity. The occasions help family members bond and perhaps catch up on family news. The annual occasion of making tamales, however difficult, is always remembered. It is also an opportunity for women to exchange newly acquired recipes. Tamale day is no less a festive tradition with the Cecilia Denogeán Esquer and Elias Esquer families, pictured here in 2004. (Elias and Cecilia D. Esquer.)

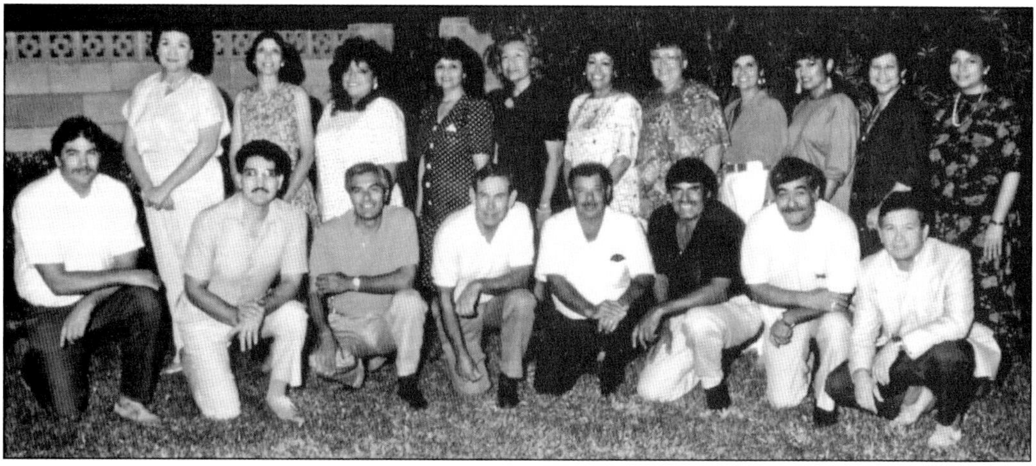

Los Amigos de Tempe has for years promoted events that celebrate their Mexican heritage and culture. In this picture, they hold a gathering in 1989. Pictured from left to right are (first row) Chris Varela, Bud Garcia, Jesse Valenzuela, Manuel Varela, George Romo, Rudy Arroyo, Robert Armoia, and Elias Esquer; (second row) Ruth Garcia, Margaret Medina, Regina Arroyo, Dolores Vareia, Terri Gladney, Terri Romo, Clara Urbano, Rachel Arroyo, Mary Armoia, Irene Gomez Hormell, and Cecilia Esquer.

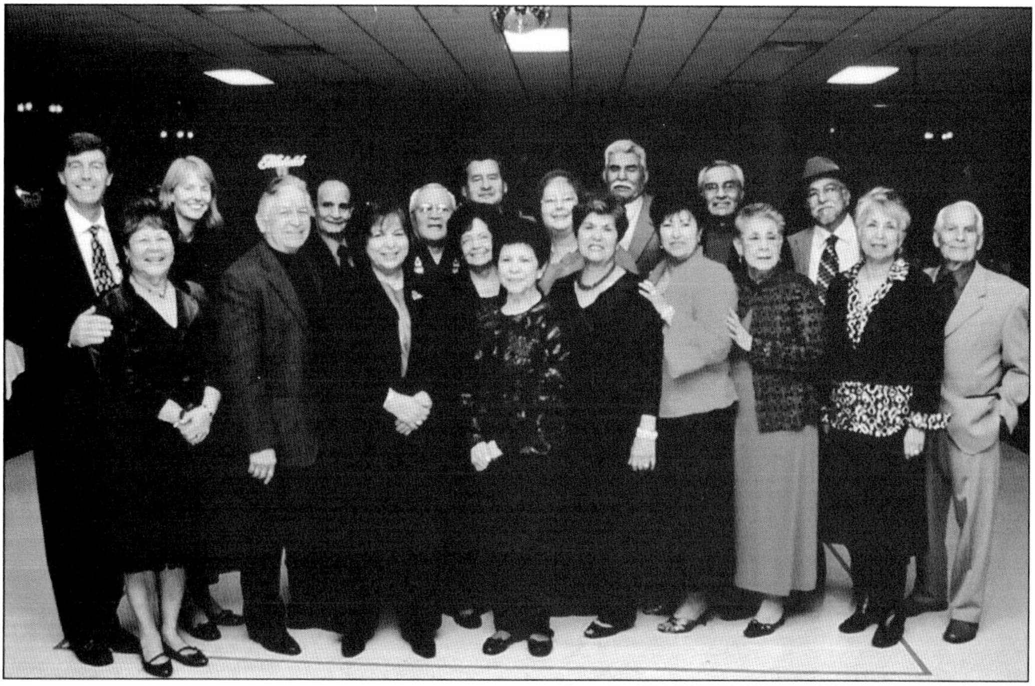

On this occasion, Los Amigos de Tempe attended a League of United Latin American Citizens dance held at the American Legion Post 41 in Phoenix for Valentine's Day in April 2008. The group honored Tempe mayor Hugh Hallman (far left).

Five

Children, Education, and Sports

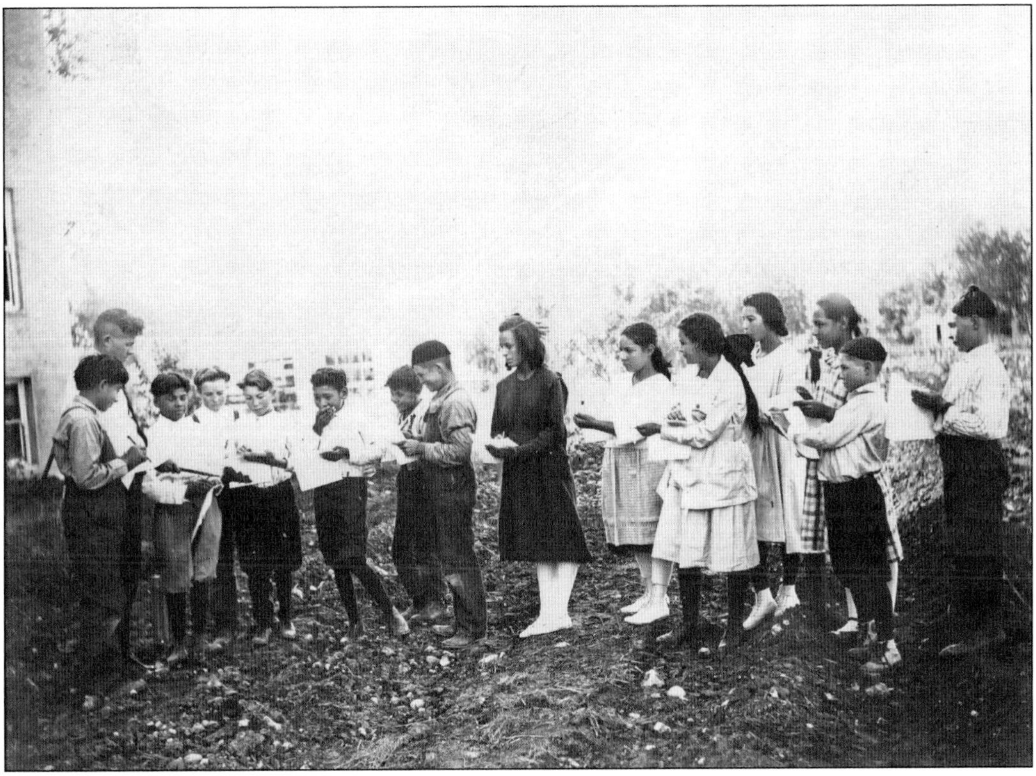

Seventh-grade students are involved in an outdoor class. It seems some food item was passed out to the students by the one holding a basket. One student (fifth from left) is taking a close look at the food, while his classmate on his left already tastes the edible. The two students to his left nervously wait their turn while student girls apprehensively hold out their hands. They may be studying the small Mexican green chili peppers grown on the nearby bushes. (AHF.)

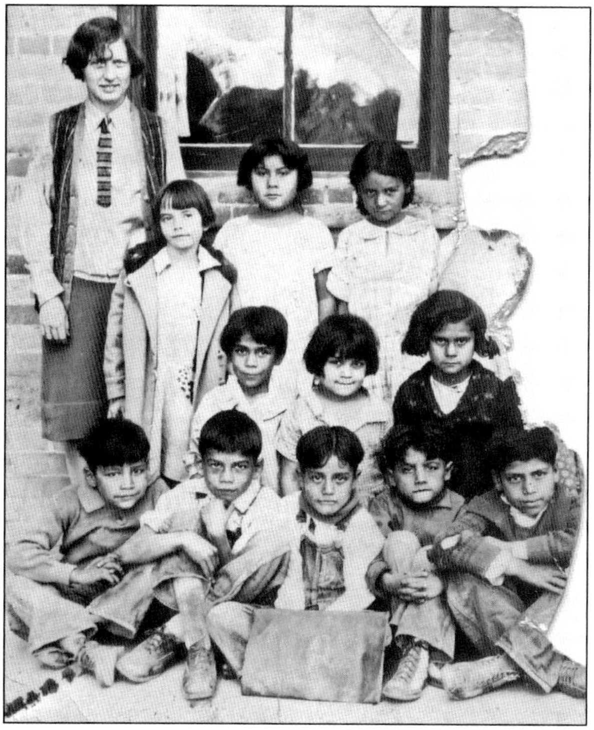

Second-grade students of the Eighth Street School (known as the Mexican School during the time of school segregation in Tempe and other towns in Arizona) place the sign identifying their class before them in 1926. The students do not smile as they face their future. The teacher standing at left is believed to be Helen Roberts, well known and highly respected in Tempe. The students are children of pioneer settlers. From left to right are (first row) Alex Calderon, Tony Sosa, David Bojorquez, and two unidentified; (second row) Susie Palomino, Margarita Morales, and unidentified; (third row) the teacher, Pauline ?, Mary Sterling, and unidentified. (Barney S. Peralta.)

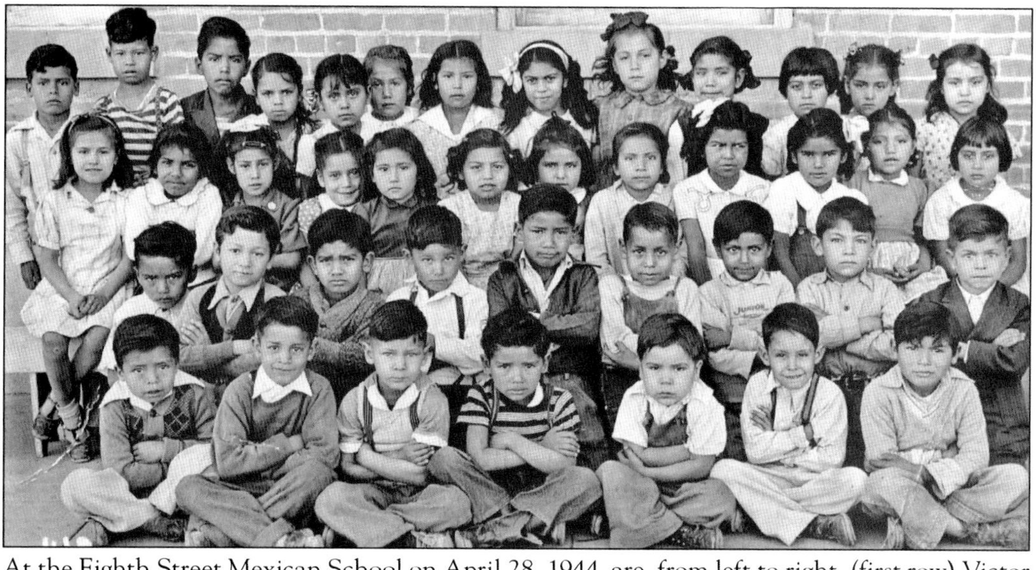

At the Eighth Street Mexican School on April 28, 1944, are, from left to right, (first row) Victor Arroyo Jr., Danny Gamboa, Philip Gamboa, unidentified, Frank Franco, Frank Martinez, and unidentified; (second row) Joe Roman, Henry Gamboa, Jose "Pepe" Gonzales, Roy Palma, Frank Verdugo, unidentified, Ralph Othon, Louie Mollon, and Floyd Acedo; (third row) unidentified, Mary Lou Roman, Esther Cruz, Rachel Burgos, Lucy Muñoz, Socorro Palma, Susie Villa, unidentified, Aurora Cortez, Mary Limon, Irene Castañeda, and Juanita Palma; (fourth row) Rudy Arroyo, Gabriel Soto, Roque Roman, Dolores Escarcega, unidentified, Mary Lou Perez, unidentified, Sally Espinoza, Ofelia Mollon, Arcenia Cota, unidentified, Lydia Limon, and Gloria Franco. (Rudy Arroyo.)

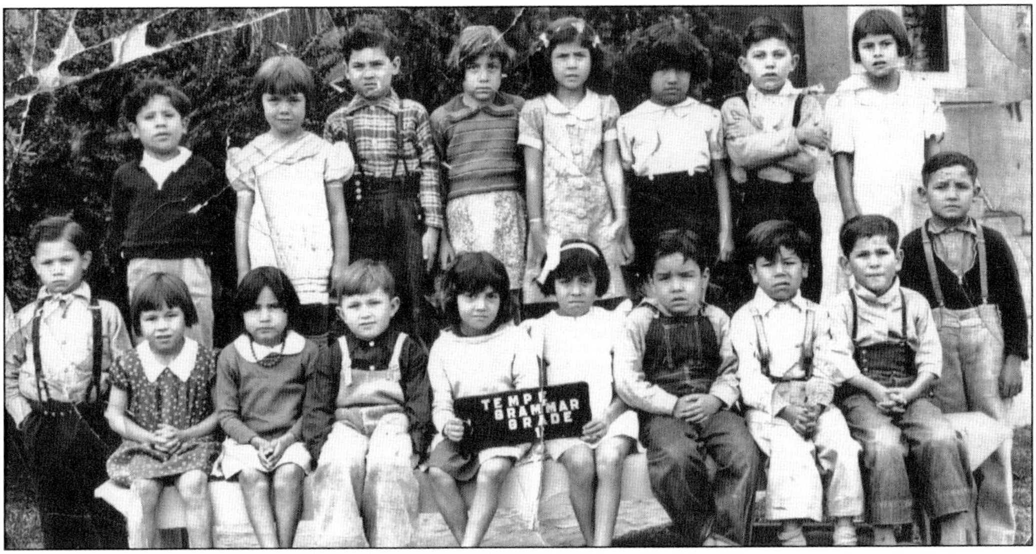

Tempe Grammar School's first grade includes (first row, seated) Alice Romo, unidentified, Antonio Ballesteros, Maggie Romero, unidentified, Eddie Arbizu, Joe Contreras, and unidentified; (second row, standing) unidentified, Gilbert Montanez, Irene Romo, unidentified, Catherine Gomez, Catalina Carbajal, Mary Arbizu, and three unidentified. In 1940, the education system at that time required Mexican children to spend two years at the first-grade level. The first year the curriculum was called the Americanization class, demanding children learn the English language, and the next year, the same children entered first grade. That is why the next picture of Tempe Grammar's first grade in 1941 includes, for the most part, the same names in this picture.

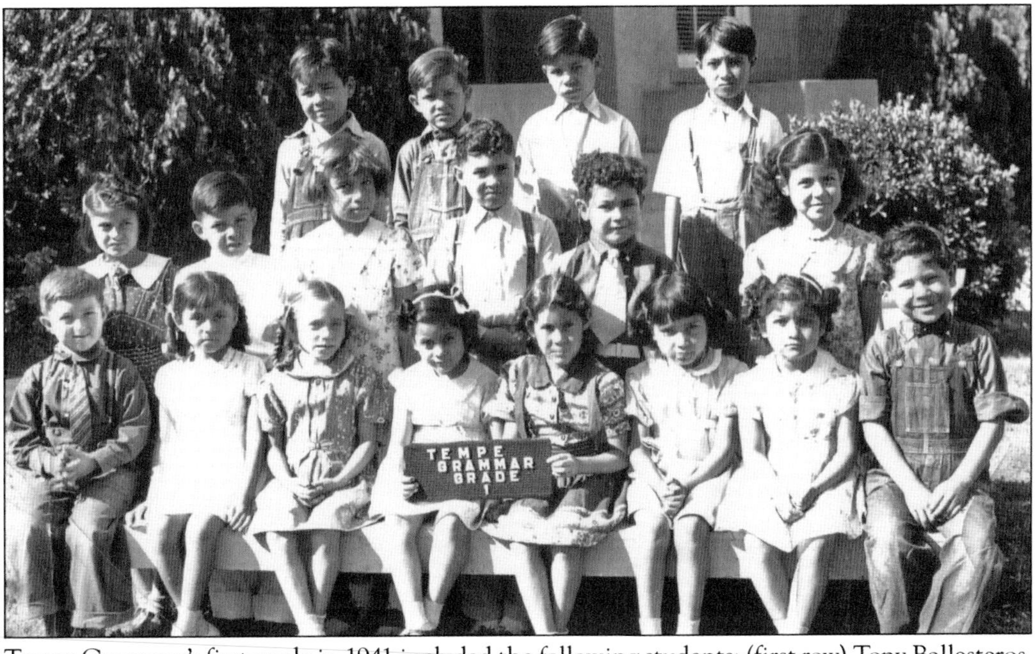

Tempe Grammar's first grade in 1941 included the following students: (first row) Tony Ballesteros, Carmen Carbajal, Irene Romo, Mary Armola, Isabel Gomez, unidentified, Betty Ayala, and Gilbert Montanez; (second row) unidentified, Billy Gomez, Catherine Gomez, two unidentified, and Catalina Carbajal; (third row) Eddie Arbizu, unidentified, Ray Rodriguez, and unidentified.

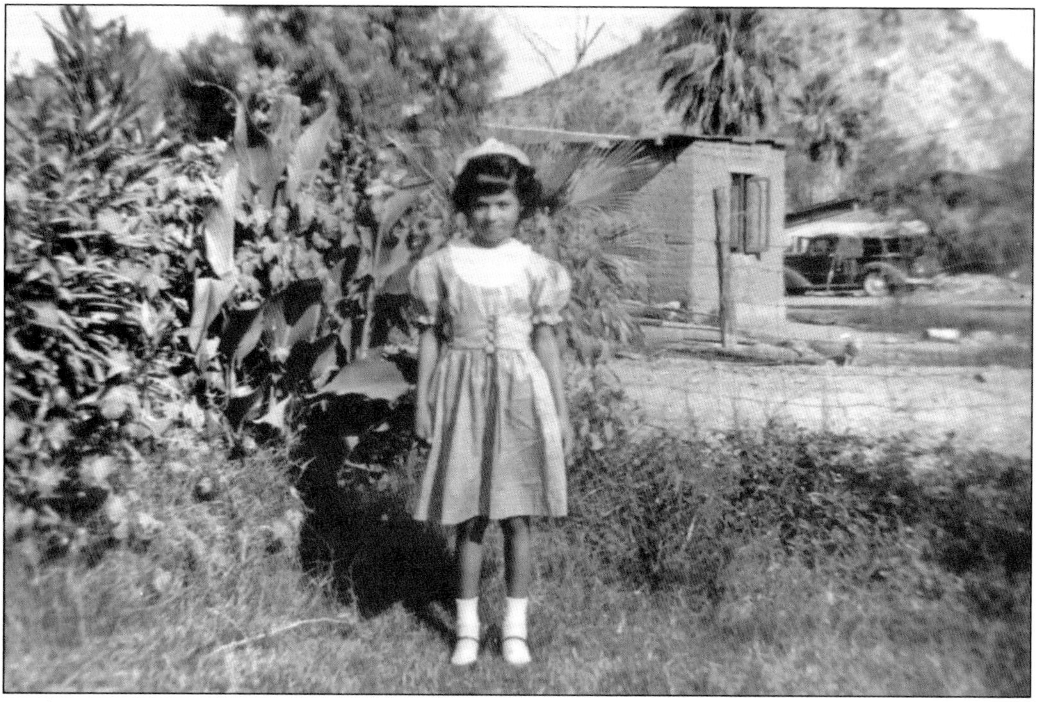

In the time of San Pablo and Mickey Mouse barrios, there were not a substantial number of children to make up a large first grade. There were vast fields, desert, lots of cacti, small adobe homes, many trees, dirt roads, and, always in the background, the majestic small butte. Gloria Tobin stands alone in her barrio, but she carried her God-given natural potential strengthened by her heritage and culture to assure her of successful accomplishments in the future. The small rental house belonged to Juan Leyvas, a brother of Victoriana Carbajal. Behind the rental house in the distance can be seen Marina Ceballos Soto's big adobe home. (Norma C. Pinate.)

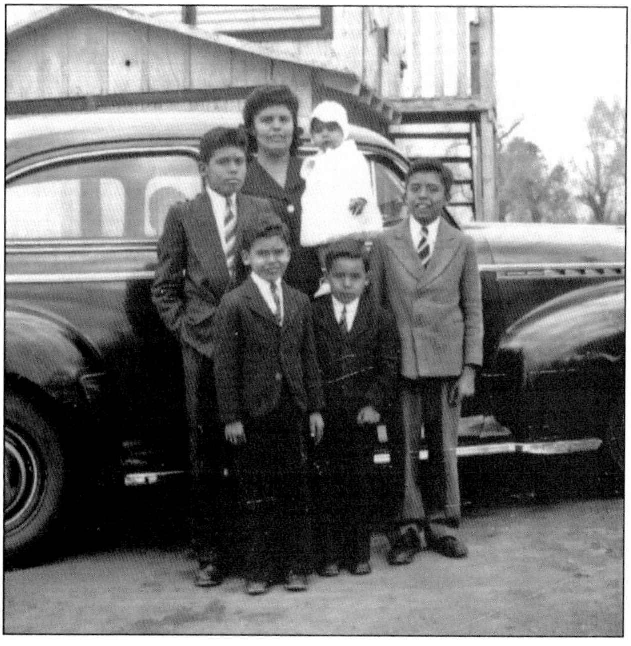

The Leonora Arroyo family includes, from left to right, (first row) Tony and Ruben; (second row) Leonora's oldest son, Rudy; Leonora holding baby Bertha; and Victor Jr.

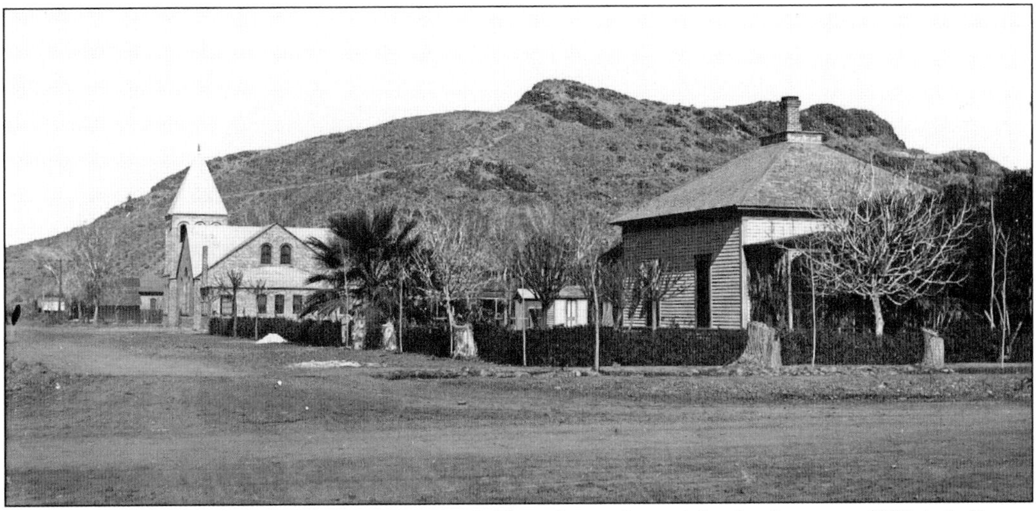

This picture shows the First Congregational Church north on Myrtle Avenue off Eighth Street (now University Drive) with the buttes close up in the north. The streets are unpaved. The photograph dates from the early 1900s, perhaps 1920. (AHF.)

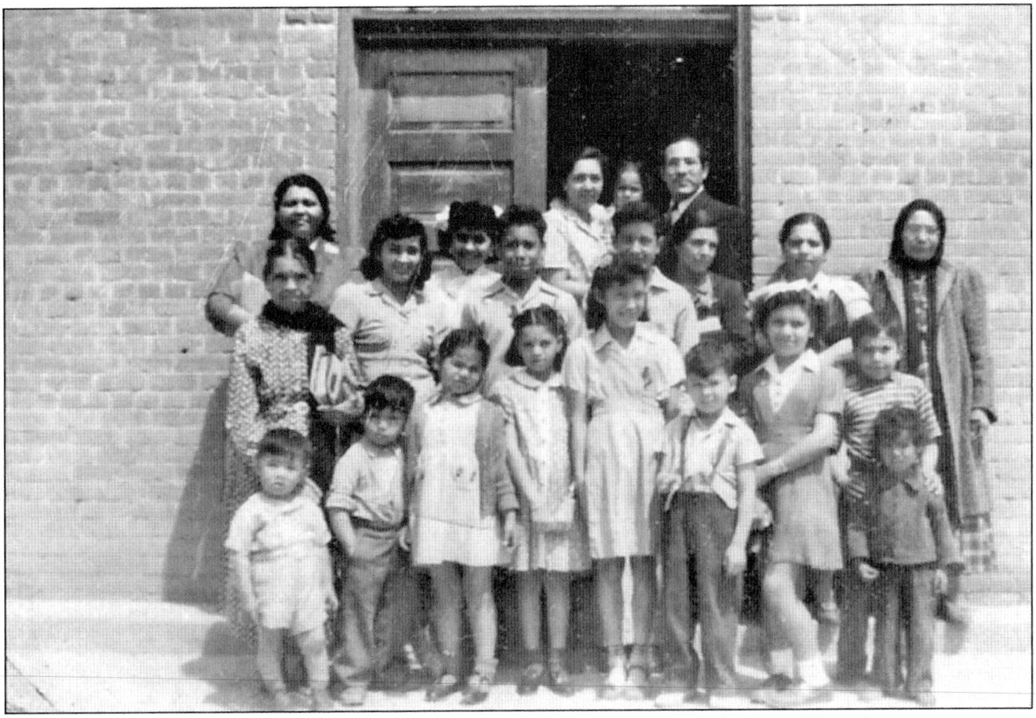

Pastor William Portillo poses with members of the Mexican Methodist Church congregation, including children, around 1942. (Rev. Mardy Olivas.)

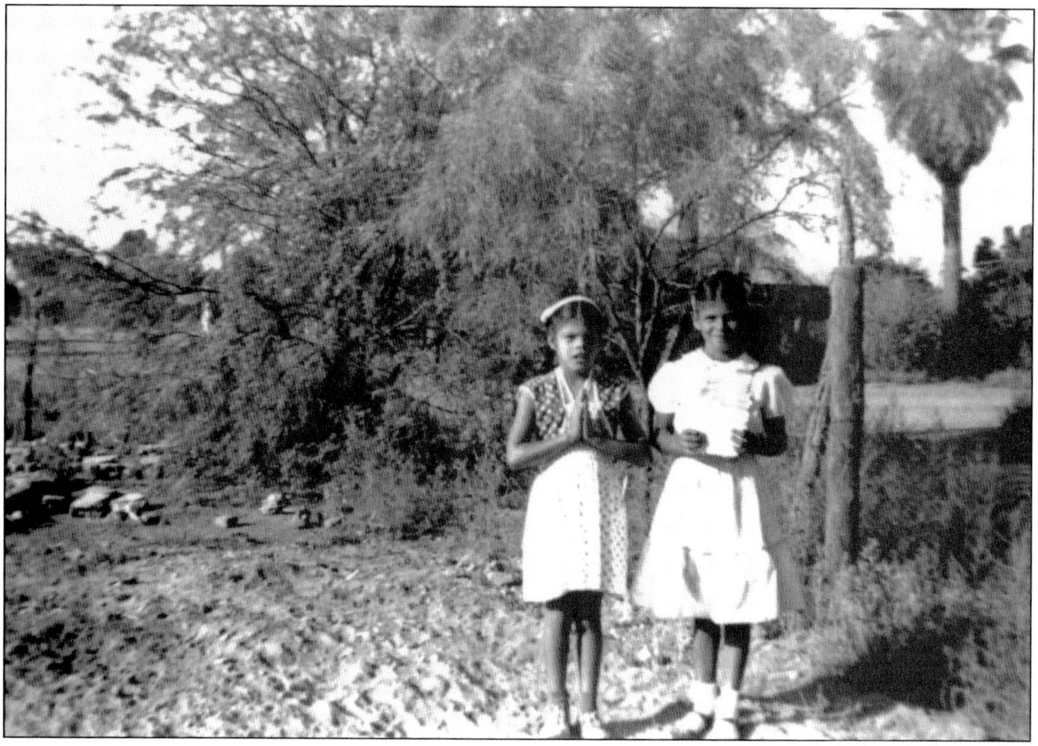

In this picture, Ruth Martinez (left) and Alice Martinez stand dressed in their Sunday best to celebrate their first Communion at the Our Lady of Mount Carmel Church. Notice the rough terrain and the great amount of sand. Not far in the background, it looks like the San Pablo canal flows through, bringing water to the crops in the fields.

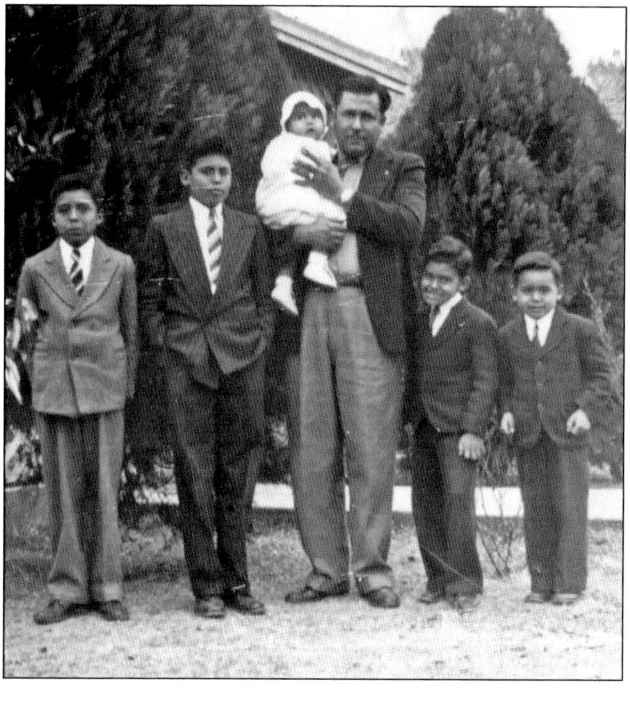

Victor Arroyo Sr. stands in the center holding his baby daughter Bertha in his arms. The young sons of Arroyo are, from left to right, Victor Jr., Rudy, Tony, and Ruben. On page 88, the children are shown with their mother, Leonora Arroyo.

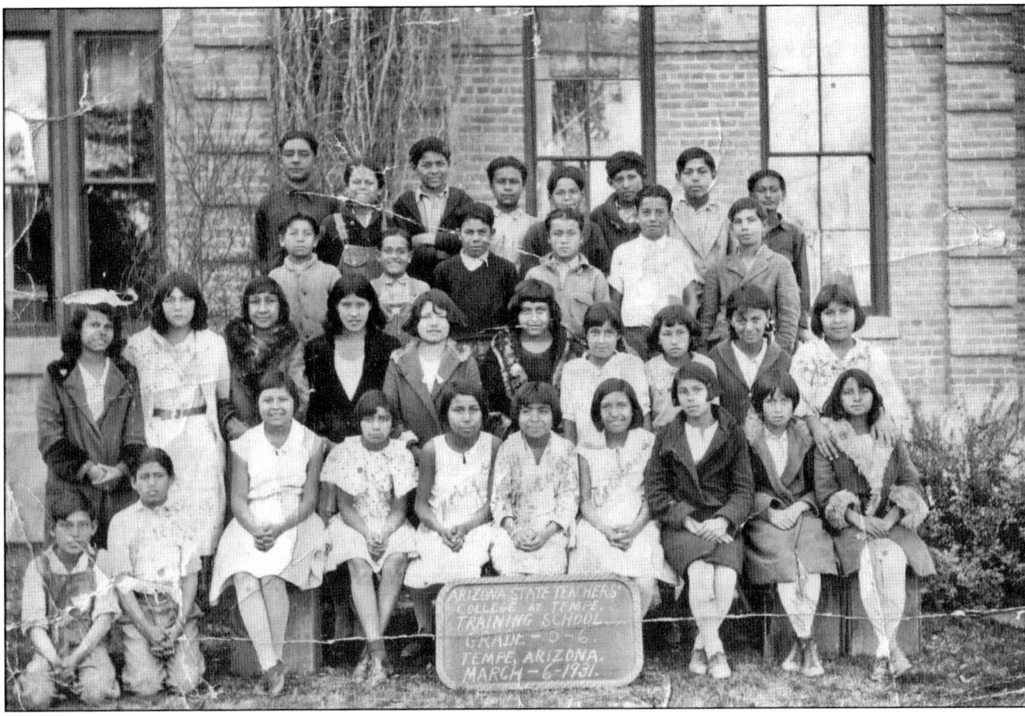

Maria Burgos's fifth and sixth grades are shown at the Tempe Training School in 1931. Pictured from left to right are (first row) 10 unidentified; (second row) two unidentified, Delia Federico, Carmen Guerra, two unidentified, Maria Burgos, Juana Luque, unidentified, and Mary Sterling; (third row) six unidentified; (fourth row) Ray Gonzales and seven unidentified.

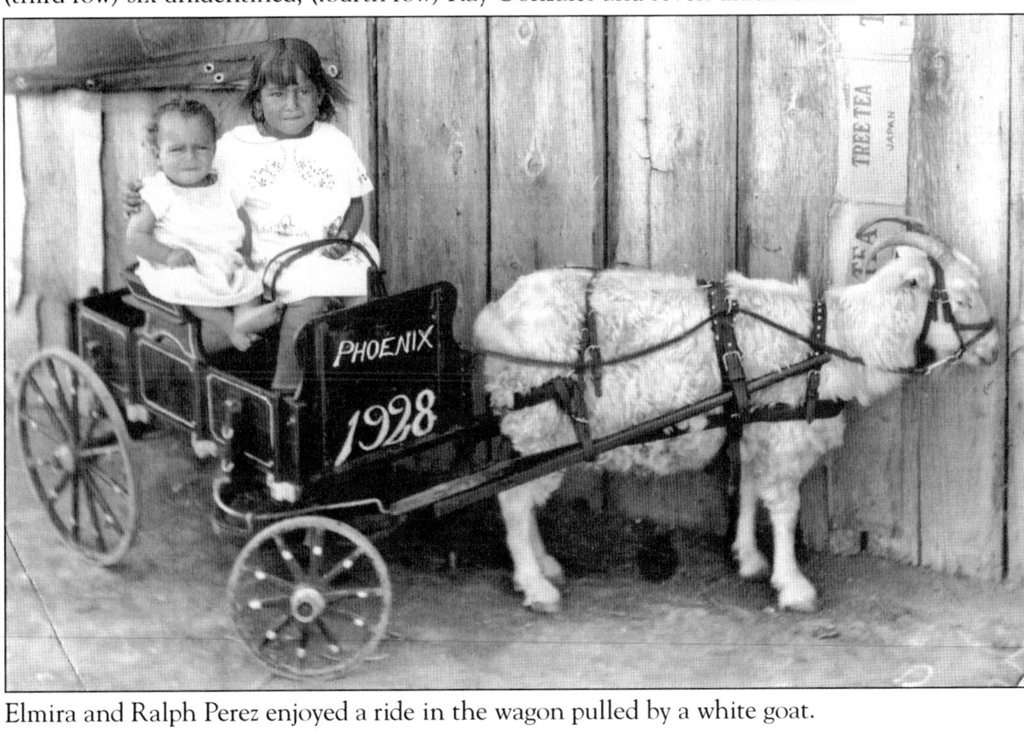

Elmira and Ralph Perez enjoyed a ride in the wagon pulled by a white goat.

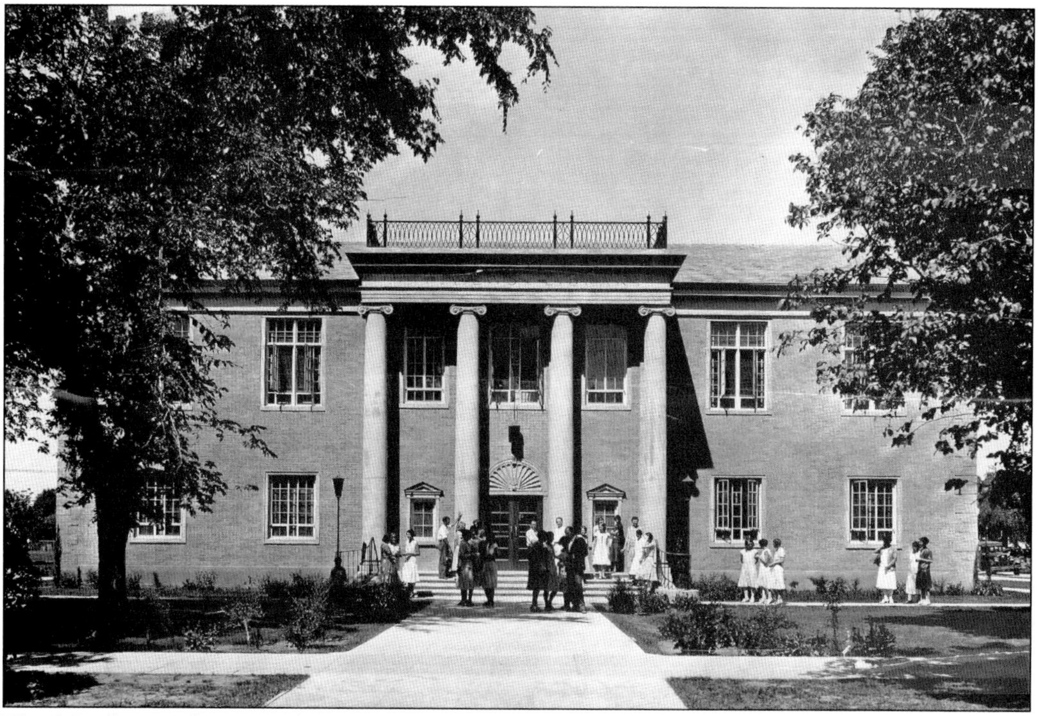

The Matthews Library at the Arizona State Teachers College, now Arizona State University, served the needs of students with aspirations of becoming teachers. (AHF.)

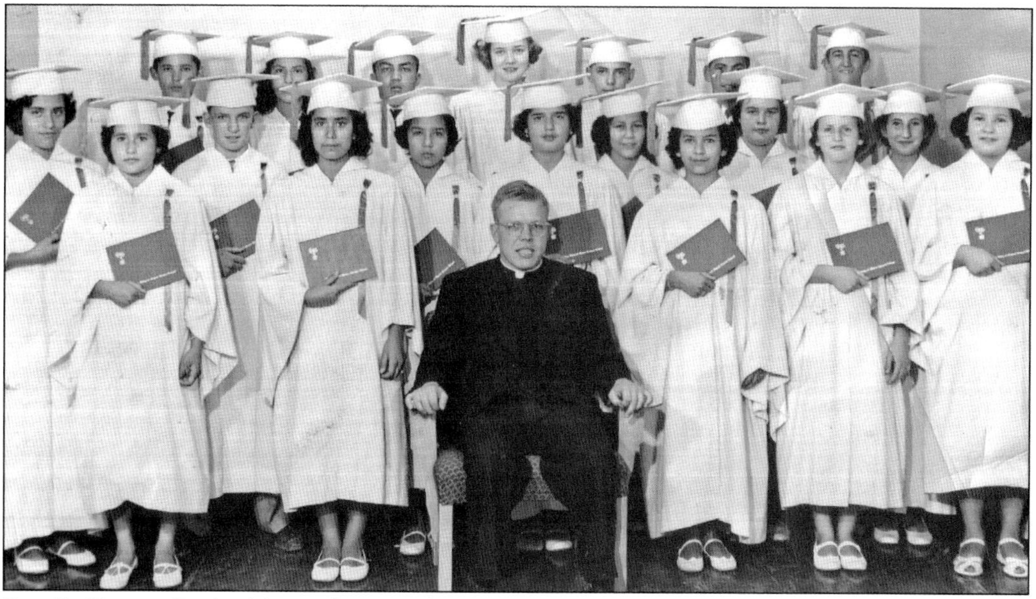

Rev. Fr. Francis Bechtel (seated) is seen here officiating at the first graduating class of Our Lady of Mount Carmel Parish in May 1952. Father Bechtel was pastor of the parish. Graduates include the following, from left to right: (first row) Lucy Muñoz, Arcenia Cota, Ofelia Rodriguez, Chloe Rader, and Mary Lou Duarte; (second row) Lydia Olimon, Charles Kittridge, Carmelita Jimenez, Rachel Corral, Irene Gomez, Carol Thomas, and Angela Capelli; (third row) Roy Palma, Patsy Gomez, Mike Alvarez, Sue Westervelt, Emil Van Utran, Joe Soto, and John Capelli.

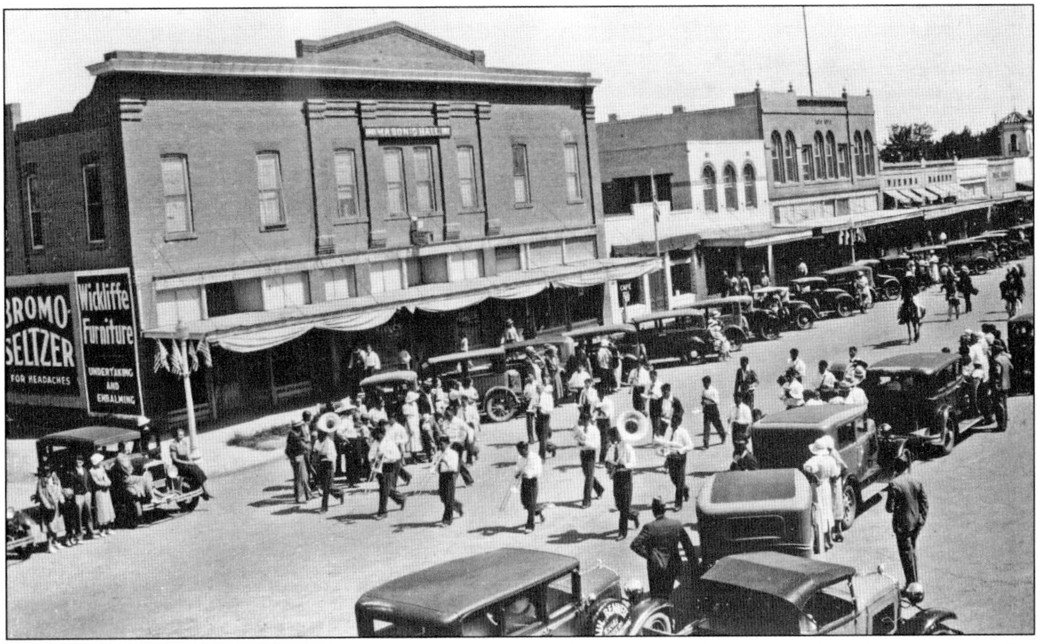

This photograph shows Mill Avenue, Tempe, in a 1928 town parade. A brass band marches on the street, cars are parked along the street, and to the rear is probably John Floyd Gomez on horseback, accompanied by Lalo Lopez, who mentored John as a vaquero. Tempe fielded its annual parade, and John Floyd served as parade marshal. (AHF.)

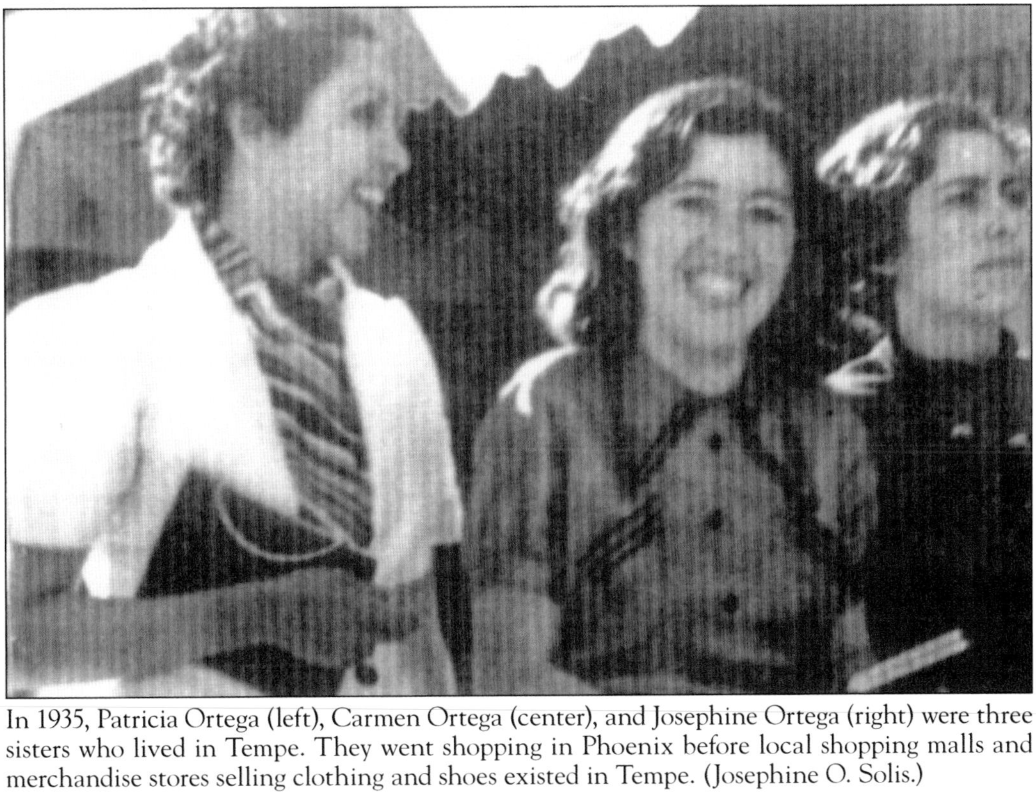

In 1935, Patricia Ortega (left), Carmen Ortega (center), and Josephine Ortega (right) were three sisters who lived in Tempe. They went shopping in Phoenix before local shopping malls and merchandise stores selling clothing and shoes existed in Tempe. (Josephine O. Solis.)

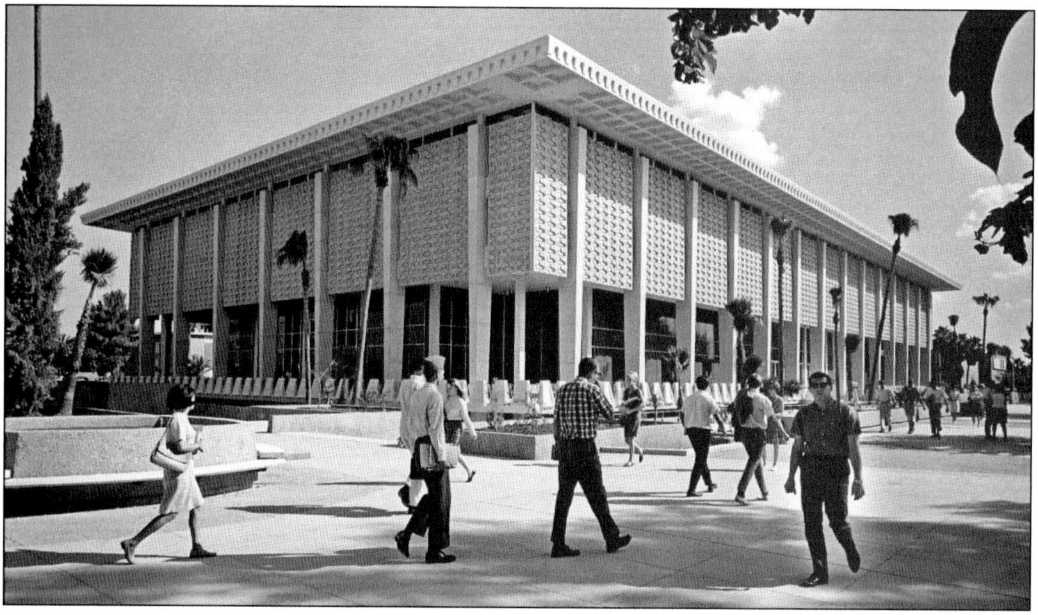

Arizona State Teachers College's Hayden Library expanded, improved, and provided a variety of information, research, and media resources throughout the years. It eventually became Arizona State University, with several campuses throughout Maricopa County. (AHF.)

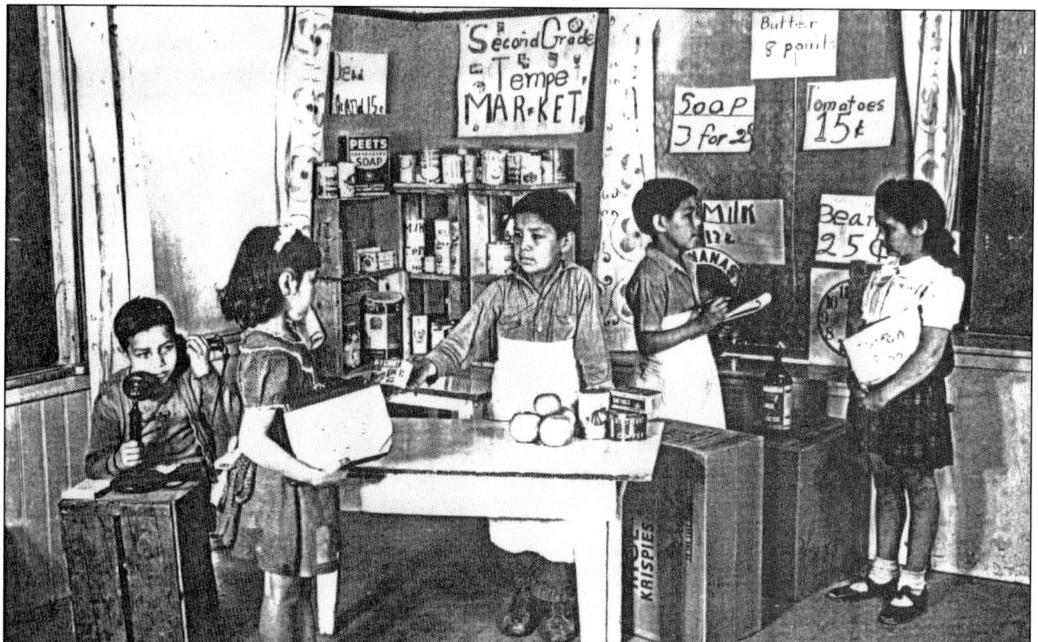

In elementary school, an effective way to help young children learn was through the project method, whereby students learned by developing a project. Here children have created a grocery store where they carry out the roles of employees and customers. Playacting bridges what each student knows into new understanding, language skills, and negotiation by involvement in a realistic situation. In this picture are, from left to right, unidentified, Mary Galaz, Jimmy Romero, Salvador Romero, and Jovita Cara Bajal.

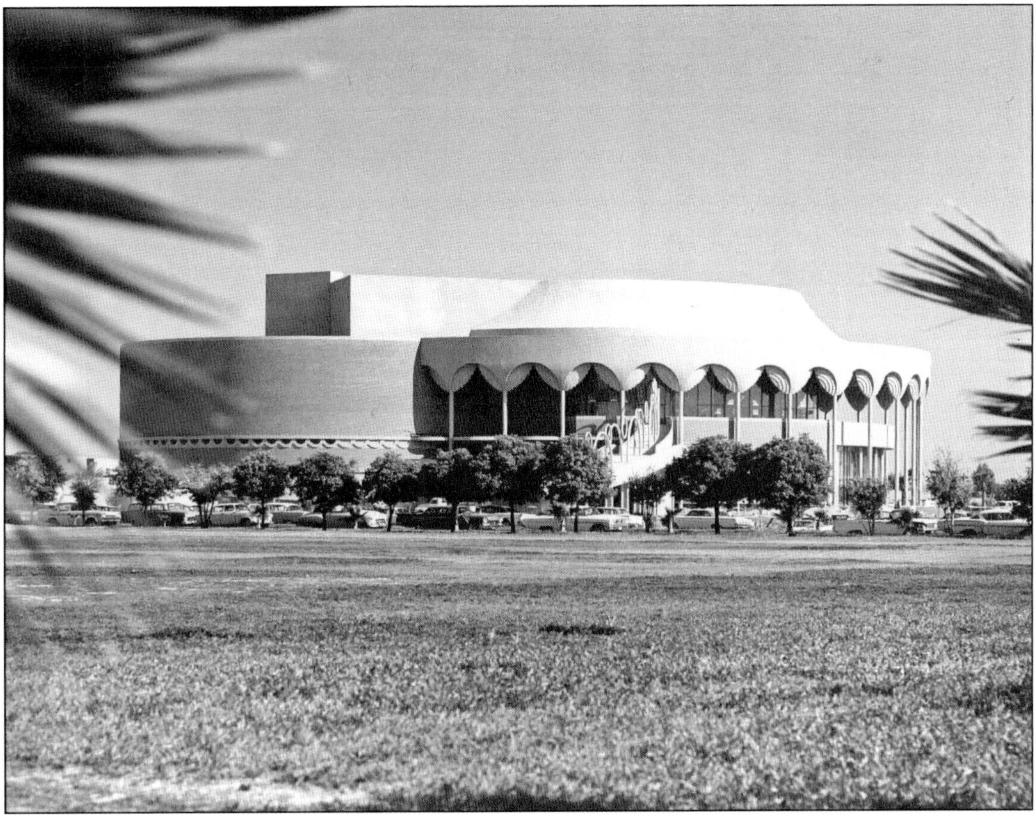

One of the most remarkable examples of architectural designs is exemplified in the Grady Gammage Auditorium on the campus of Arizona State University in Tempe. (AHF.)

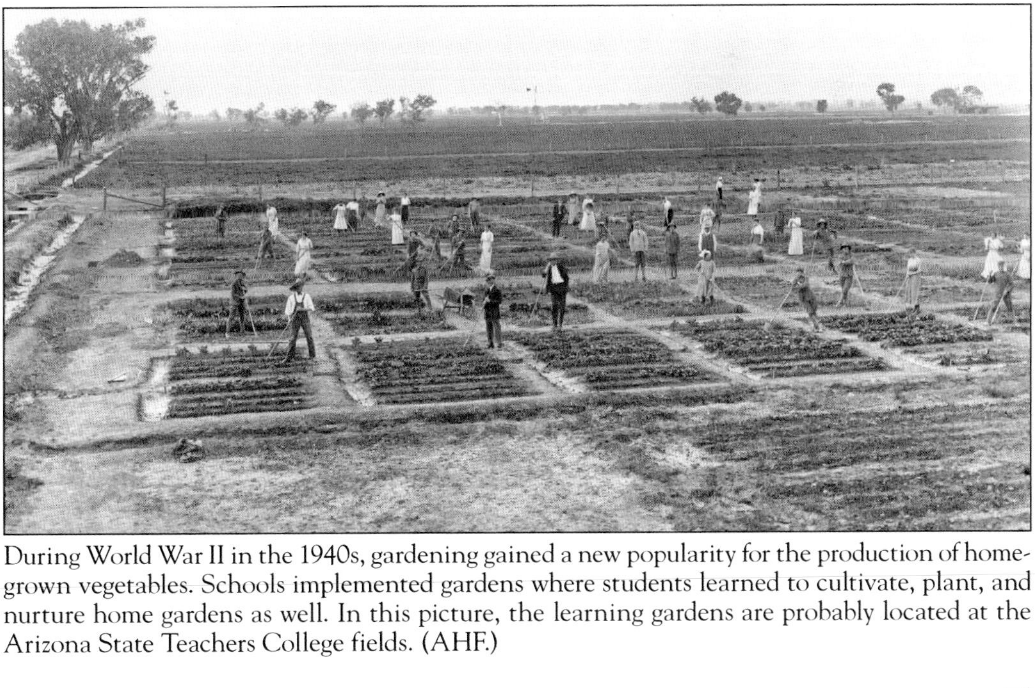

During World War II in the 1940s, gardening gained a new popularity for the production of home-grown vegetables. Schools implemented gardens where students learned to cultivate, plant, and nurture home gardens as well. In this picture, the learning gardens are probably located at the Arizona State Teachers College fields. (AHF.)

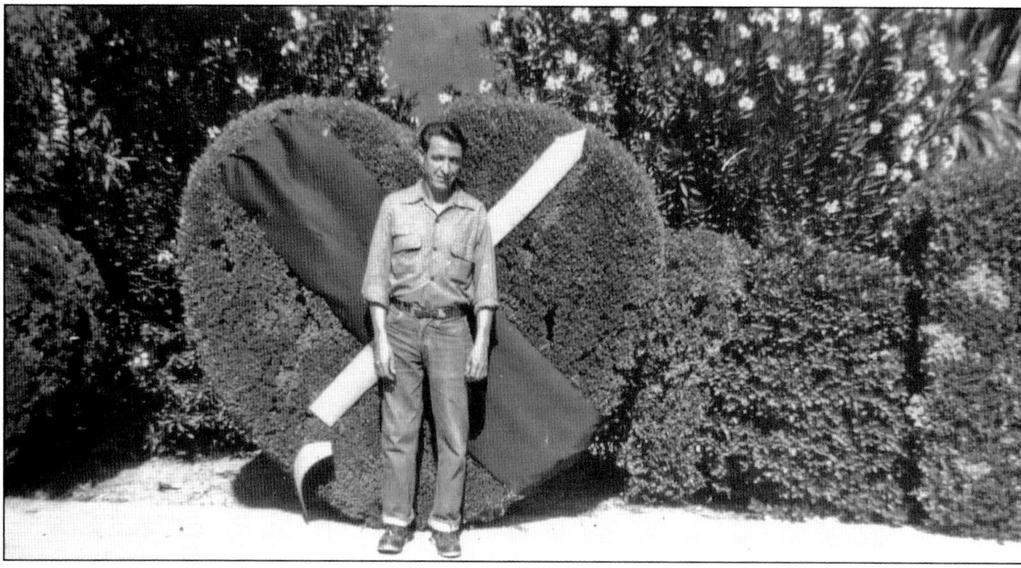

David Jaimez is pictured in 1955. He worked for Arizona State Teachers College, and later when the school became Arizona State University (ASU), for 42 years. A number of Mexican American workers kept the garden fields, the campus landscape, and the buildings well maintained. (Norma C. Pinate.)

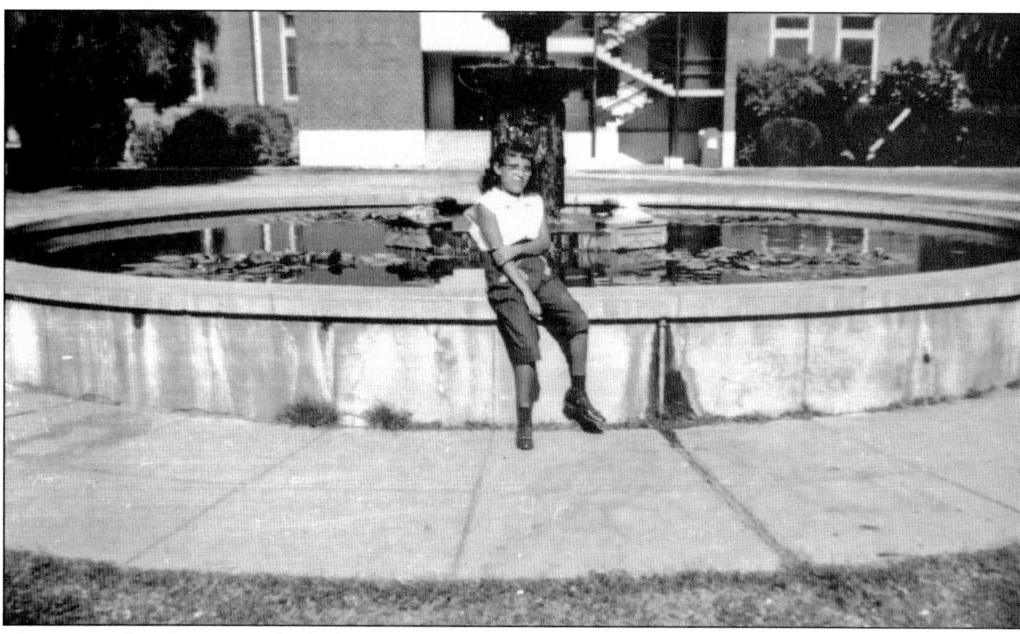

Norma Carbajal, age 10, had the run of today's Arizona State University campus. One of her favorite places to sit and rest was the ASU fountain and pond; she is shown here in 1955. (Norma C. Pinate.)

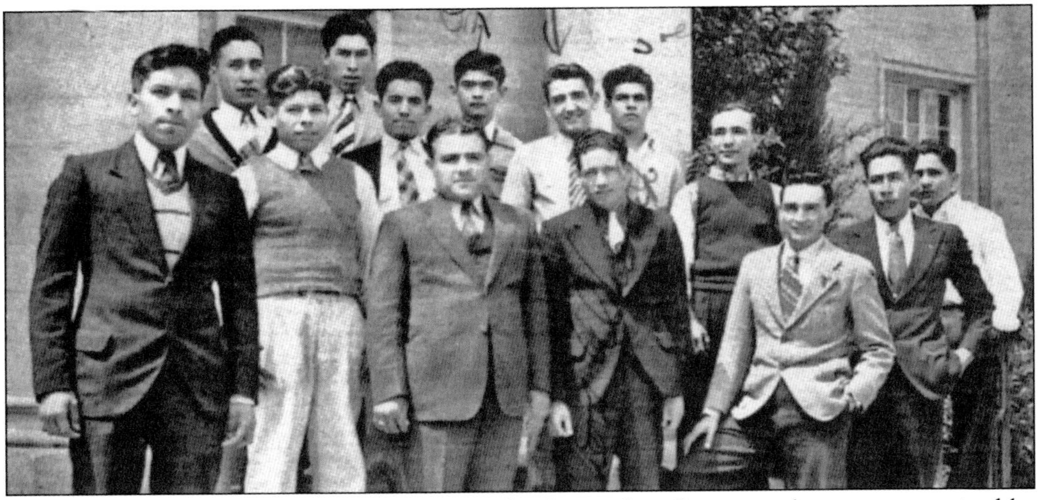

During the first semester of the 1937–1938 school year, Los Conquistadores was organized by Spanish-speaking students of the Arizona State Teachers College. Los Conquistadores intended to establish friendly relations among its members and with other students on the campus. Faculty members Irma Wilson and Wilbur Dutton were advisers. Pictured here are (first row) Hilario Alvarado, president; Fred Teyechea, vice president; Albert Alvarado, publicity agent; ? Timbres; and ? Salazar; (second row) ? Alva, ? Munoz, Tony Vicente, Fernando Ortega, and ? Rivera; (third row) Victor Ortega, Gilbert Orrantia, Albert Ramirez, and ? Garcia. Carmen Reynoso, secretary, is not pictured. Most, if not all, of these students served in World War II. Gilbert Orrantia served as a combat pilot in the Army Air Corps (prior to the creation of the U.S. Air Force). Fernando Ortega served in the U.S. Army Intelligence Corps, and after the war, he served for years as superintendent of the elementary school district in Florence, Arizona. (Gilbert Orrantia.)

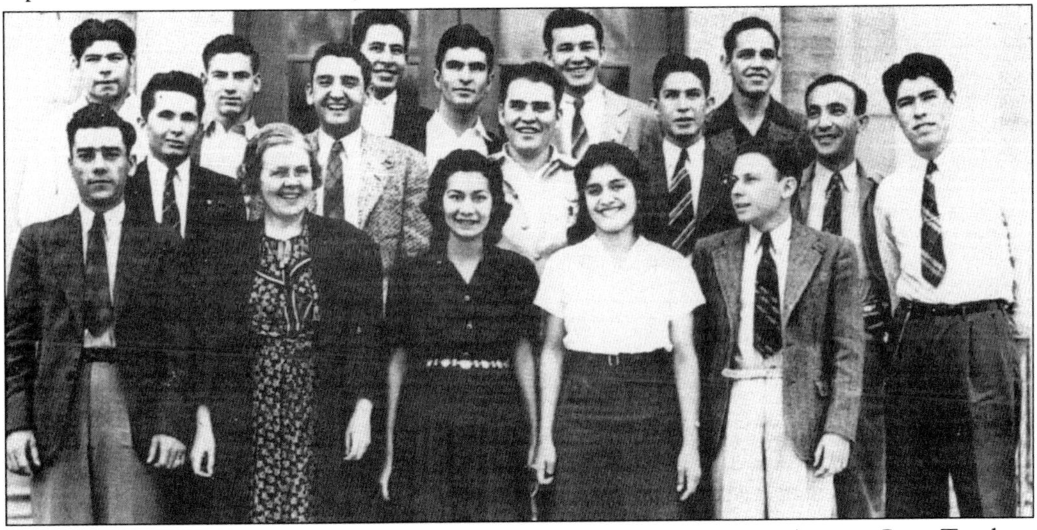

Los Conquistadores of 1940–1941 continued as a student organization at Arizona State Teachers College, now ASU, and fostered friendship and social relationships among students. Los Conquistadores sponsored Mexican Youth Conferences, a dance, a breakfast in honor of seniors, and a picnic that year. Irma Wilson of the foreign language department served as faculty adviser for the organization. Pictured from left to right are, using last names only, (first row) Diaz, Prof. Irma Wilson, Gonzales, Muñoz, Arevalo, and Orrantia; (second row) Felix, Vicente, Saucedo, Mendoza, and Ortega; (third row) Alva, Soto, Salazar, Soza, Andrade, and Marquez. (Gilbert Orrantia.)

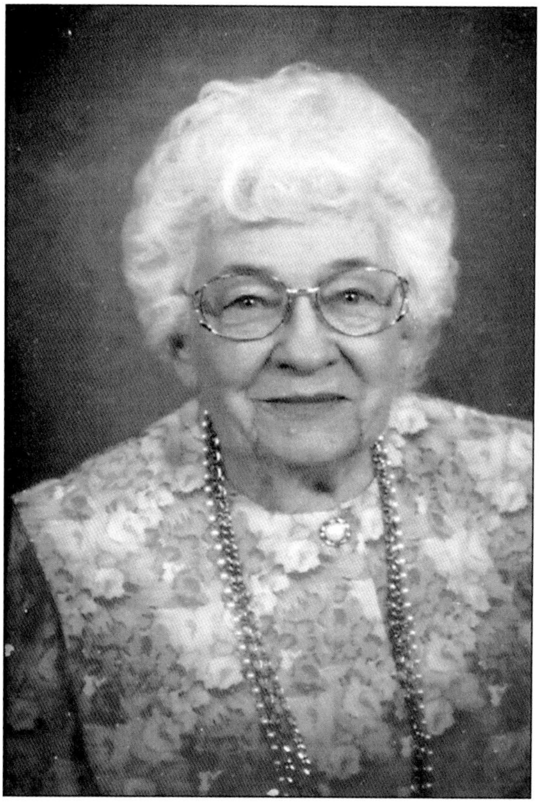

Mary Alice (Fike) Pigg, pictured at the age of 90 in 2000, was born on April 13, 1910, when Arizona was a territory, and died on October 21, 2005, at the age of 95. Pigg is remembered and revered by her family, friends, and countless students she helped along the learning process. She taught at the old Rural School, which served children who, for the most part, lived in the ranches when there were only empty fields and ranches east of Rural Road. She had an illustrious 35 years of teaching in the valley. In 1985, Mary Alice was recognized as Tempe All-American Woman, and she was honored as a Tempe Legend by the Tempe Historical Society in March 2004. Mayor Hugh Hallman declared April 13, 2005, "Mary Alice Pigg Day" for the city of Tempe. (Dr. JoAnne Pigg and Mary Lynn Pigg Younger.)

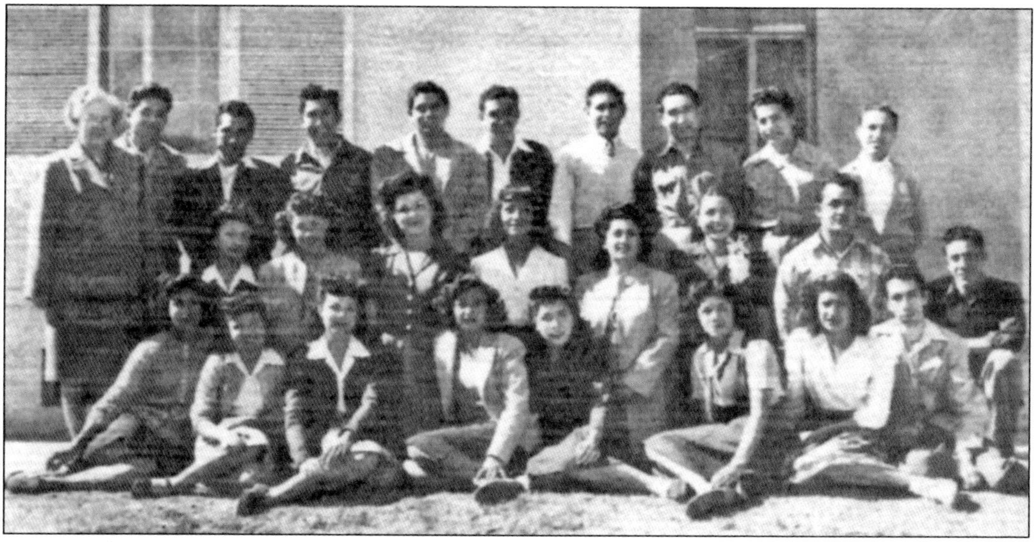

At every level of education, Mexican American students strived to excel at a new language and a different culture while keeping their own heritage. This picture of Los Conquistadores of 1945–1946 showed that more young Mexican American women had enrolled at Arizona State Teachers College, now ASU. Early Mexican women had graduated from the school when it was the Normal School in the 1920s, prior to becoming ASTC. The first Mexican American teachers in the valley were sisters Mary and Inez Gomez, who taught in the Litchfield and Goodyear areas. (Gilbert Orrantia.)

At the high school level, Mexican American youth participated in sports throughout the state, including in Tempe. In this c. 1947 picture, Dan Gamboa jumps for a layup to score two points, but Danny Peralta runs to rebound. (Gilbert Montanez.)

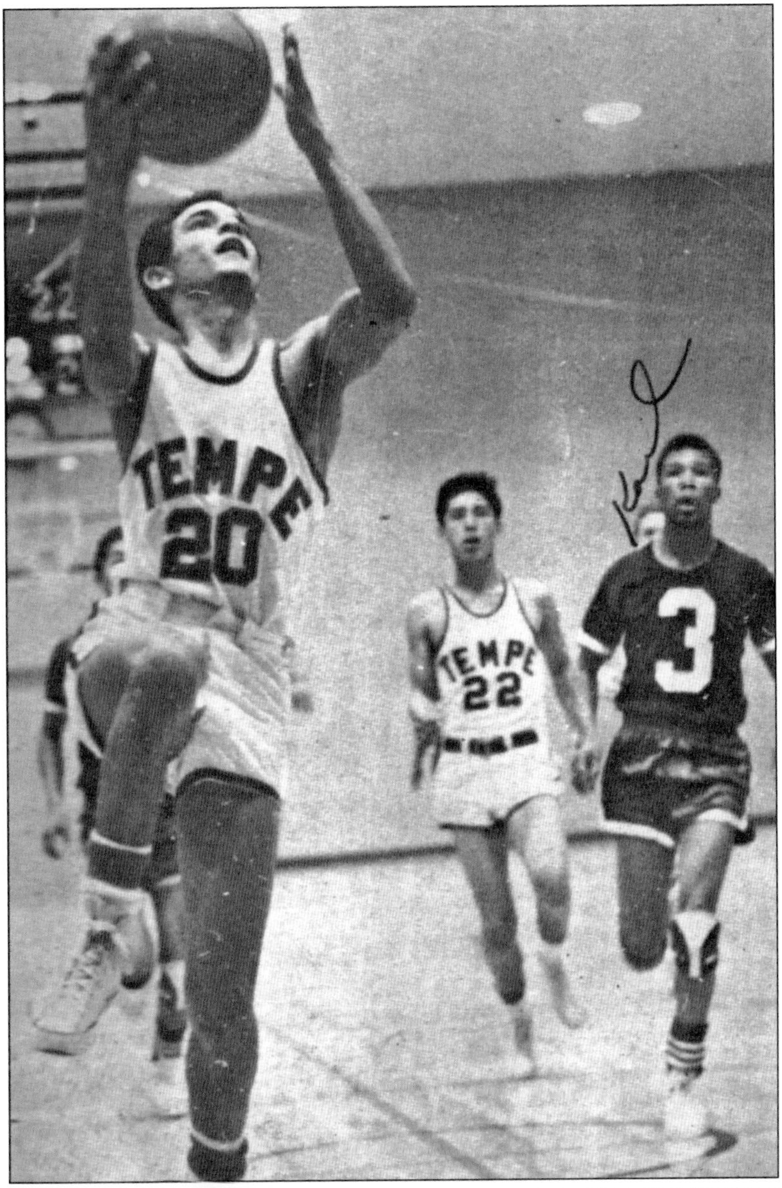

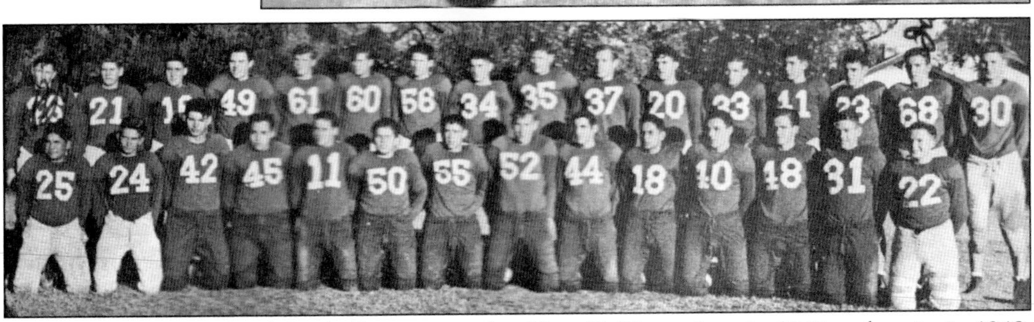

The Tempe High School football team was the Class D Champions in 1947 and again in 1948. (Gilbert Montanez.)

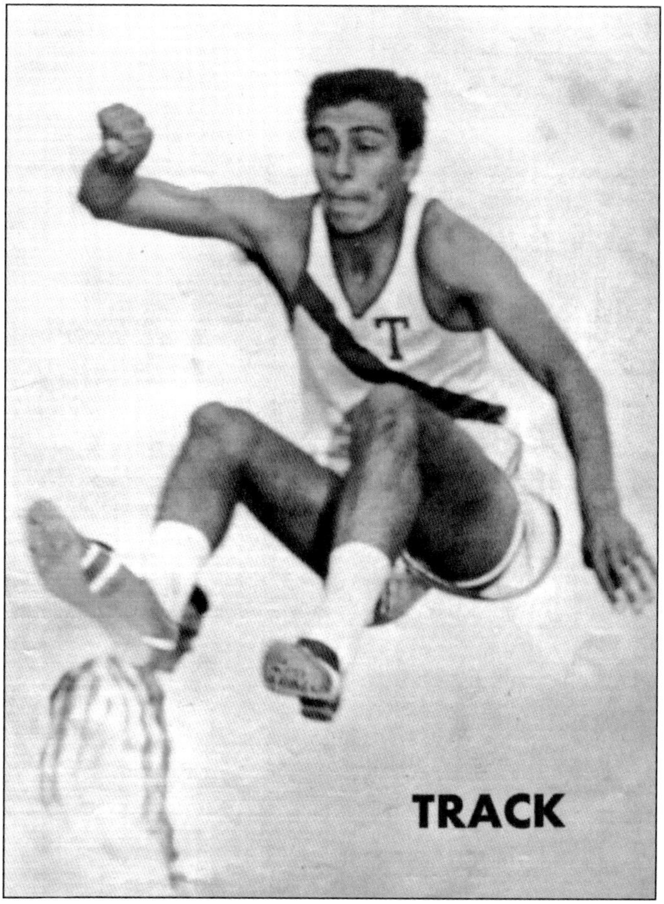

Jesse Valenzuela of Tempe High School participated in track and field in 1957. In this picture from the school annual, the *Horizon*, Jesse leaps in a broad jump for 23 feet. (Jesse Valenzuela.)

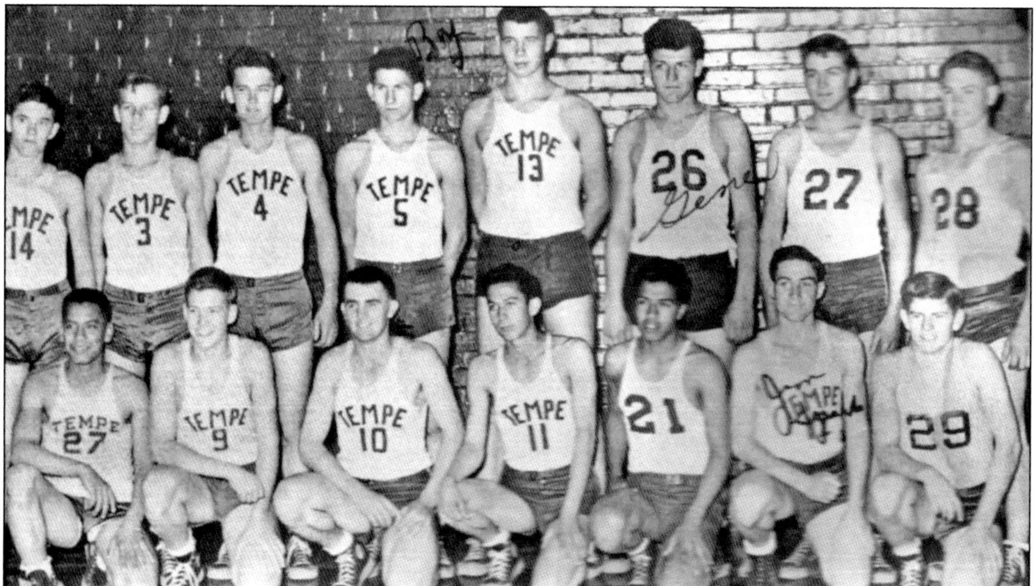

This picture shows the Tempe High School basketball team of 1947. (Gilbert Montanez.)

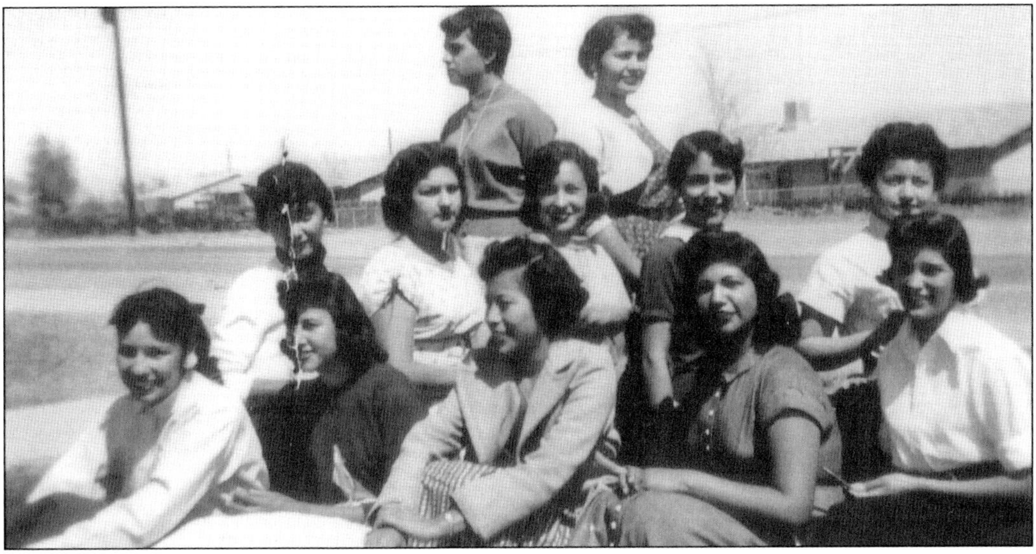

The bond between barrio neighbors goes beyond going to school together and sharing experiences, beyond knowing every neighbor and who can be trusted, beyond borrowing a cup of sugar or a spoonful of lard. It is an intimate friendship from years of social events, making tamales for Christmas, going hunting, drinking beer, and having a party. The bond exists because of family relations and strong religious connections the Mexican culture has: orphans welcomed into a family who become sons and daughters called *hijos de crencia*, *compadres y comadres* (co-fathers and co-mothers), and *padrinos* (sponsors at baptisms and marriages). Traditions and customs are integrated into a culture, such as naming children, and form an integral part of religious culture—for example, Encarnacion (Incarnation) and Trinidad (Trinity). Their religion of 3,000 years is carried within their very flesh. In this picture is a group of Tempe girls, friends of photographer Clara Urbano.

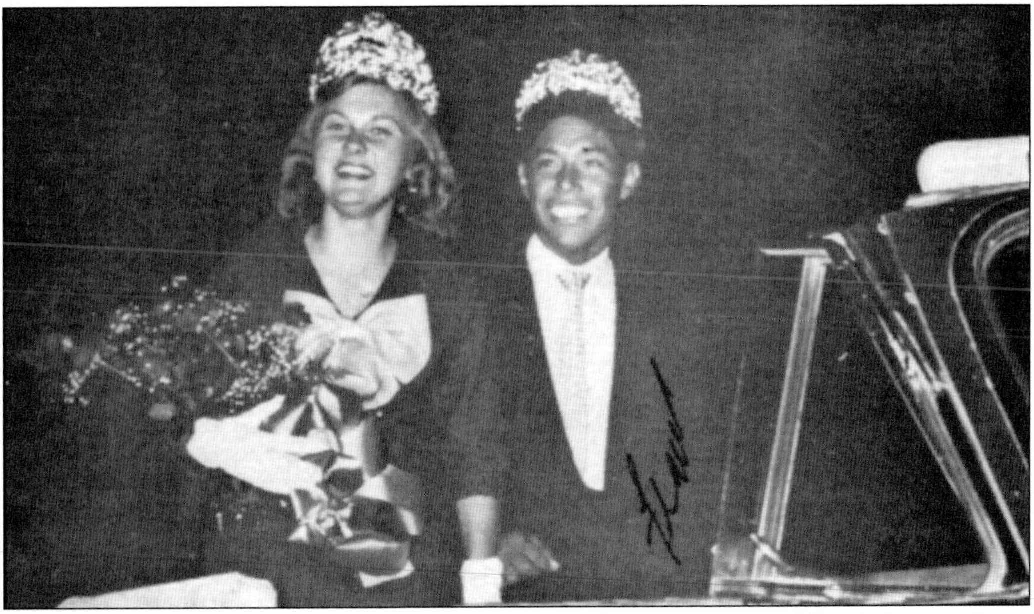

Tempe High School Homecoming Day presents Jerri Glover as queen and Frank Lopez as king. They were chosen to reign as king and queen by the students in 1955. (Jesse Valenzuela.)

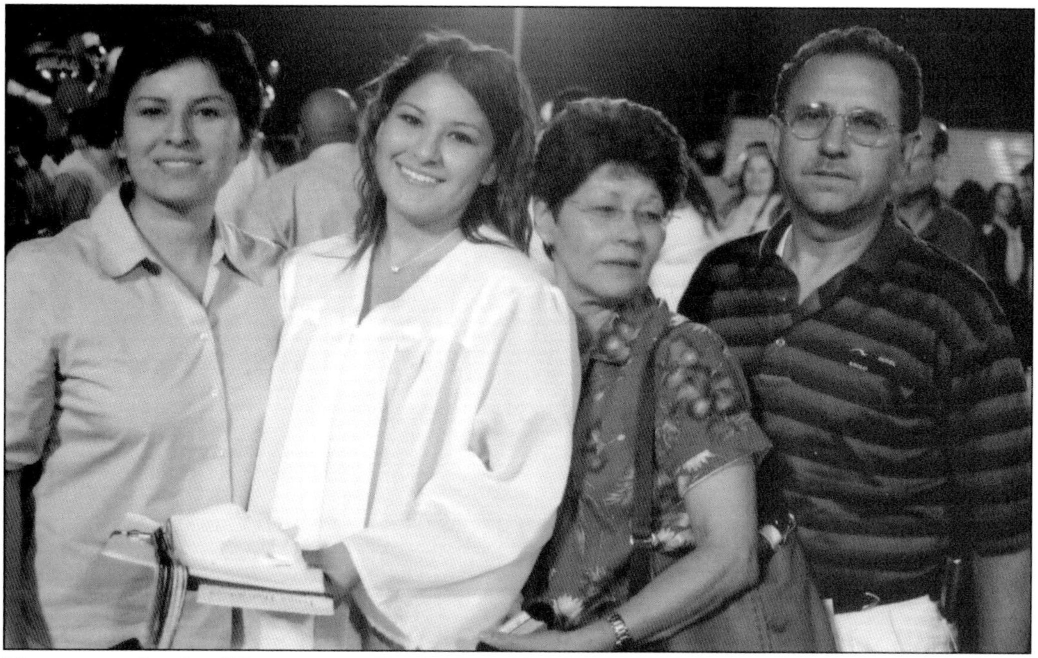

The many schools of Tempe provide educational opportunities for all its young citizens. In this photograph, Sunnie Minjarez graduates from Tempe High School in May 2004. From left to right are Sunnie's mother, Monica V. Minjarez; Sunnie; and Sunnie's grandparents Rumaldo and Isabel Minjarez from Denver, Colorado. (Author's collection.)

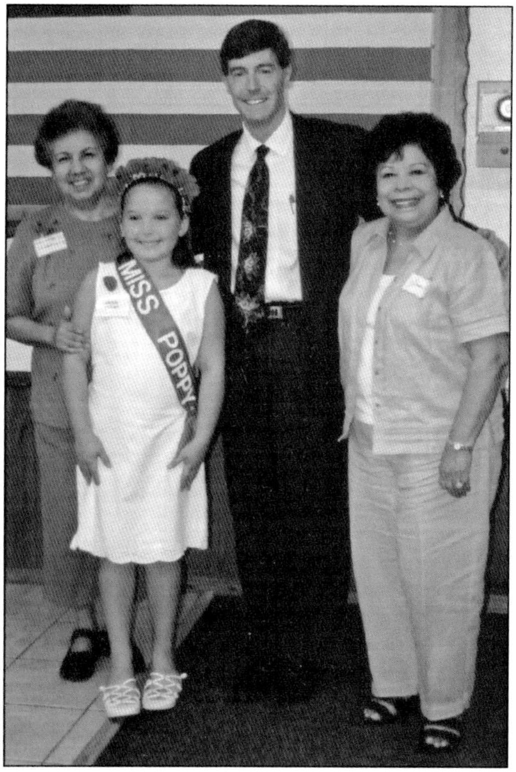

The American Legion Post No. 2 of Tempe in 2003 sponsored the Americanism Banquet to recognize auxiliary past presidents. BriAnna Sweetie Marie Schrimpe was appointed as "Poppy Girl" to present each past president with a flower. This picture shows, from left to right, Erlinda Varela Schweller, auxiliary treasurer; BriAnna; Tempe mayor Hugh Hallman; and Josie R. Vega, auxiliary member. (Erlinda Varela Schweller.)

Josie Ortega Solis (left) and her cousins Leo Enriquez and Margie Berumen celebrate their first Communion, demonstrating an example of a strong, integrated religious tradition in the Mexican American culture. (Josie O. Solis.)

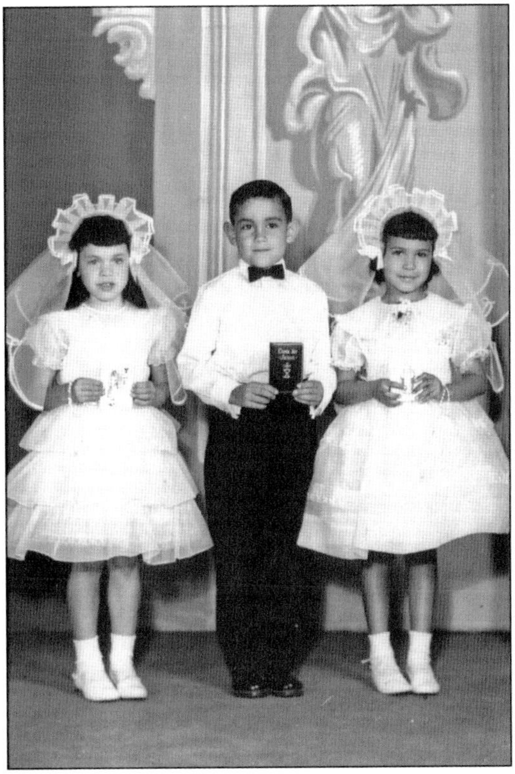

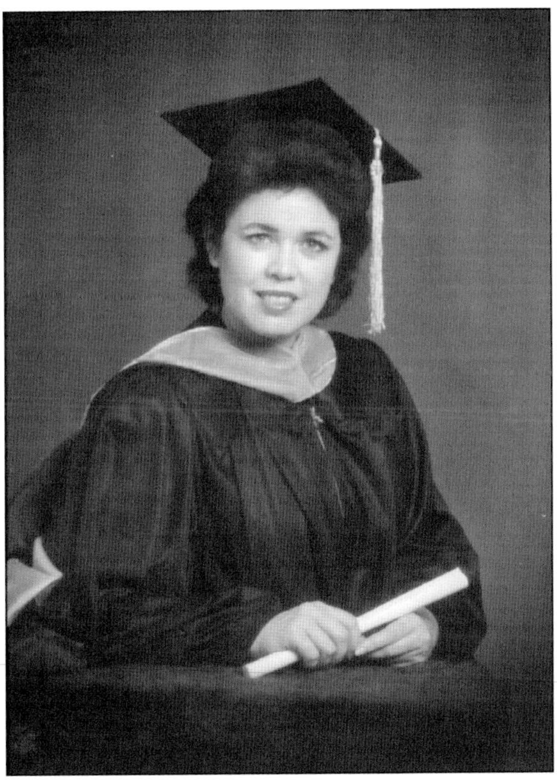

In 1983, Josie Ortega Solis earned her master's degree in psychology from Arizona State University. Education represents another tradition of Mexican Americans, who, when they overcome the hardships of hard work in the fields and in the mines, turn their attention to supporting their children in educational pursuits. (Josie O. Solis.)

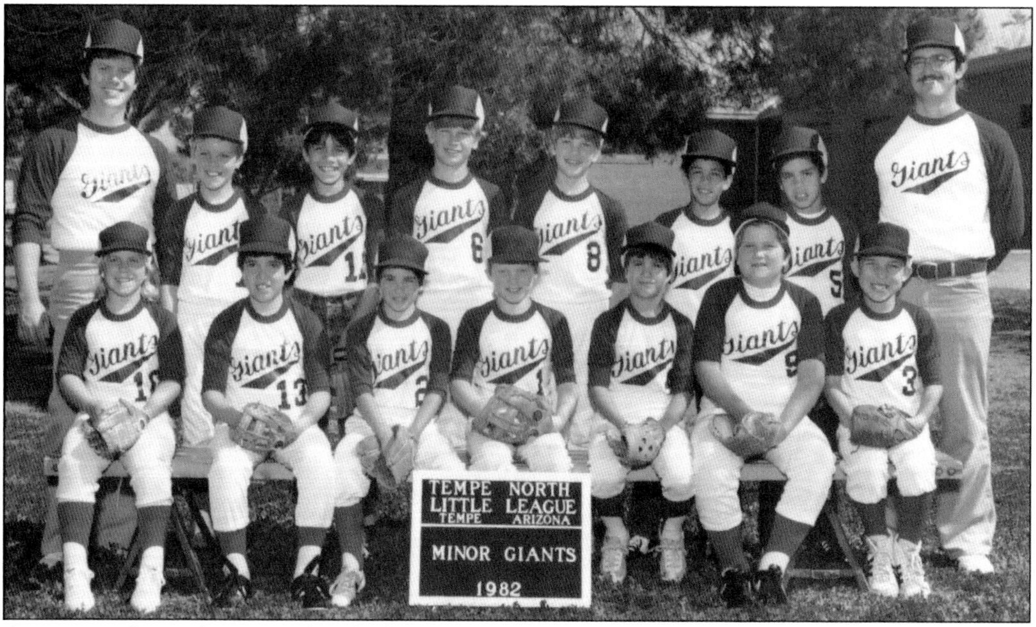

A picture of a Little League baseball team shows the Tempe North Minor Giants in 1982. The picture includes Basilio Coracides, an architect born in Mexico. He graduated from Arizona State University. Pictured from left to right are (first row) four unidentified, Nico Coracides, unidentified, and Arturo Galven; (second row) two unidentified, Anthony Chavez, Josh Olson, Jake Olson, Nickolas Chavez, Alfonso Chavez, and coach Basilio Coracides. (Josie O. Solis.)

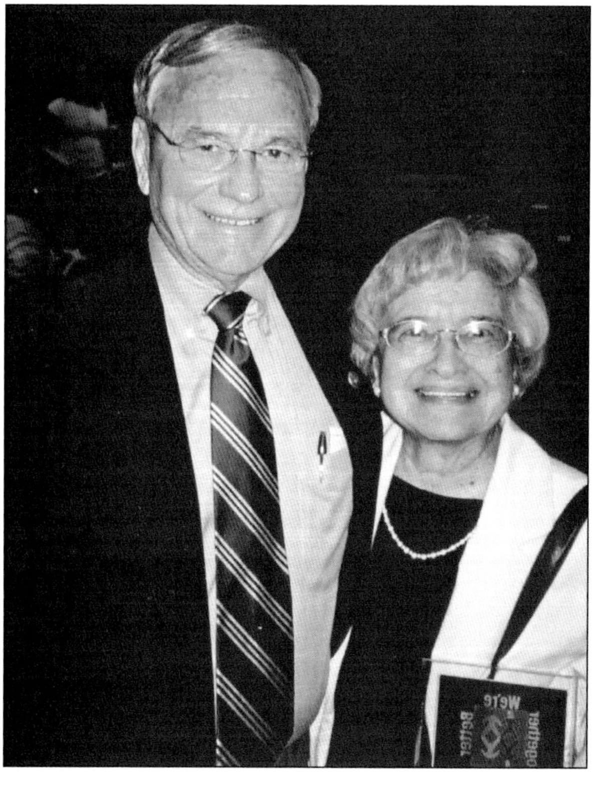

Senator Harry Mitchell served as a teacher in Tempe for many years; he then served as mayor of Tempe for many years. Now he serves Tempe, the state of Arizona, and the United States in the U.S. Senate. Here he is with Narcisa M. Espinoza when she represented the interests of the National Association of Retired Government Employees. (Narcisa M. Espinoza.)

Six

LEGACY AND REMEMBRANCES

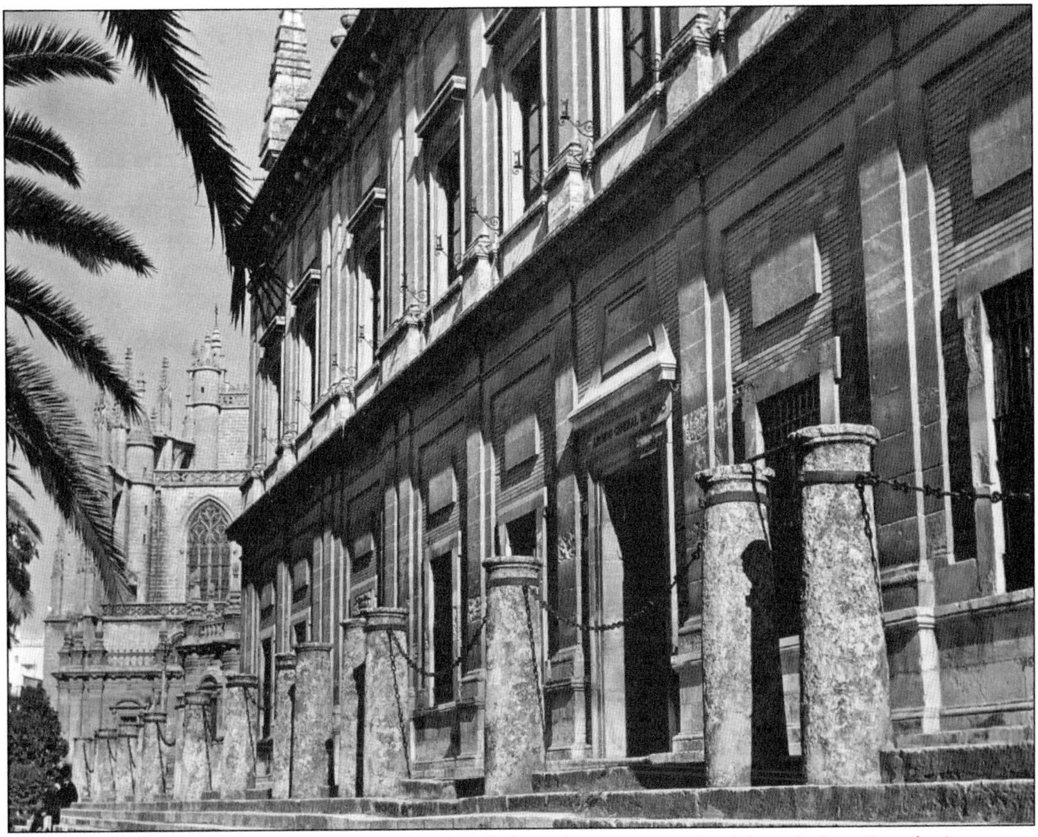

Spain was where the footprints to the New World began in 1492. They led to South America, first named "America" by a German mapmaker, and to Argentina, where the word "Americano" was first used in designation of a people in 1526 and later translated into the English "American." Although Spain was a small country comprised of a few kingdoms and a small population of approximately eight million, Spain governed the New World with the purpose of Christianizing its people, civilizing the new political entities into a European mold, and creating economies through a mercantile system that would pay back its investments. The records of all this enterprise are housed in the Archivo General de Indies, the government of the Indies archives in Seville, Spain. Records kept in this building concern the footprints of 22 Spanish-speaking countries, including Mexico, and the U.S. Southwest, Texas, Louisiana, and Florida. (AHF.)

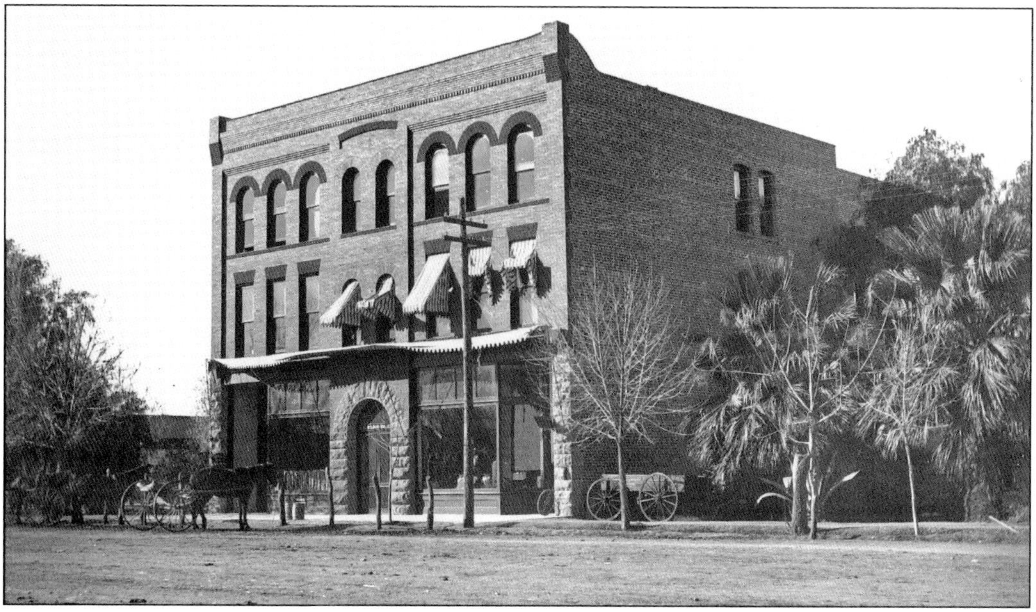

The Hodnett Building in Tempe presents a different type of architecture than the Spanish and Arabic influences commonly seen in buildings in the Southwest. The square and narrow box brick reminds one of the Chicago style. (AHF.)

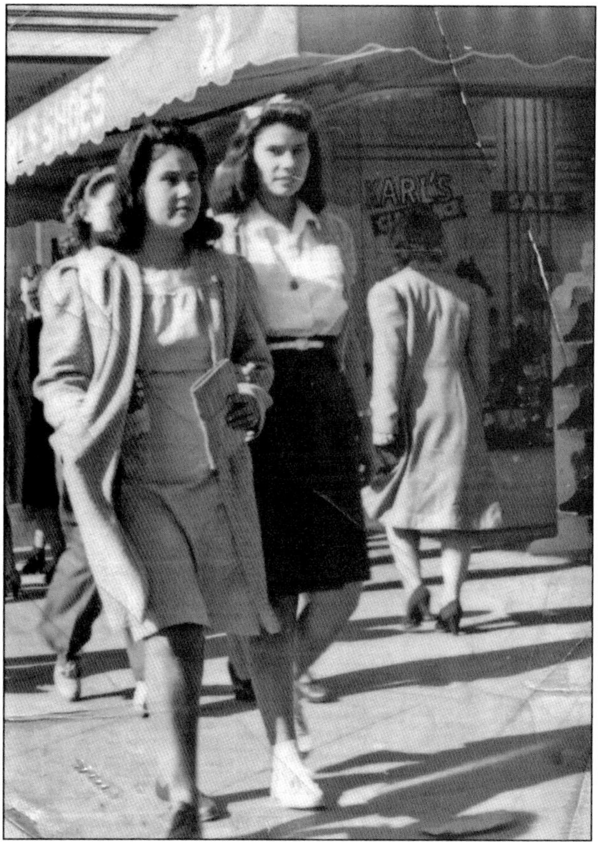

Mary Burgos (left) and Ramona Burgos (right), sisters and the daughters of Juliana and Francisco "Chico" Burgos, shop in downtown Phoenix at a time when there were no large clothing stores or malls in Tempe.

The Alianza Hispano Americana, founded in Tucson in 1895, spread to many towns and cities of the Southwest. The Spanish American Lodge in Tempe, pictured in 1915, is believed to be same organization as the Alianza Hispano Americana. It was located on Dewey and Normal Streets in San Pablo. In the downstairs of the same building lived Joe Soto, and upstairs was the meeting hall. In that same meeting room, puppet shows were held for kids.

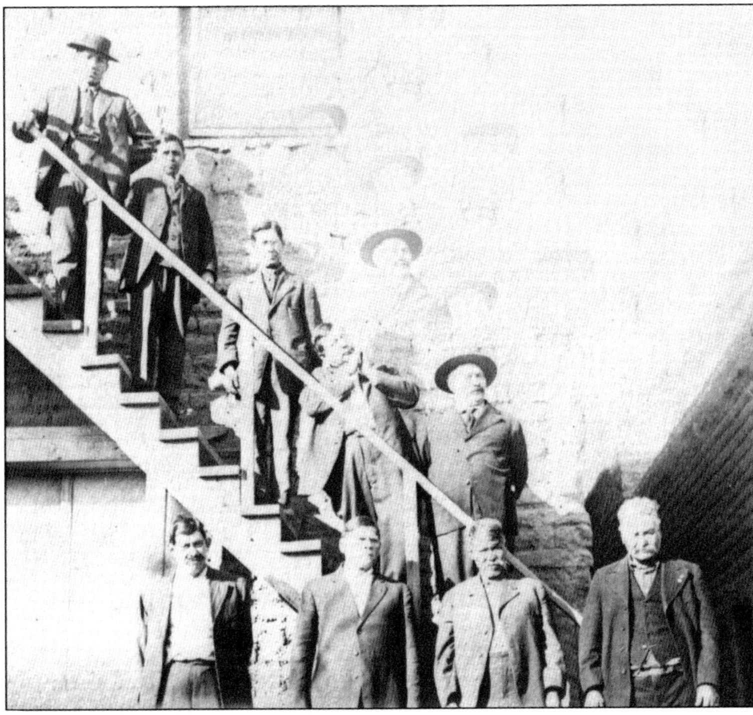

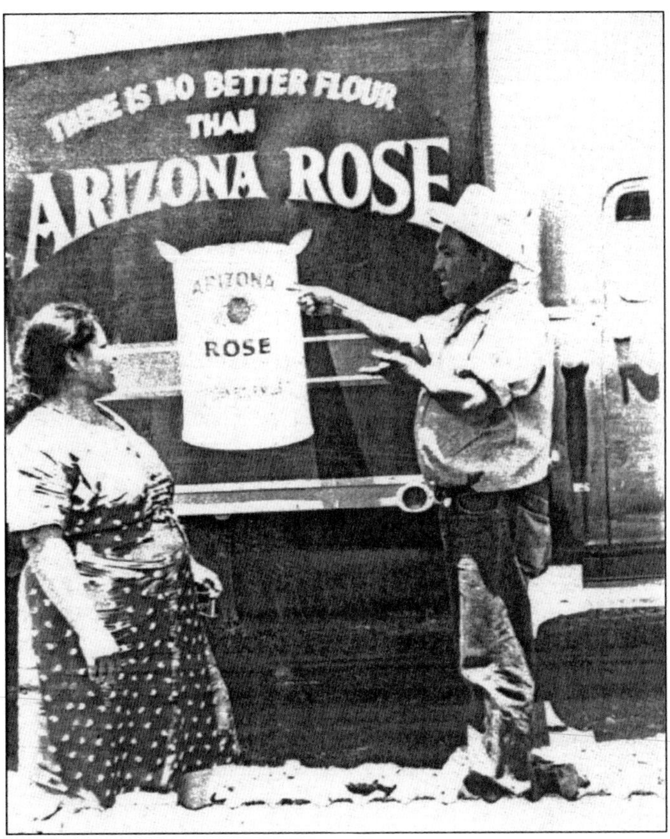

Both Victoria Soto Leon and Gene Romero Leon worked at the Hayden Four Mill in the 1950s.

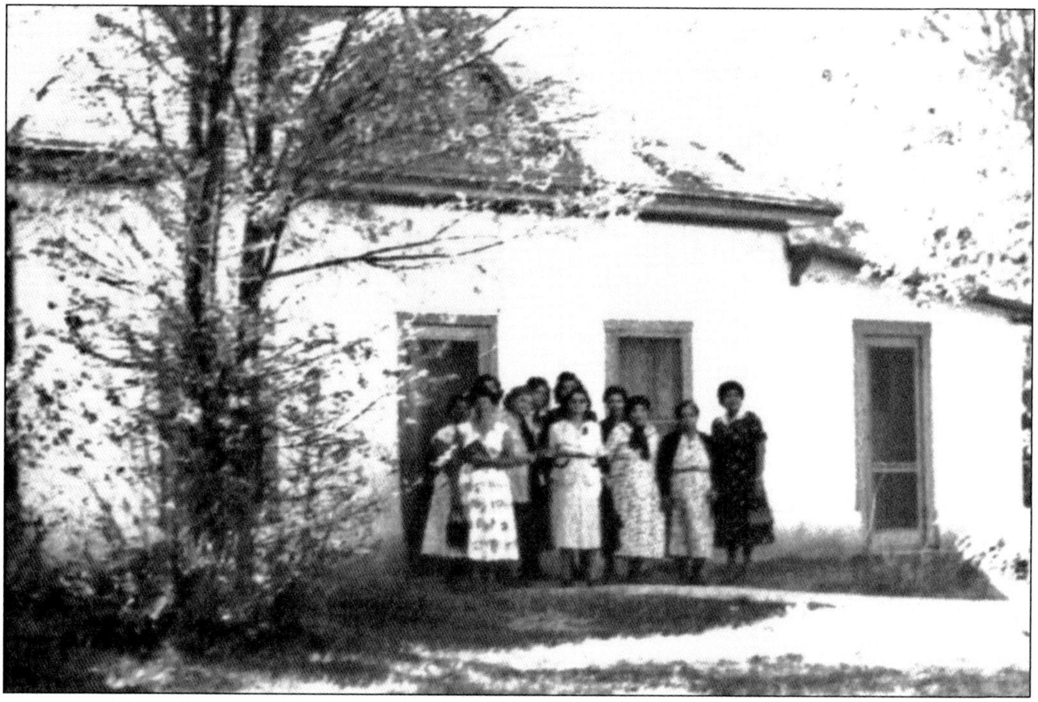

A group of women friends gathers in front of the Elias Rodriguez House on Eighth Street in Tempe in November 1955. The house was built in the late 1800s. Pictured from left to right are (first row) Helen Gracia, Carmela Reyes, Elizabeth Rodriguez, Cuca Gamboa, Rosa Perez, and Sarah Garcia; (second row) unidentified, Lena Gray, Mary Compoy, Dolores Rodriguez, and Fernanda Gamboa (Mrs. Johnny Gamboa).

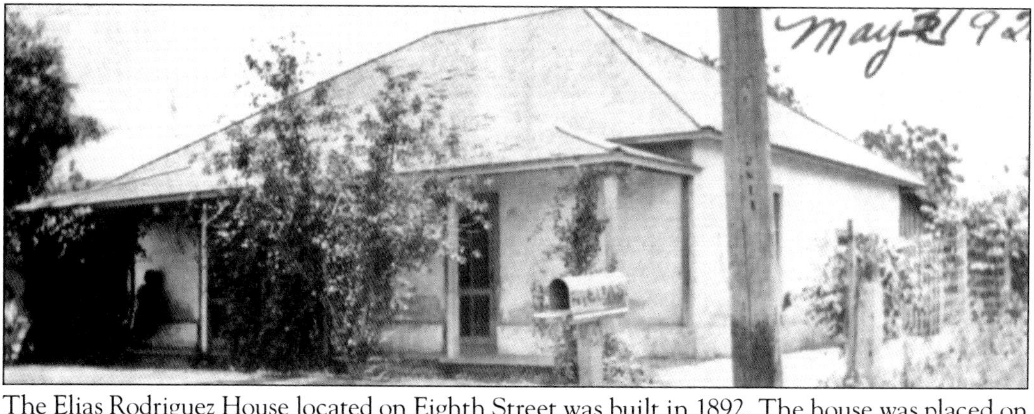

The Elias Rodriguez House located on Eighth Street was built in 1892. The house was placed on the National Register of Historic Places in 1984. Later the house was stabilized and advertised for viewing. It is 116 years old. (City of Tempe.)

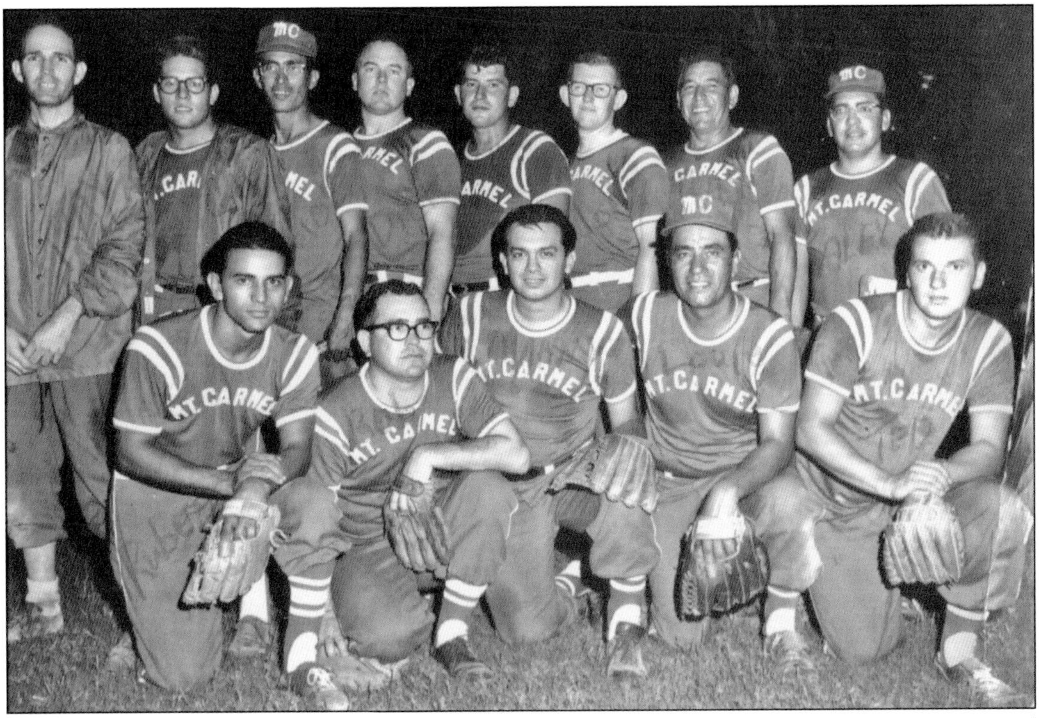

The Our Lady of Mount Carmel (OLMC) baseball team participated in the Mesa League around 1959. The OLMC team created unity by representing Mount Carmel Parish in a baseball league. The only player identified in this picture is Cano Perez (second row, far right).

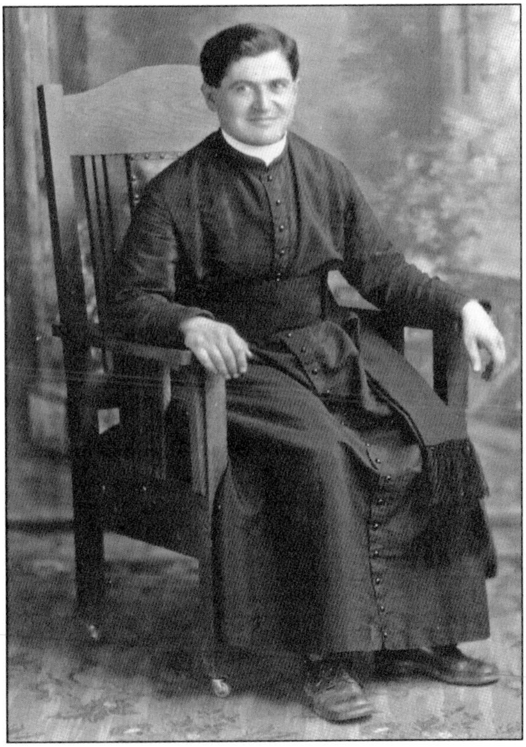

Padre Jesus M. Almudo served in Tempe. This picture was dated July 3, 1930. Padre Jesus, as he was commonly known, was a priest at Our Lady of Mount Carmel and was noted for serving the Mexican faithful. A missionary priest, he came from St. Mary's in Phoenix to serve the Nuestra Señora del Carmen (Our Lady of Mount Carmel) mission church. He recruited people to join the church, and he promoted the Mexican faith traditions in the 1920s. He originally came from Spain and is thought to have been a Claretian missionary.

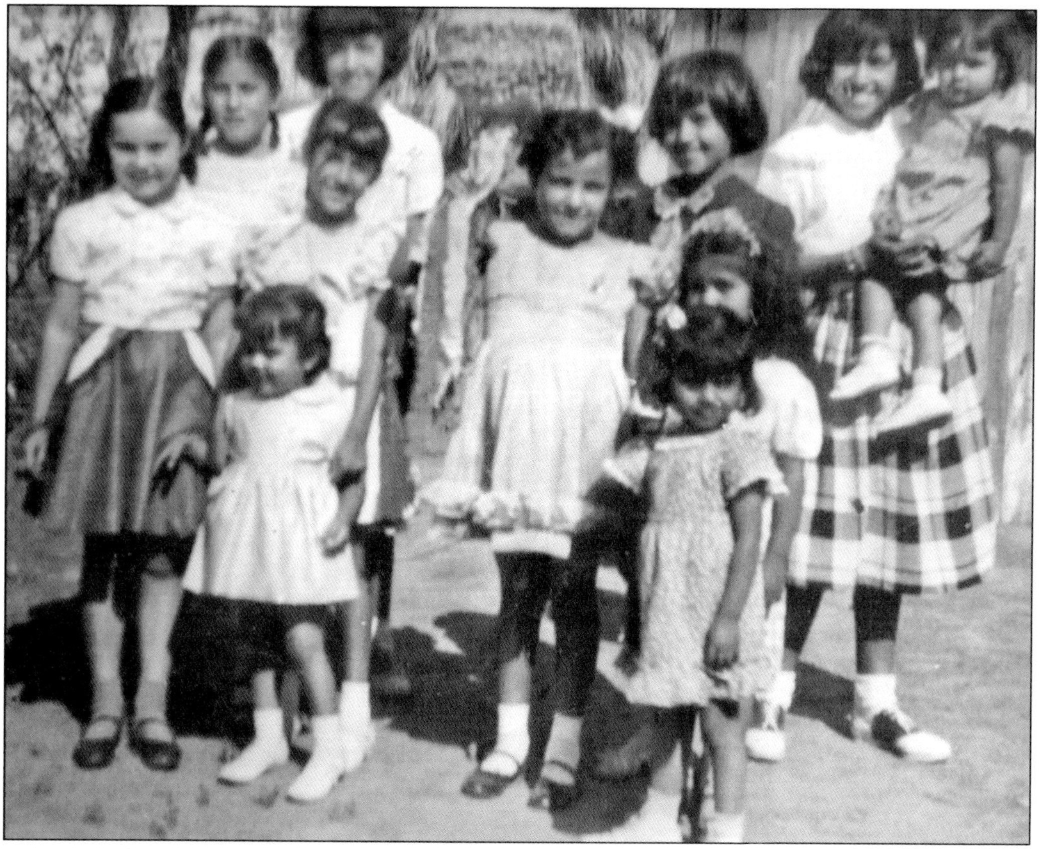

Norma Carbajal (second row, third from left) and other children celebrate Norma's birthday in the Mickey Mouse barrio in 1953. (Norma C. Pinate.)

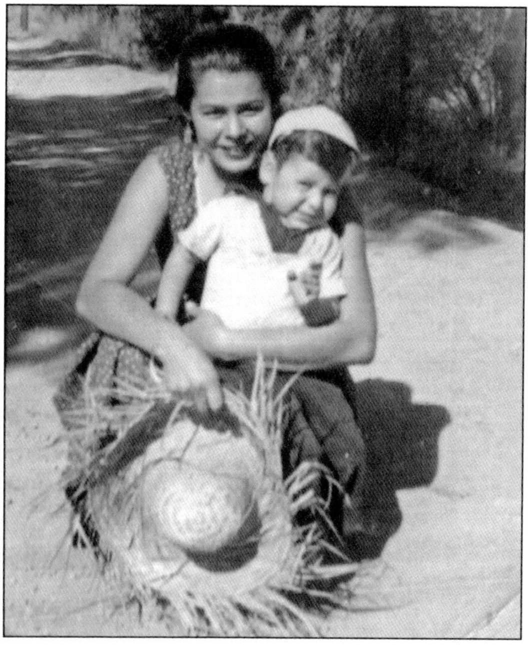

Helen Gomez Tramont held her hat and embraced her young son Louie Tremont as they stroll on Quarry Road in the Mickey Mouse barrio. One can see the dirt road leading to the quarry on the north side of the west butte prior to the Carriage Bridge, before cars came into being. The dirt road still existed after new roads and bridges had come to serve the transportation needs of a growing Tempe. One can see the barrio scenery of abundant brush and trees along the road. The picture was taken in 1953.

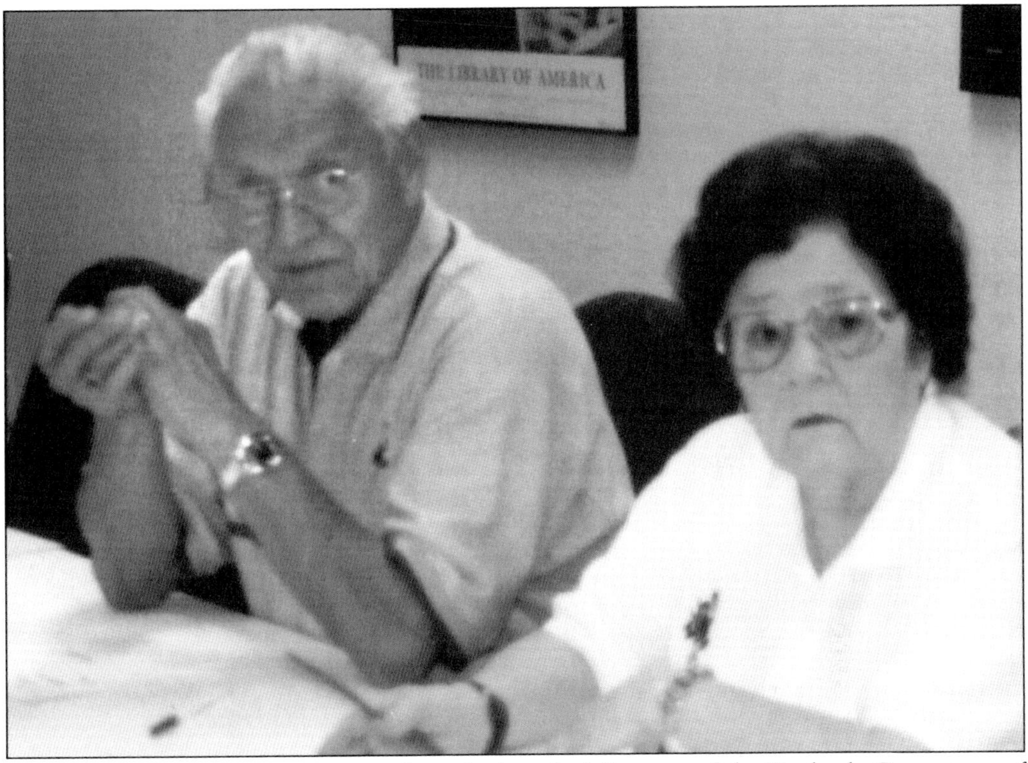

Ernest and Lillie Parra Moraga served on the board of directors of the Tardeada Committee of Tempe. This picture was taken in 2003. (Author's collection.)

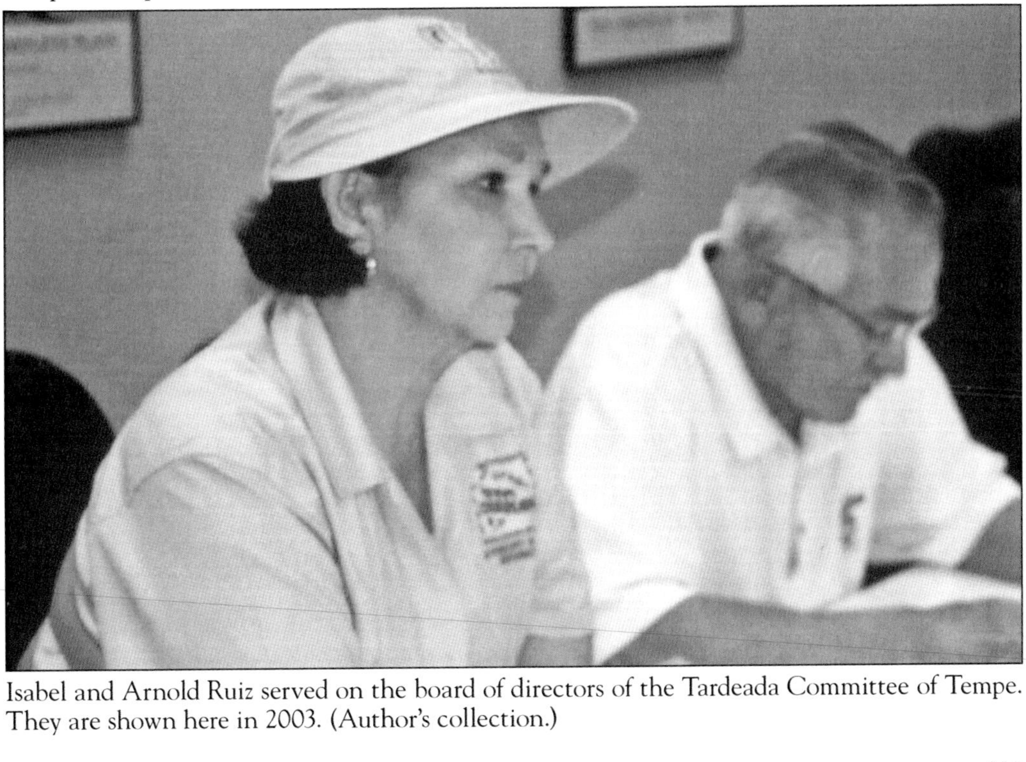

Isabel and Arnold Ruiz served on the board of directors of the Tardeada Committee of Tempe. They are shown here in 2003. (Author's collection.)

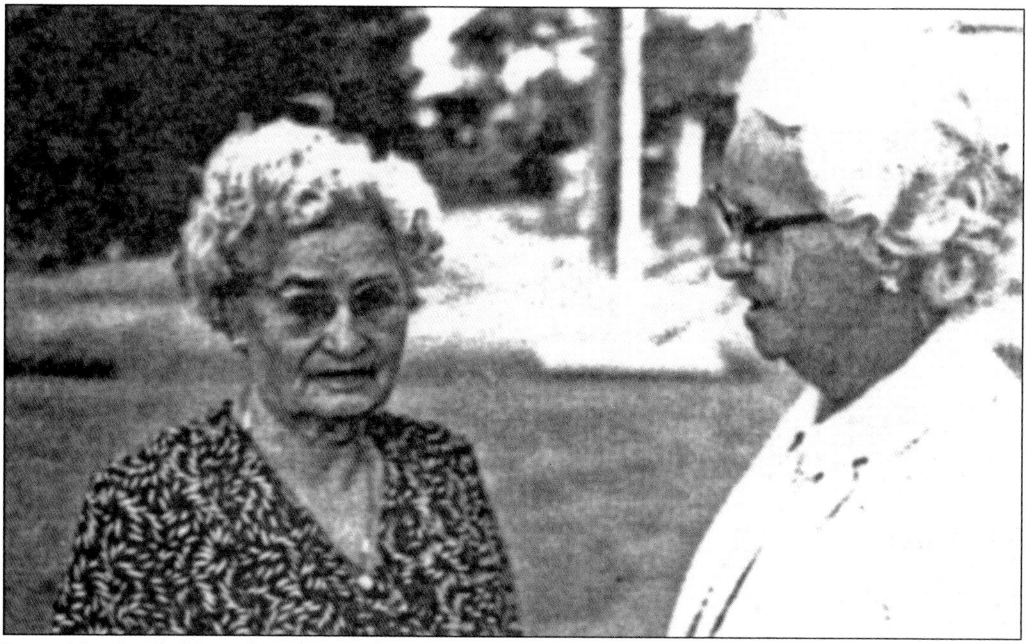

Lupe Varela (left) and Helen Roberts, teacher at the Tempe Eighth Street School, hold a conversation. Both were icons of service to poor schoolchildren of the Mexican School (as this school was called because it was segregated). Individuals were expected to perform much of the social work needed before public social work began. Mrs. Roberts supplied clothes and shoes for many barrio children so they could attend school. Lupe helped Our Lady of Mount Carmel School at Eighth Street and College Avenue, which served the barrios. The school later moved to Sixth Street and College Avenue next to the convent of Blessed Virgin Mary Sisters from Des Moines, Iowa. Sr. Mary Lucille served as the first principal of the school. Other teachers were Sr. Mary Bertilla and Sr. Mary Valeria.

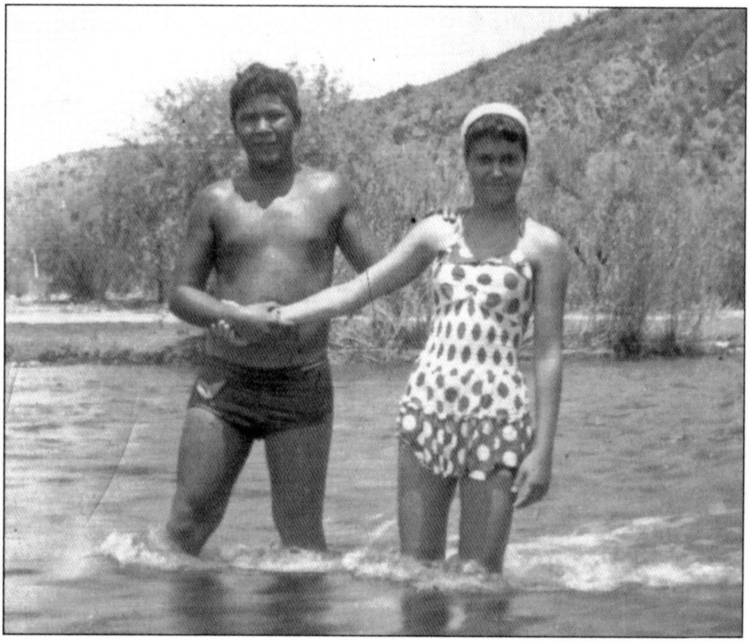

Floyd Gomez Jr. and Lucille Tramont, sister-in-law of Helen Gomez Tramont, enjoy themselves, splashing and swimming at a favorite swimming place called Blue Point on the Salt River, northeast of Mesa. Blue Point was a place where Mexican families also went to have picnics.

Mary Sterling Peralta is pictured in 1950. Mary's grandmother Isabel Guzman Rivera came from California to Tempe in 1890. Isabel settled at Rural Road and the railroad tracks (today it is Rural Road and Tyler Street). Isabel's daughter Maria Guzman Carillo was born in Tempe in 1894. Maria married Joseph Sterling in Tempe on 1913. Joseph and Maria had their wedding at Irene Rodriguez's house (the Rodriguez House now on the National Register of Historic Places). Maria died while giving birth to Mary Sterling on January 17, 1919, in Phoenix. When she was two years old, Mary was brought to Tempe so Isabel Guzman Rivera could raise her. (Barney S. Peralta.)

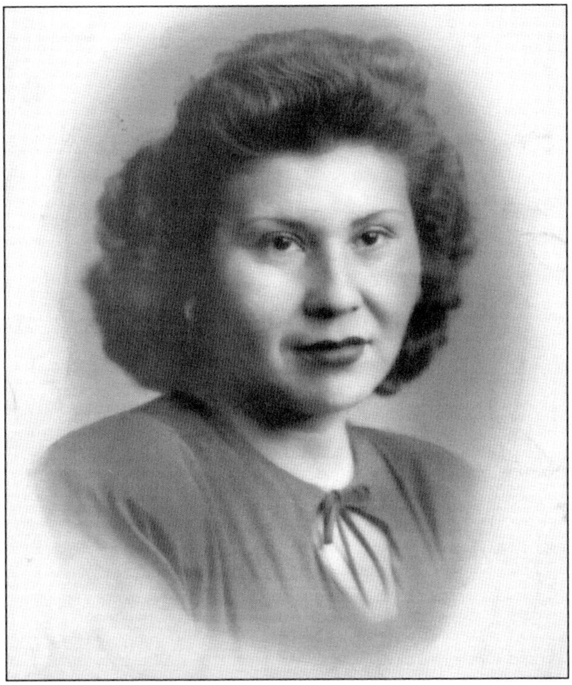

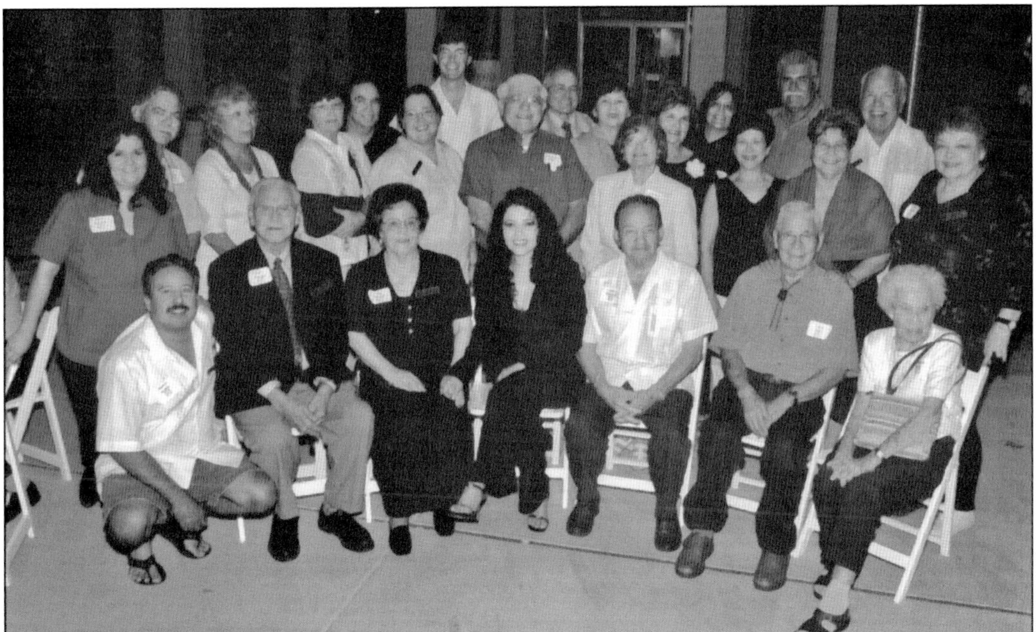

The Tardeada Advisory Committee and a few guests are pictured at the 2003 Tardeada in Tempe. The Tardeada is an evening of celebration with music, dance, and food with friends and neighbors. In the days of San Pablo and other early barrios, *tardeadas* were held in homes and backyards. The neighborhoods' own musicians provided the music. The food was potluck style. The dance area was the hard dirt yard itself, having been sprinkled with water and swept clean. During these *tardeadas*, social relations were cemented and young people met in a safe and approved manner. (Author's collection.)

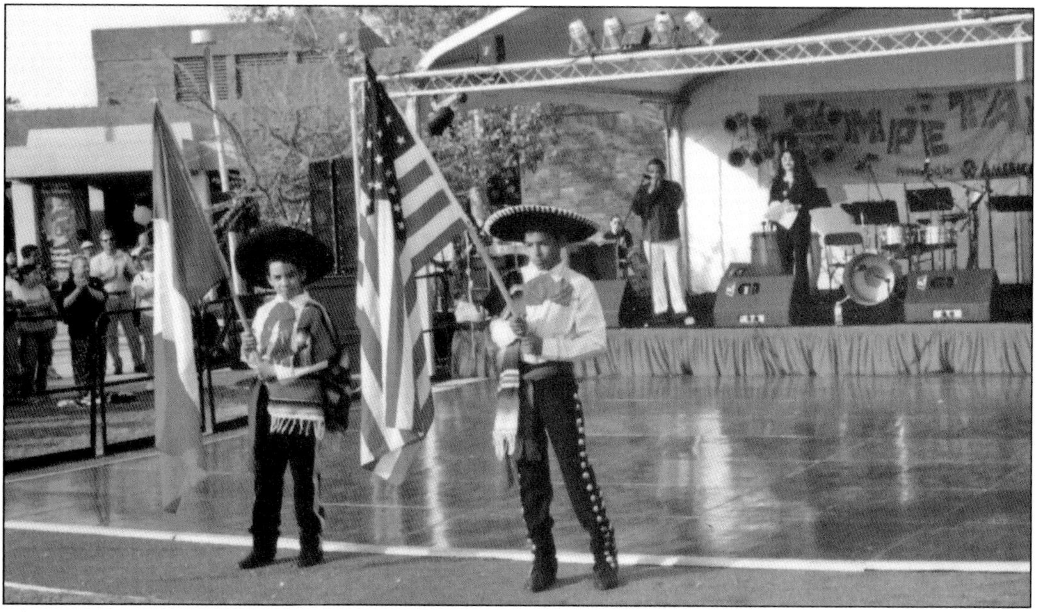

The stage program at the *tardeadas* in Tempe is held every second Sunday in October during Hispanic Heritage Month, designated by U.S. president Lyndon B. Johnson in 1968. The City of Tempe has sponsored the Tardeada for the last 10 years. Tardeada Committee members Tony Gutierrez and his daughter Normalicia Blanco have chaired the entertainment committee and are responsible for obtaining music and dance performers. The public also dances and observes the festivities. Other members of the Tardeada Committee perform duties necessary to accomplish the event. Staff members of the diversity department provide administrative and advisory assistance.

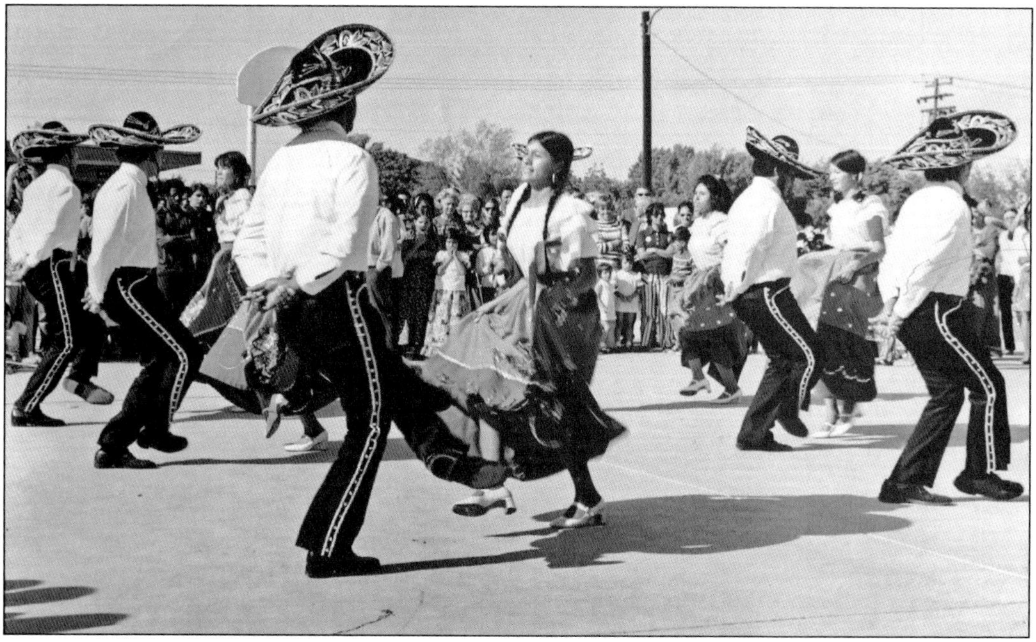

A performance of the Mexican dance "El Jarabe Tapatio" is an example of cultural dances exhibited at the Tardeada. This dance, however, was performed during the Tempe Centennial Celebration. (Photograph by Jan Young; Irene Gomez Hormell.)

Sipie Martinez, an accomplished bandleader for many years, played at the Tardeadas on Friday nights for special guests and the Tardeada Committee and families prior to the Sunday when the Tardeada would be held. Sipie's band included Dr. George Sanchez, on trumpet, an optometrist in Tempe and a longtime past member of the Tempe Elementary School Board of Directors, who had an administrative building named after him. Dr. Joe Sanchez of Miami, Arizona, a dentist, is another member of the band and a brother of Dr. George Sanchez. Sipie Martinez of Miami, Arizona, passed away on July 25, 2008. He performed music into his 94th year. (Samuel Obregon.)

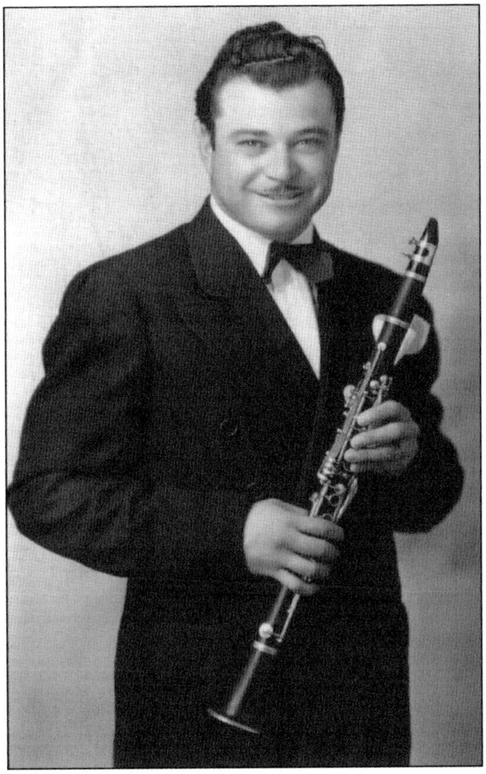

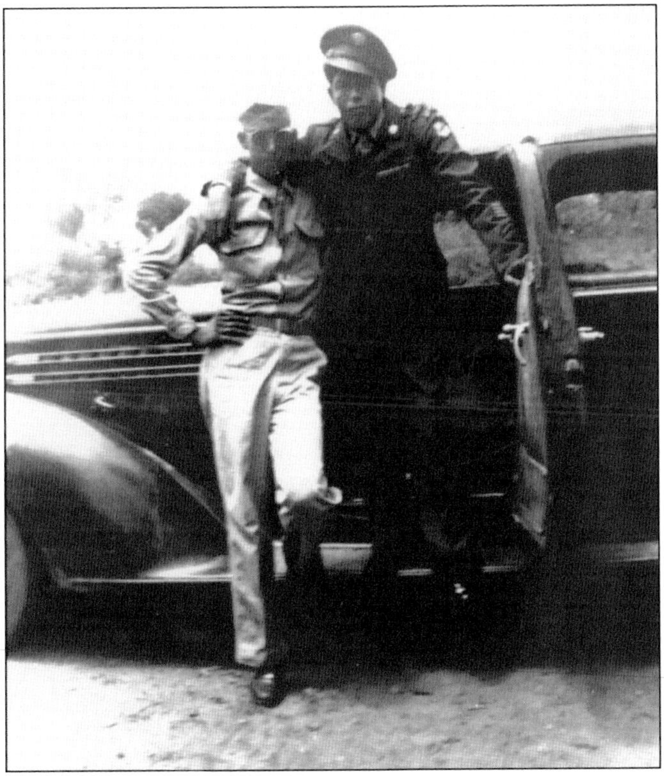

Pictured are World War II servicemen and friends on leave in Tempe, Luis Burgos (left) and Andy Martinez (right), visiting the barrio San Pablo on their furlough at the end of the war in 1945.

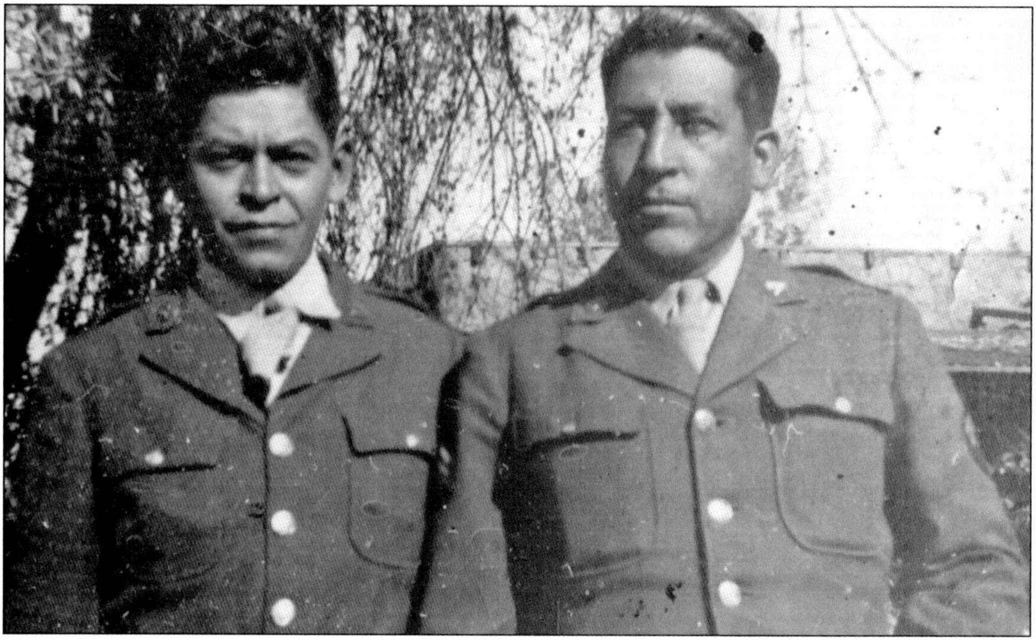

Floyd "Chino" Soto (left) and Gabriel Carbajal (right) both fought in World War II. Floyd gave up his life in 1944 while in action on July 2, 1944, in France and was honored with a Purple Heart. Gabriel Carbajal returned home. He was the son of Victoriana Carbajal and the brother of Artemisa Carbajal. (Norma C. Pinate.)

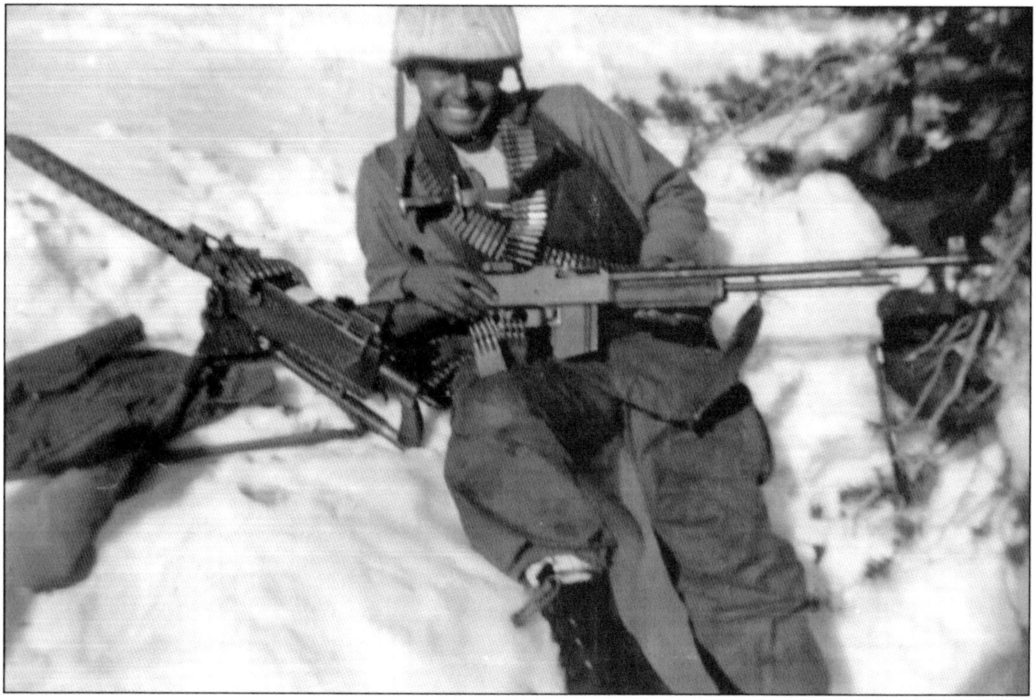

Rudy Arroyo served in the marines in 1957. In this picture, he is shown in training. Rudy graduated from Tempe High School on May 29, 1956. He married Rachel Burgos on October 19, 1958. Rudy and Rachel have a family in Tempe.

Luis "Louie" Gonzales, son of Francisco and Lupe Gonzales, lived in the Mickey Mouse barrio. He served at the end of World War II in Korea. Luis was sports minded and played with the Our Lady of Mount Carmel baseball team in the 1950s.

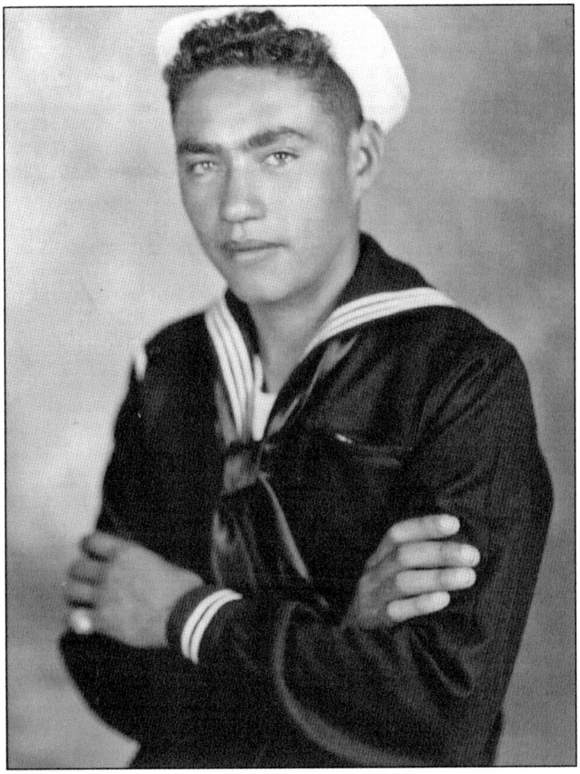

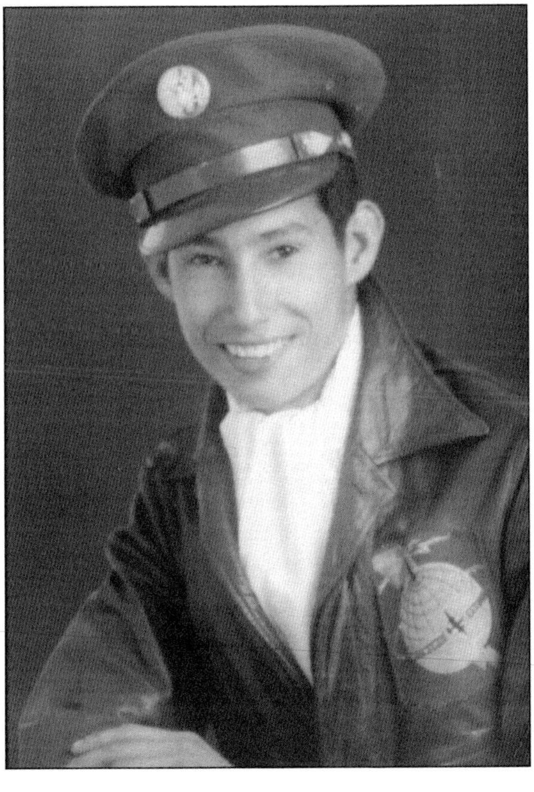

Luis "Louie" Gonzales Burgos, son of Francisco Burgos and Juliana Gonzales Burgos, was a nephew of Candelaria Rios Guerrero. Luis, an army paratrooper, served during World War II in Korea.

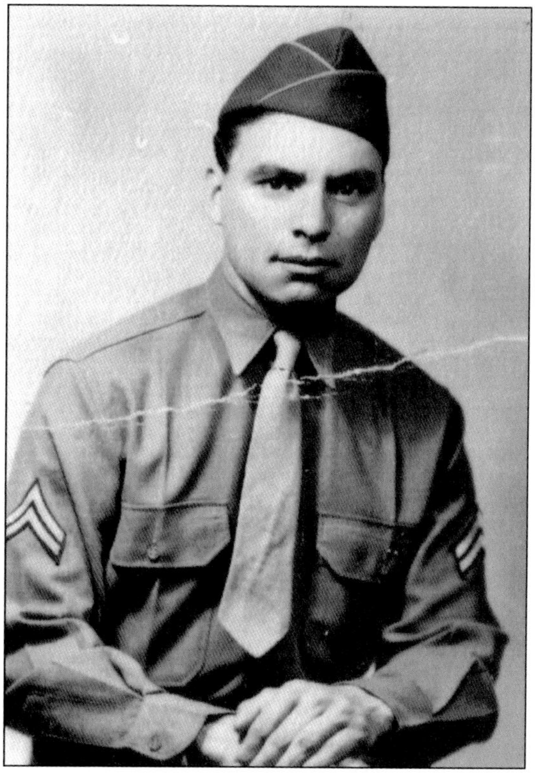

Juan Lopez served during World War II and gave up his life during active duty in Italy in 1943. Juan's sister Leonor was the wife of Victor Arroyo Sr. and mother of Rudy Arroyo.

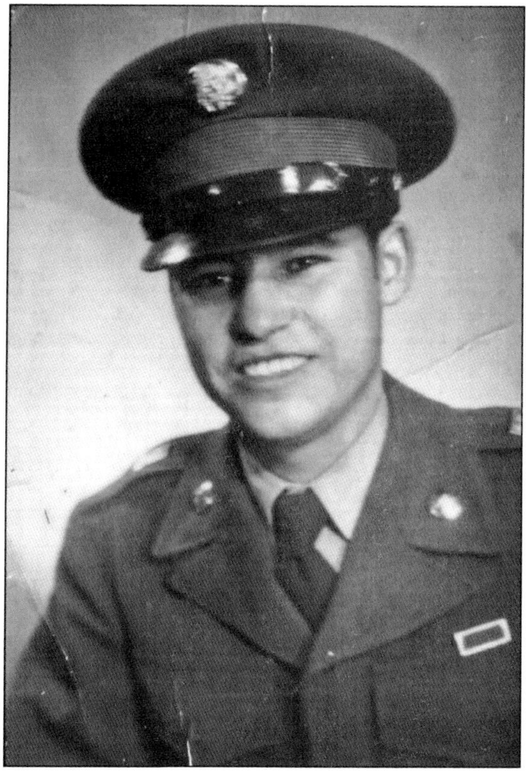

The youngest son of Juliana and Francisco Burgos, Frank Burgos Jr. served in Korea in the 1950s.

Chris Cresencio Varela served his country when assigned to a scout section of the 3rd Armored Division C Troop 12th Cavalry motorized infantry unit. After his time in the service, he married Pat Galaz, and they became the parents of Cathy and Christina. Cathy, in time, became the mother of Christopher, and Christina became the mother of Fiona.

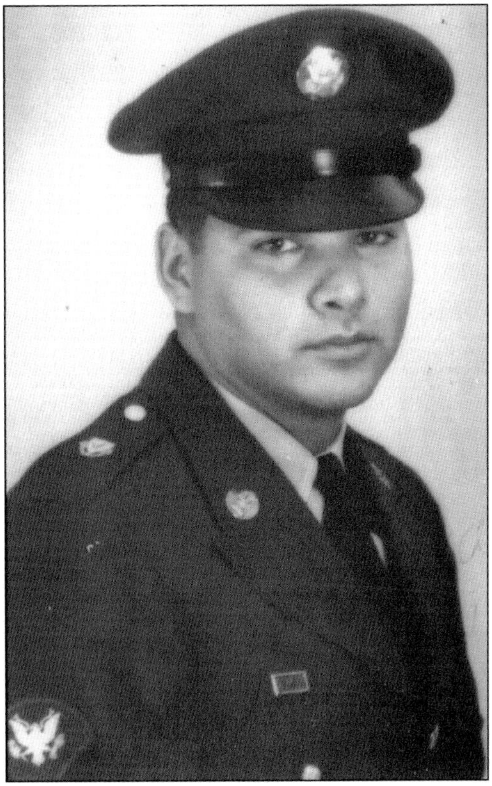

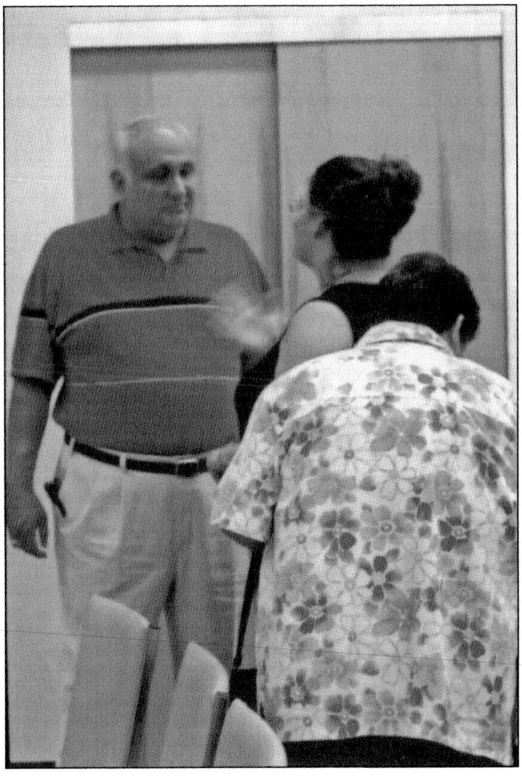

Tempe city councilmember Ben Arredondo, grandson of Ceriaco Arredondo, who pioneered in Tempe around 1900, is shown participating in a program at the Escalante Community Center during the presentation of the oral history booklets about the neighborhoods Victory Acres and Escalante. As a youth, Ben Arredondo and his father's family lived in a ranch on Transmission Road (today University Drive) near Victory Acres. Council member Arredondo, along with all the city council members and Mayor Hugh Hallman, has been supportive of the Tardeada and other Mexican cultural events.

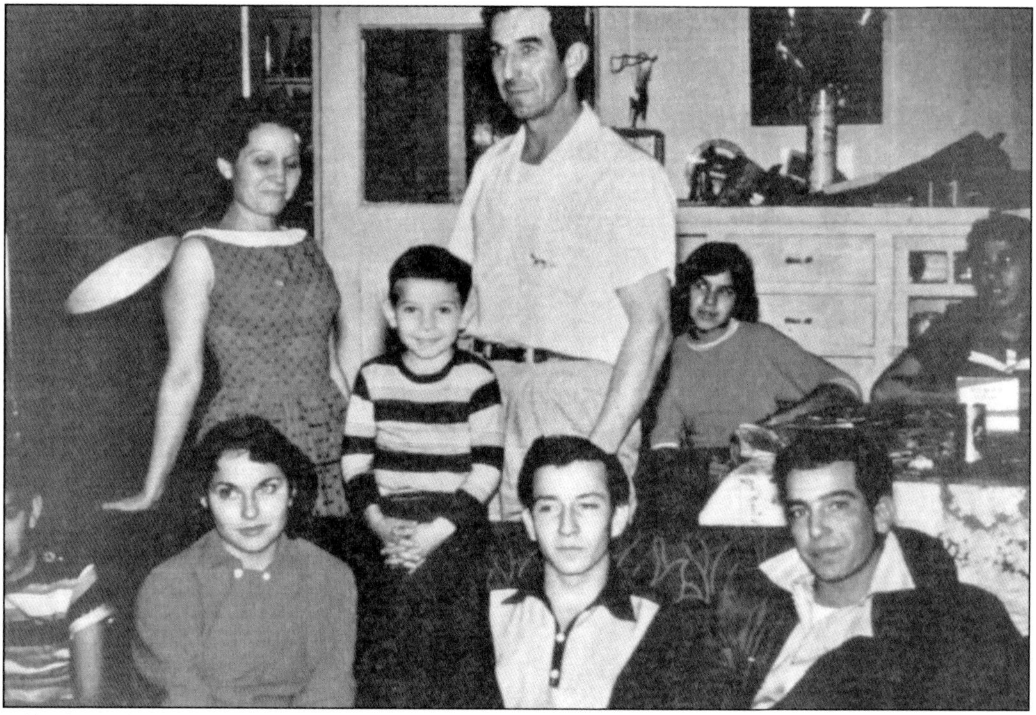

Alfredo "Felo" Guaderrama and his wife, Helen, both standing behind the sofa, are pictured with their family. From left to right in the first row are Armida, Georgie, Alfred Jr., and Jose. In the background are young friends visiting. Felo, who had operated a heavy truck business in New Mexico, moved to Tempe in the early 1950s and was the first Hispanic to open a Schwinn bicycle business, the Tempe Cyclery Shop.

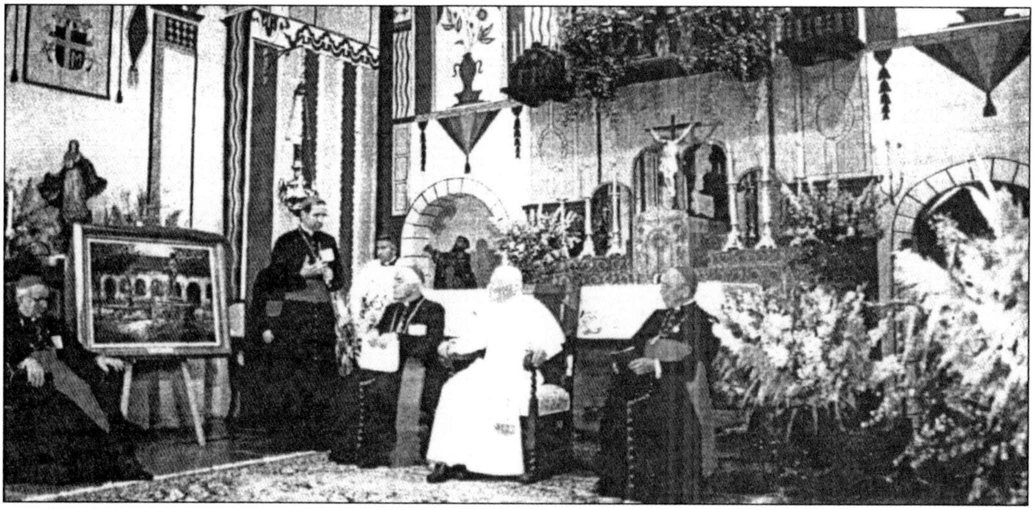

Cardinal Roger Mahony, archbishop of Los Angeles, presented a painting of the San Fernando Mission to Pope John Paul II when he visited the United States to meet with the 325 Catholic bishops on September 16, 1987. The meeting took place at the San Fernando Mission. The governor of California had commissioned artist Ben Abril to paint the mission for the pope. Abril is the oldest son of Ventura Abril and Sarah Varela Abril of Tempe. Sarah is the first daughter of Cresencio and Lupe Acedo Varela.

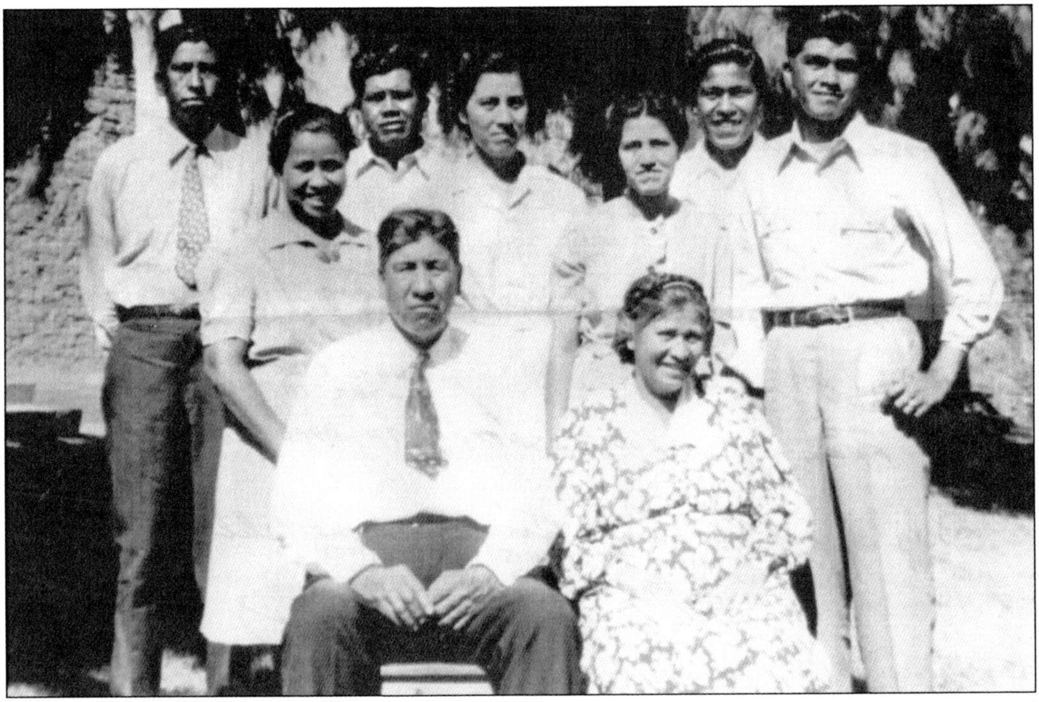

Joe Obregon's family lived in Tempe in the 1940s. Family members also lived in Phoenix and California but kept a heartfelt remembrance of Tempe barrios, heritage, and culture. From left to right are (first row) Hilario V. Obregon and Maria P. Obregon; (second row) Hilaria, Rita, Adelina (born 1914), and Tony (born 1925); (third row) Frank (born 1912), Rosario, and Joe (born 1928). Those individuals with noted birth dates were still alive in 2008. (Joe Obregon.)

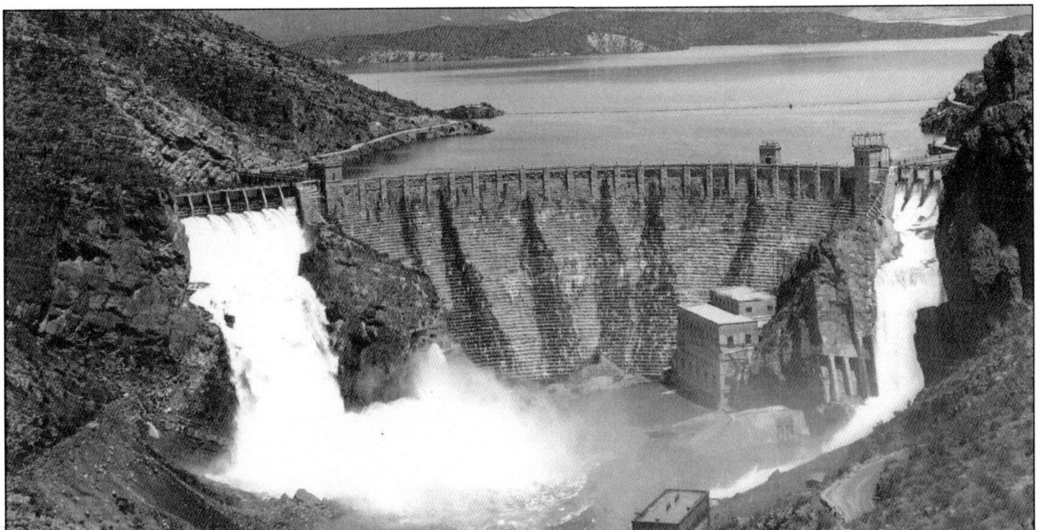

Tempe-based freighters, in the days of large wooden wagons and mule trains, helped supply materials needed to build the Roosevelt Dam, pictured in 1941. Jose Ruiz worked on the Roosevelt Dam. Walter Wilson Jones, father-in-law of Jesus Aros Gomez, had a freight company doing business from Yuma to Prescott. Gomez leased his mules to be used in work hauling and leased them to water users working to build canals. (AHF.)

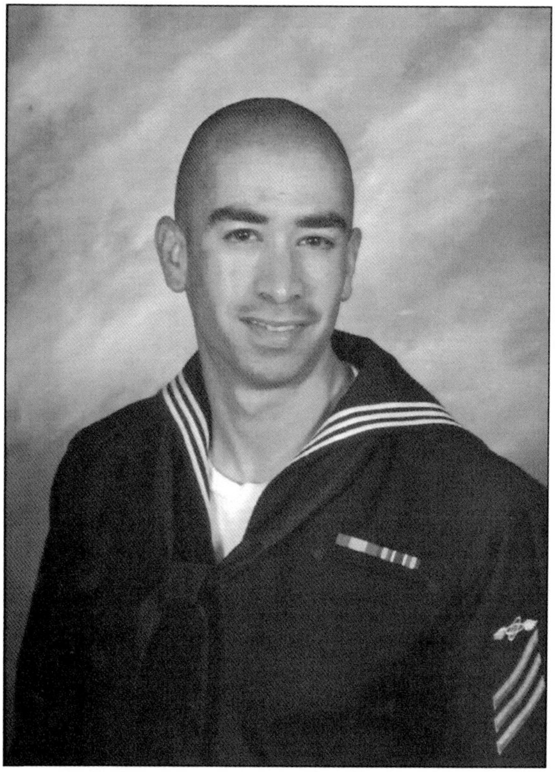

Nick Solis Chavez from Tempe serves in the U.S. Navy as an air technology specialist. (Josie O. Solis.)

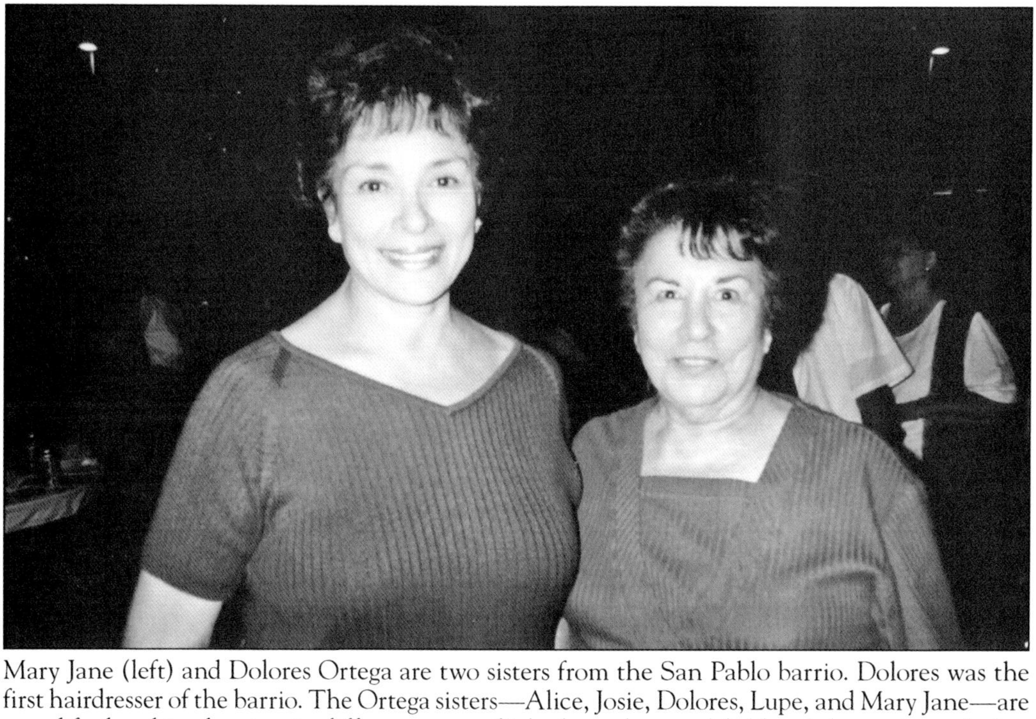

Mary Jane (left) and Dolores Ortega are two sisters from the San Pablo barrio. Dolores was the first hairdresser of the barrio. The Ortega sisters—Alice, Josie, Dolores, Lupe, and Mary Jane—are noted for breaking barriers in different areas of jobs from the usual field and domestic work that marginalized Mexican women in the past.

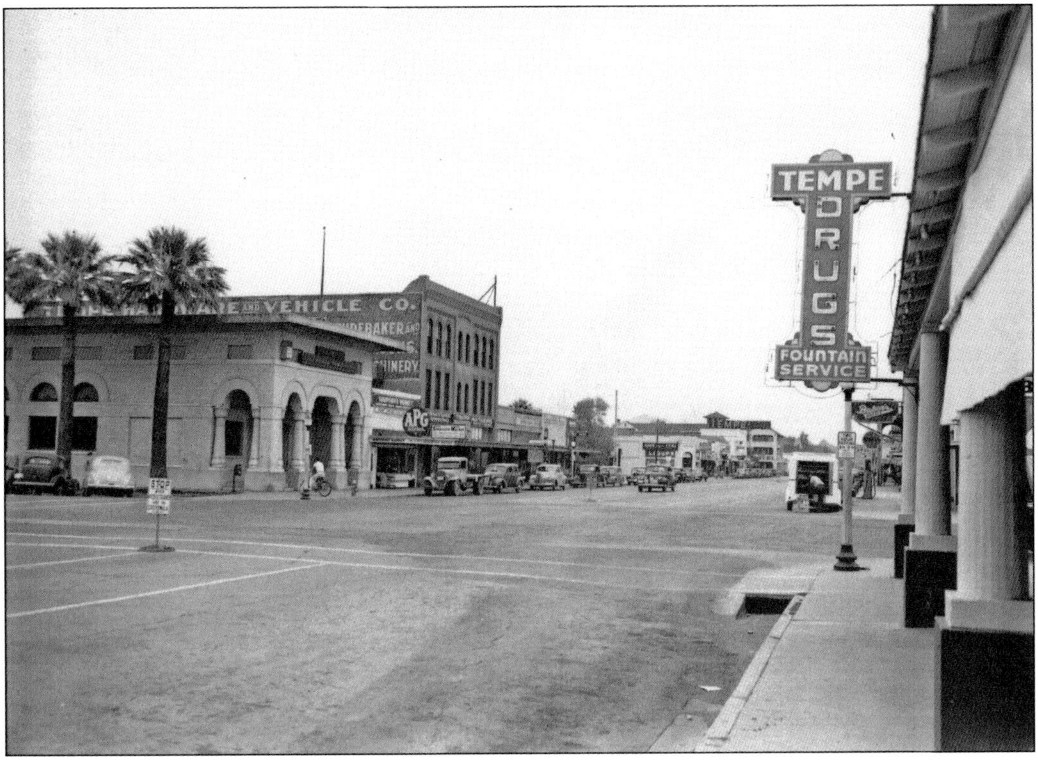

First National Bank on Mill Avenue is a remembrance that reveals the past and graces the present as it stands on a now paved and busy Mill Avenue in Tempe. This picture shows the Curry Building next to the First National Bank. On Sixth Street and Mill Avenue next to the Curry building was the *Tempe Daily News* and the Miller Store. Also on the right side is the Tempe Drugs Fountain Service. (ASU.)

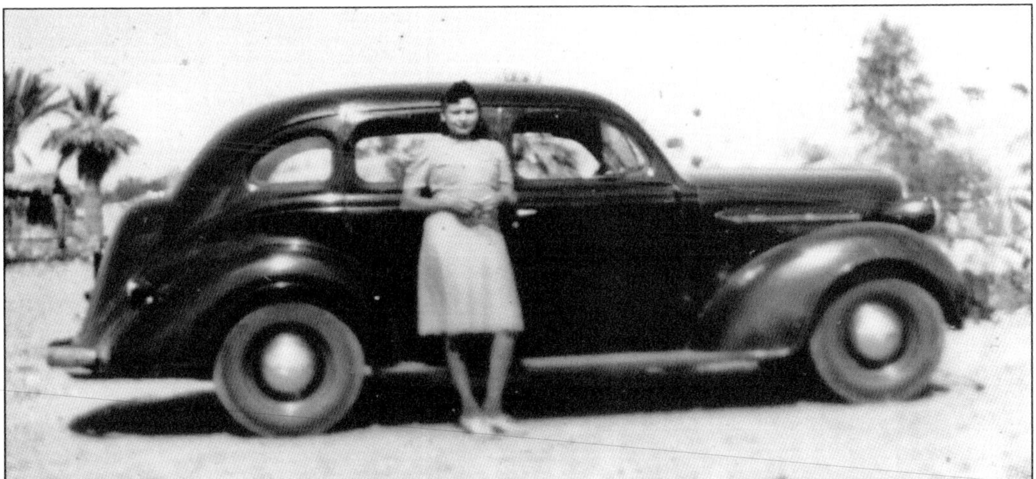

Belen Soza Carbajal enjoys a bright c. 1938 day in front of her family home in the Mickey Mouse barrio at the foot of the Tempe Butte. (Norma C. Pinate.)

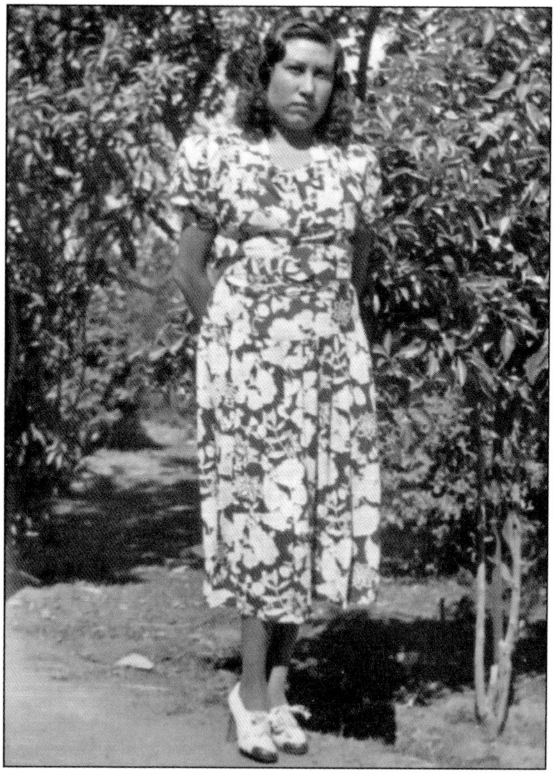

Arty Carbajal stands in front of her trees in the Mickey Mouse barrio in 1944. (Norma C. Pinate.)

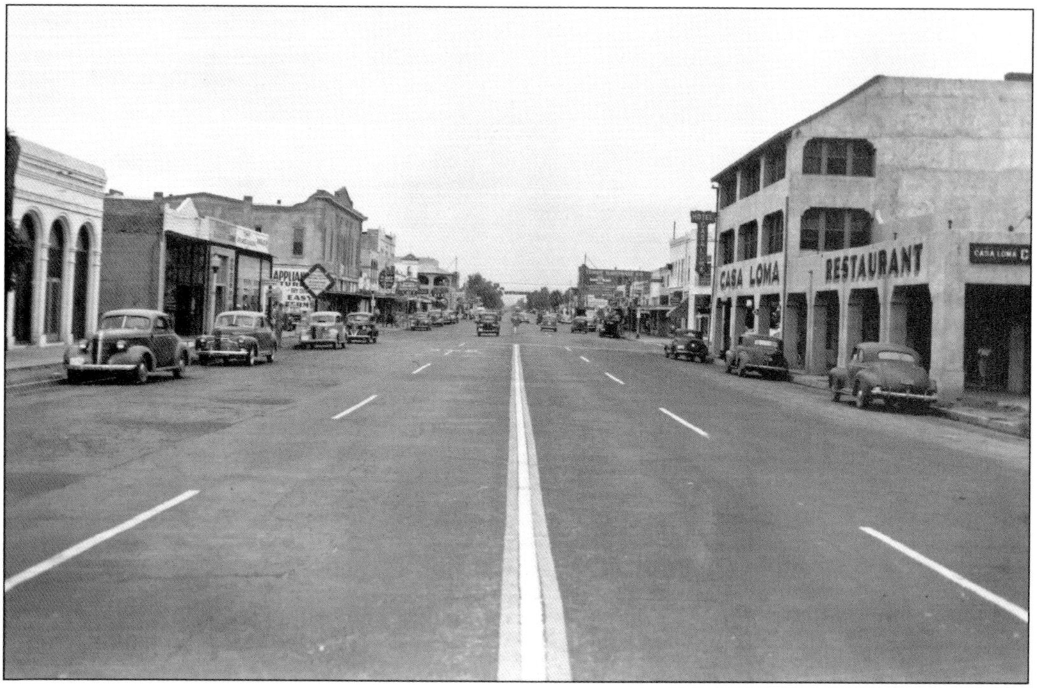

The Casa Loma Hotel and Restaurant on the right side of Mill Avenue is on the west side of the street. South and on the east side of the street is the First National Bank. Mill Avenue is freshly paved and painted, with two lanes facing north and two lanes going south. (ASU.)

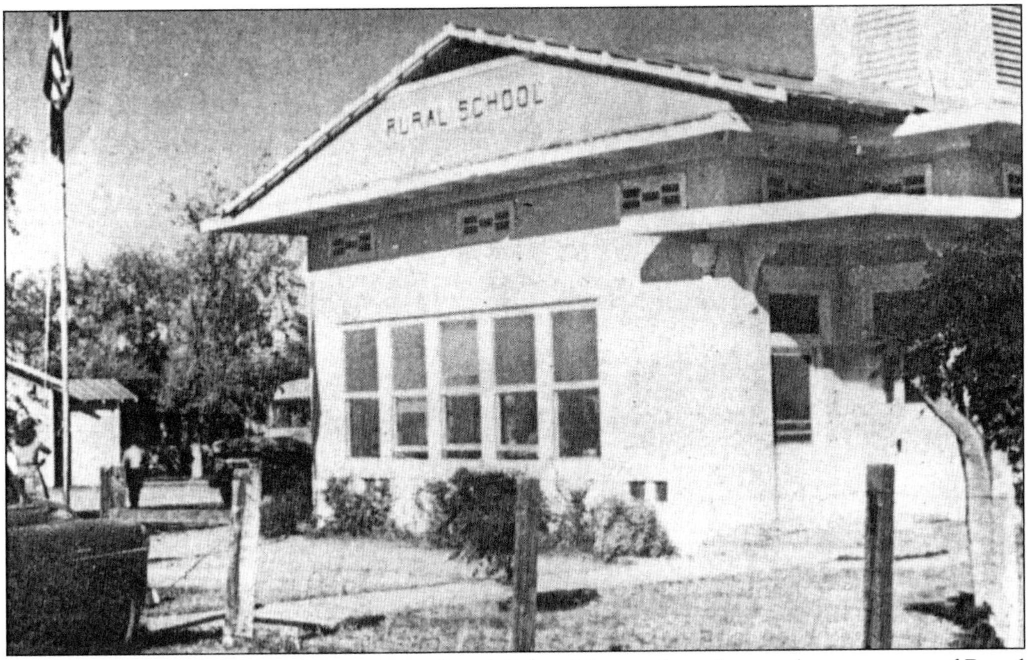

Another remembrance in Tempe is the Rural School located on the northeast corner of Rural Road and Southern Avenue. It served children who lived on ranches south of Southern. Most were Mexican children whose parents worked on farms and ranches. A longtime teacher, Mary Alice Pigg taught at Rural School.

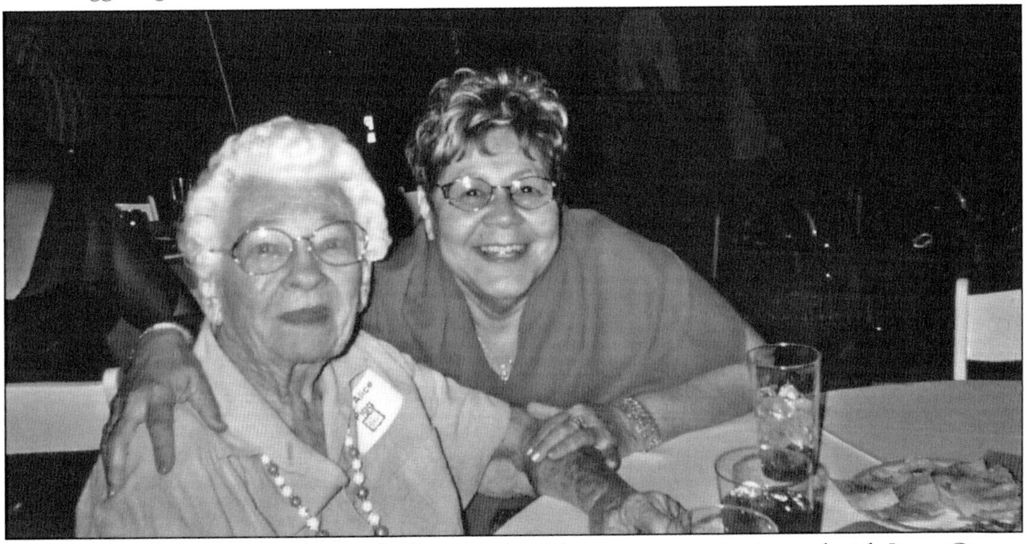

Mary Alice Pigg (left), a teacher at the Rural School for many years, is pictured with Irene Gomez Hormell, who considered Pigg her mentor and friend. Joe Pigg, Mary Alice's husband, owned Joe Pigg's Eat and Drink Sandwiches Shop near the Mexican barrio. He also had the first auto stage line, Fike Stagecoach Company. Mary Alice's family, the Fikes, came to Tempe in the late 1800s. Pigg was an artist and active in many community activities through her church and the city. Mary Alice was involved with the Tempe Historical Museum. The family lived in the barrio on Dewey Street and College Avenue, where Joe had his restaurant as well. Irene Gomez Hormell came from an old pioneer family herself. She is noted for her storytelling and knowledge about Tempe.

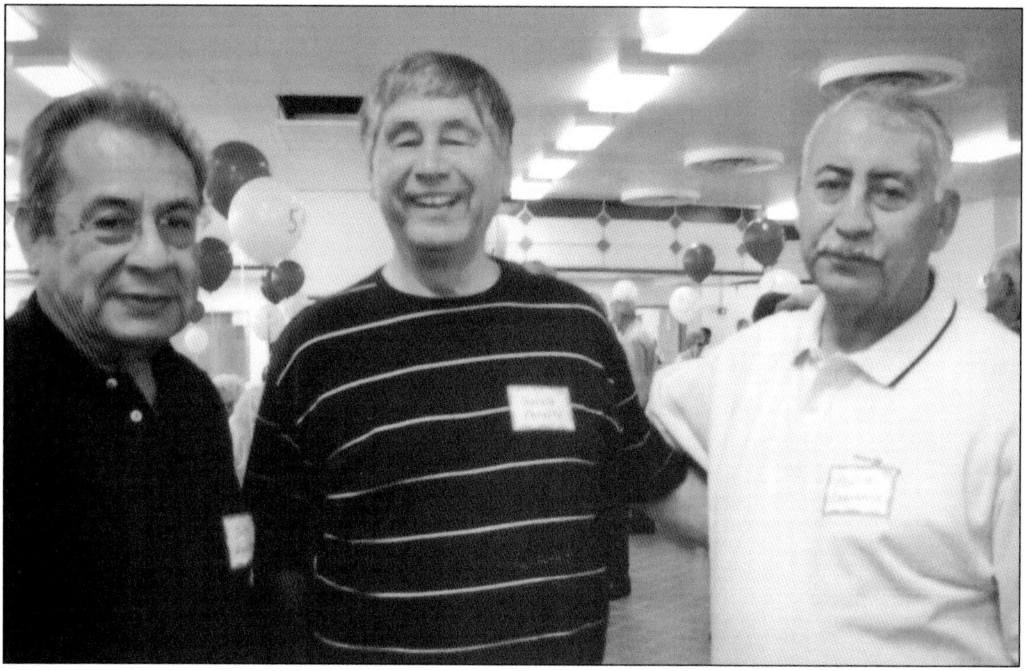

This photograph shows members of old pioneer families who have many remembrances to share when they get together. From left to right are John Aguilar, Gerald Peralta, and Paul Chavarria Jr. Paul is the son of Pablo Chavarria Sr. and Eulalia Guerra Chavarria. Gerald is the son of Geraldo Peralta and Jean Soza Peralta. Gerald's grandmother Maria Soza Mendez had a restaurant on Dewey Street around 1954.

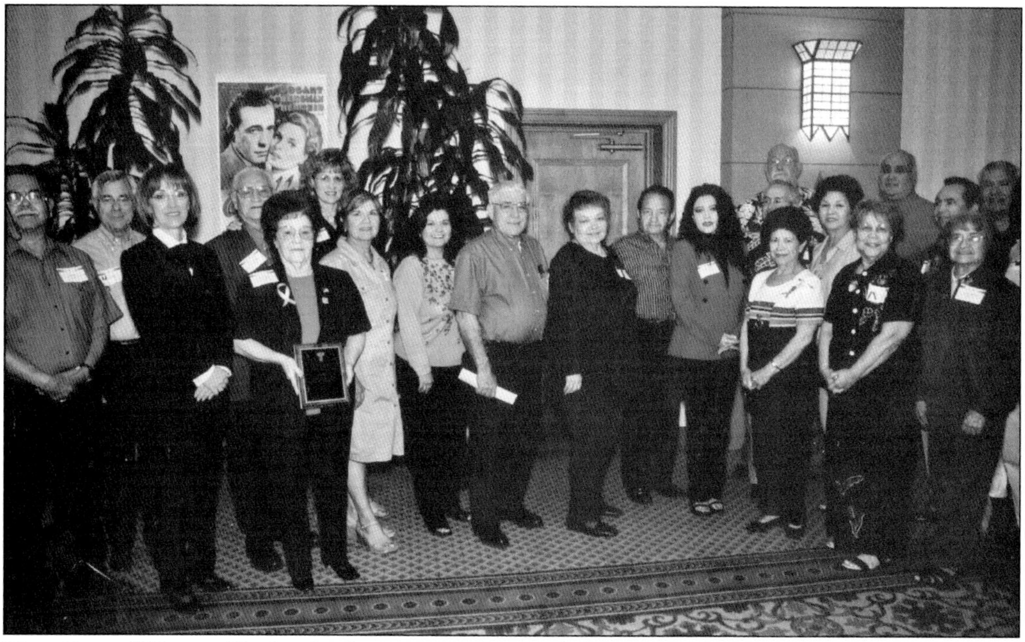

The City of Tempe Tardeada Committee received the 2006 Diversity Award from the city government for its work in promoting and guiding the annual Tardeada Festival on the second Sunday of October for the last several years. (City of Tempe.)

Another remembrance is Johnny Martinez's love of sports and his contributions to Tempe as an employee of the city. Here Johnny celebrates with the Arizona Diamondbacks' left field baseball star Luis "Gonzo" Gonzalez at the dedication of the Tempe Beach Park. The Diamondbacks won the 2001 World Series over the New York Yankees. (Johnny Martinez.)

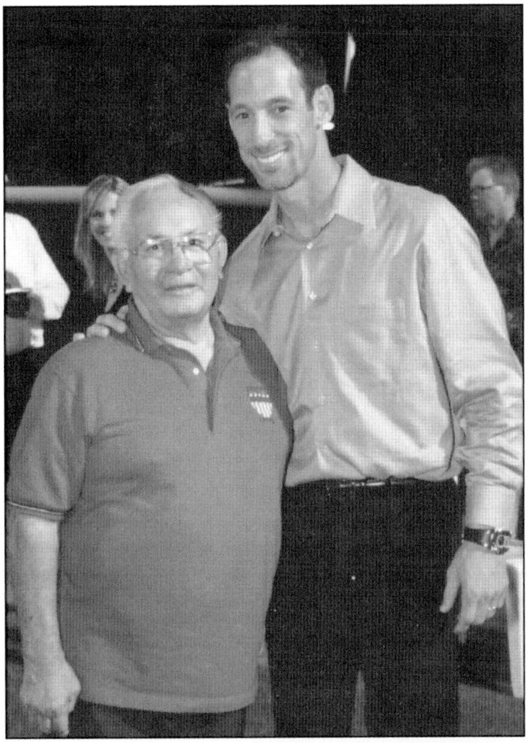

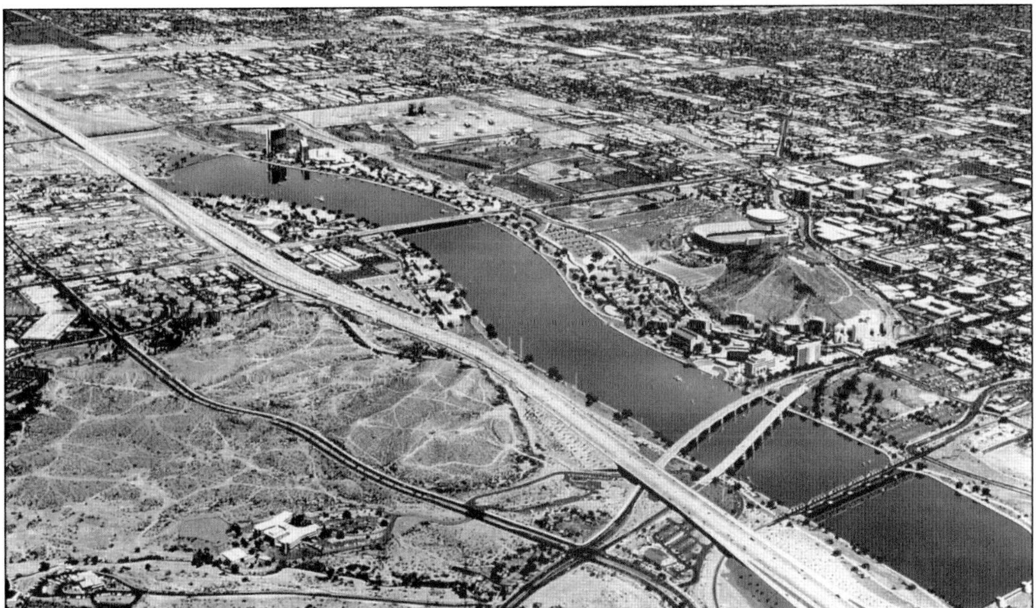

This has been a remembrance of Tempe's footprints of Mexican pioneers and settlers, and their walk through a historical path from the early 1800s to the 21st century. Now all of Tempe's citizens look to a new future of development of their God-given potential, strengthened by their combined heritage, traditions, and cultures that make a nation of immigrants strong and free. This aerial view of Rio Salado Town Lake by artist Julian Clark was given to Johnny Martinez by the city before his retirement. (Johnny Martinez.)

Across America, People are Discovering Something Wonderful. *Their Heritage.*

Arcadia Publishing is the leading local history publisher in the United States. With more than 4,000 titles in print and hundreds of new titles released every year, Arcadia has extensive specialized experience chronicling the history of communities and celebrating America's hidden stories, bringing to life the people, places, and events from the past. To discover the history of other communities across the nation, please visit:

www.arcadiapublishing.com

Customized search tools allow you to find regional history books about the town where you grew up, the cities where your friends and family live, the town where your parents met, or even that retirement spot you've been dreaming about.

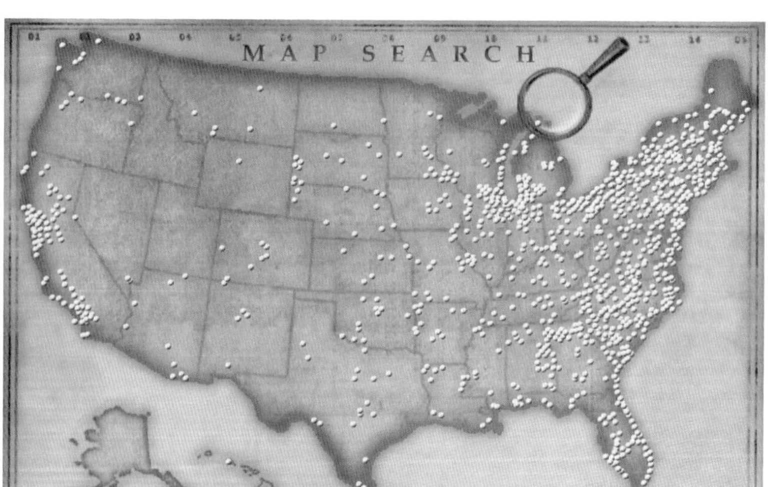